KIPLING'S MYTHS OF LOVE AND DEATH

Also by Nora Crook

SHELLEY'S VENOMED MELODY (*with Derek Guiton*)

Kipling's Myths of Love and Death

NORA CROOK

Cambridgeshire College of Arts and Technology

MACMILLAN

First published 1989

Published by
THE MACMILLAN PRESS LTD
Houndmills, Basingstoke, Hampshire RG21 2XS
and London
Companies and representatives
throughout the world

Typeset by
Wessex Typesetters
(Division of The Eastern Press Ltd)
Frome, Somerset

Printed in Hong Kong

British Library Cataloguing in Publication Data
Crook, Nora
Kipling's myths of love and death.
1. English literature. Kipling, Rudyard, 1865–1936—
Critical studies   I. Title
828'.809
ISBN 0–333–45482–0

To the Five who told me to read Kipling and read Kipling
with me

Keith Kim Lisa Rick Ted

Mox adparebat idolon

'And how think you of the Seven Devils?' the Abbot went on. *These melted into convoluted flower or flame-like bodies, ranging in colour from phosphorescent green to the black purple of outworn iniquity, whose hearts could be traced beating through their substance. But, for sign of hope and the sane workings of life, to be regained, the deep border was of conventionalised spring flowers and birds, all crowned by a kingfisher in haste, atilt through a clump of yellow iris.*

('The Eye of Allah')

Little words are sometimes of great import in cases of history as well as of law. Evagius tells us . . . that in the Emperor Leo's reign, Constantinople was set on fire by a malignant and wicked Devil in the shape of a woman . . . or by a poor woman at the instigation of the Devil.

(Robert Southey, 'If', *Omniana*)

Nobody seems to have understood what I mean by most of the stories I write.

(Rudyard Kipling, as reported by Thelma Cazalet Keir)

Contents

List of Plates

Note on Texts

Citations of Kipling's prose works and of the verse included in them are based on the Macmillan Pocket Edition, which has the same page numbers as, for example, the red-cloth 'Elephant's Head' volumes of the Uniform Edition (1899–1938), the Library Edition (1950) and the Centenary Edition (1965), though there are variants in spelling and punctuation. I have used the authorised edition of *Abaft the Funnel* (New York: Doubleday, Page, 1909) and Haining (see List of Abbreviations) for collected prose not appearing in the above editions. For most other verse, I have used *The Definitive Edition of Rudyard Kipling's Verse* (Hodder and Stoughton, 1940).

Chaucer references are taken from *The Riverside Chaucer*, ed. Larry D. Benson (Oxford: Oxford University Press, 1988). Quotations from John Ruskin are taken from *The Works*, ed E. T. Cook and A. Wedderburn, 39 vols (1903–12). Quotations from Swinburne are taken from *Swinburne's Collected Poetical Works*, 2 vols (Heinemann, 1924).

List of Abbreviations

Dates in parentheses are of book publications. Unless otherwise stated, place of publication is London.

AF	*Abaft the Funnel* (1909)
AR	*Actions and Reactions* (1909)
BW	*A Book of Words* (1928)
DC	*Debits and Credits* (1926)
D of C	*A Diversity of Creatures* (1917)
DV	*The Definitive Edition of Rudyard Kipling's Verse* (1940)
DW	*The Day's Work* (1898)
EV	*Early Verse by Rudyard Kipling, 1879–1889*, ed. Andrew Rutherford, pbk edn (Oxford: Oxford University Press, 1986)
Haining	*The Complete Supernatural Stories of Rudyard Kipling*, ed. Peter Haining (Allen, 1987)
JB	*The Jungle Book* (1894)
JB2	*The Second Jungle Book* (1896)
JSS	*Just So Stories* (1902)
KI	*Kipling's India, Uncollected Sketches 1884–88*, ed. Thomas Pinney (Macmillan, 1986)
LF	*The Light that Failed* (1890)
LH	*Life's Handicap* (1891)
LR	*Limits and Renewals* (1932)
LST	*Land and Sea Tales* (1923)
LT	*Letters of Travel* (1920)
MI	*Many Inventions* (1893)
OBK	*O Beloved Kids: Letters of Kipling to his Children*, ed. Eliot Gilbert (Weidenfeld and Nicolson, 1983)
PT	*Plain Tales from the Hills* (1888)
RF	*Rewards and Fairies* (1910)
SC	*Stalky & Co.* (1899)
SF	*Souvenirs of France* (1933)
SM	*Something of Myself* (1937)
SS	*From Sea to Sea*, 2 vols (1899)
ST	*Soldiers Three* (1888)
TD	*Traffics and Discoveries* (1904)
TSD	*Thy Servant a Dog* (1938 edn)
WWW	*Wee Willie Winkie* (1888)

Introduction and Acknowledgements

The flurry of publications and reviews following the fiftieth anniversary of Kipling's death has provided an occasion for the literary world formally to jettison the outdated image of the children's writer yoked to the imperialist. This hybrid is replaced by that of the man with a good deal more than a mere 'two sides to his head'. The Kipling for our times is a 'gentle–violent' man, a complex and baffling personality, if 'personality' is the word for a writer whose impulses to be Keats's 'chameleon poet', to have 'no self' and to 'live in gusto, be it foul or fair' are checked by a corresponding need to create stable Edens and erect a 'carapace in which he could shield his vulnerable and uncertain identity'. In the schema, the imperialism emerges as both cause and palliative of Kipling's fear of Great Darkness and the Breaking Strain. Simultaneously, Kipling the short-story writer has become more interesting as a 'case'. He is both a craftsman who treats writing as a species of intellectual wordsmithery, 'cherished by practising writers as a supreme technician', and a Romantic believer in the artist's inspirational Daemon. He is increasingly seen as a proto-modernist or even proto-post-modernist, a literary ancestor of Joyce and Eliot on the one hand and of Borges and Eco on the other.[1]

This multi-faceted Kipling is just as controversial as the old laureate of Empire, but today the divisions tend to centre round hermeneutics. Some of his short stories, such as the notorious 'Mrs Bathurst', have, from the day they were written, defied explication, even on the simple level of 'What really happened?' Others give rise to a diversity of interpretation because readers cannot decide (for instance) whether Kipling is ironically distancing himself from the narrator or whether he is writing a comic celebration or a savage satire. But even stories where the narrative presents no obvious difficulties are more difficult than they seem. The received idea is that he started out simple and vivid, becoming elliptical and cryptic as he got older, and like his admired Jane Austen refused to write 'for such dull elves / As have not a great deal of ingenuity themselves'. The straightforwardness of the early Kipling has, however, been much exaggerated.

It is in this climate that I present this study – an attempt to interpret some of Kipling's most dense and problematic tales, approaching them through his famous (or notorious) allusiveness. The study focuses on three writers: Dante, Chaucer and Swinburne. All three were read by him intensively at school and remained with him throughout his life, though you might not think so if you merely judged by the number of times he mentions them by name. I have not bound myself to refer to these authors alone, which would be a procedure grossly simplifying Kipling's intertextuality. Dante, for instance, is interwoven with Milton, the Bible and classical mythology. Allusion-spotting, which I don't regard as a literary can-opener that infallibly enables one to get at the goodies inside a story, is used only inasmuch as it serves the purpose of interpretation or illumination of narrative strategies, after which I avail myself of other means.

Nevertheless a self-denying ordinance is operating; I should have liked to take on board other authors whose importance in Kipling's work is arguably greater – Browning and Poe spring immediately to mind – and to discuss the significance of his considerable reading of female writers (Austen, Barrett Browning, Lydia Sigourney, Christina Rossetti, Jean Ingelow, Margaret Gatty, Juliana Ewing, Margaret Oliphant, 'Gyp') during his formative years. I should have liked to extend the argument into an exploration of how family magazines introduced middle-class Victorian children to adult writers such as Dante. However, this book is not a cultural history of the period 1870–1930 (though it may contribute to one). It is not a source-hunt or a demonstration of Kipling's wide reading, which Ann Weygandt's pioneering study of 1939 established once and for all, or a treatment of the interesting subject of Kipling and women. To follow too many trails would blur the focus of the book, which began with my trying to understand particular stories. It was only after the three writers had emerged as threads in Kipling's texture that I noticed a certain coherence in the triad, two of them being genuine medieval poets and the third having a tendency to pose as one. Since Dante and Chaucer were mediated through nineteenth-century Romanticism and antiquarianism, all three could be described as 'Victorian medieval poets' when related to Kipling. There is also a sense in which Kipling himself makes a fourth.

The bias of this study is towards Kipling the prose poet and adult writer. Inasmuch as Kipling's writing is one and indivisible, this produces a distortion. In omitting to do justice to his *surface* qualities, to the pleasure of reading his evocation of atmosphere and situation, to the innocent and lucid Kipling, this book lacks a dimension which constitutes his chief charm for many readers. They *will* find here the Kipling of the Chaucerian 'derke fantasye', the Thomas who harps down in Hell, the fashioner of Daedalian labyrinths and Minotaurs, the natural supernaturalist, the Last Romantic writer who declared that his chief subjects were 'Life and Death and Men and Women and Love and Fate'. (I don't think that this places Kipling above history, for to announce these as one's subjects is itself to be participating in nineteenth-century myth-making.) I hope that this limited study of a protean author may modify readers' total apprehensions of the whole; that it may spark off a corresponding pleasurable activity in their mind, and prompt them to supply the missing breadth.

Two preparatory chapters exemplify a certain way of approach and place Kipling in a context of Victorian exegesis. He was a bookish man, and trained to read in a very late-Victorian way, which Chapter 2 sets forth. The ambiance of Carlyle, Ruskin and the Pre-Raphaelites in which he grew up, and the popularising of their work, provided an education in looking closely into things, in seeing Nature as a book, the British Flag as a veil screening mysteries, man as walking in a forest of symbols. Chapter 3 attempts to show some of the possible results of the above perspective on the interpretation of five stories.

Then follow chapters on Kipling's use of the three authors named. Each has a corresponding major tale, to which that author is especially relevant – Dante to 'Mrs Bathurst', Chaucer to 'Mary Postgate' and Swinburne to 'The Madonna of the Trenches'. There is also a substantial interlude on 'The Strange Ride of Morrowbie Jukes', and short discussions of other tales. These are the satellites of which the first three mentioned are orbs, for the purposes of this argument. Each major tale has at its heart the figure of a demonic woman.

Although I often write of Kipling laying 'clues', the process by which these readings were arrived at was not a deductive, linear one, but closer to the intuitive leaps recommended by Kipling's Pyecroft: 'I used to think seein' and hearin' was the only regulation aids to ascertainin' facts, but as we get older we get more accommodatin'.' But, when attempting to rationalise the leaps, it seemed to me that Kipling had in each case provided an alternative route, suspended a rope-bridge over the chasm, often composed of the texts of older authors. I have been forced to describe the rope-bridge in order to persuade, but in doing so I risk making Kipling sound like someone who wrote only for the few who had read what he had read. There is a counter-argument to that: Kipling's favourite authors – Horace, Browning, Stevenson – must necessarily have been less esoteric than they appear today. But that is only a part-answer. It would be truer to say that the *essentials* of these readings I put forward may be arrived at without the help of the 'bridge'. I suspect that they often *have* been arrived at by individuals but just happen not to have been published.

But the esoteric Kipling cannot simply be discounted. In these pages I shall develop a theory that some of Kipling's tales are 'yarns' in several senses – entangling webs for the unwary disguised as pastimes. True, his work has become more liable to misunderstanding as the context in which it was written has receded. Contextualisation is still incomplete and fragmented, though this is changing. It is possible (for instance) that, if 'The Village that Voted the Earth was Flat' and 'The Vortex' had not been divorced from the year of the Marconi scandals and the preliminaries to the First World War, their meanings might not have been turned upside-down by some modern critics. But the fact remains that contemporaries do not seem to have perceived their pessimism either, and that says something about the kind of writer Kipling is. Hugh Brogan has observed that 'you re-read a story you thought you knew well and you find that it means something quite different'.[2] There are many writers of whom this is true, but none, I think, to the same degree as Kipling. Which is peculiar.

Kipling made a famous plea that his posthumous critics should 'Seek not to question other than/The books I leave behind'. This is usually seen as an embargo on biographical investigation, but it also assumes that readers *will* 'question' his works – that is, investigate their secret meanings. He is an inveterate punster, and 'the books I leave behind' can refer not only to the books he wrote, but also to those he read, the mental library that can be constructed from his writings, and which, like his physical library and all other possessions, he had to leave behind when he died. He is, I think, giving readers permission to question these in order to interpret his work. This is one of Kipling's legacies; like the dying man in the Aesop fable he tells us that a 'treasure' lies buried in that field (the story-as-gem is another favourite metaphor of his). Like the offspring, we may find a 'treasure' other than that sought in investigating the books he read. Kipling wants to make readers of us all and to keep up literature, not to hoard his riches.

To confirm one's inferences about the books he read, however, it is sometimes necessary to go beyond the evidence of the fiction, and to make use of private letters, memoirs, *obiter dicta*, the contents of his library. This last must be treated with some caution. In the endnotes there are frequent statements that this or that book is in Kipling's library at Bateman's, his Sussex home. As far as is known, the library is as Kipling left it when he died, and most of the books contain his book-plate. Some have marginal markings. However, it is seldom possible to tell the exact date that Kipling acquired or read a particular book, nor is it always certain whether a very worn book was read extensively by him, or by his father, or whether he acquired it second-hand.

His posthumous autobiography *Something of Myself* must, of course, be counted among 'the books I leave behind' and is now at last living down the gibe of deserving to be retitled 'Practically Nothing of Myself'. As Richard Holmes's sensitive introduction to the 1987 Penguin reprint recognises, almost every episode of this fiction of his own life is chosen to illuminate some aspect of his art, and, though lacking his final revisions, it is structured as if it were one of his own short novels. But the account given in *Something of Myself* of his literary indebtedness needs amplification from external evidence.[3]

Kipling borrowed the Rabelaisian coinage 'metagrobolise' (puzzle, mystify), and, describing the genesis of his novel *The Light that Failed*, gave it a special sense: to create a work of art out of the concealed metamorphosis of another, a process which could be unconscious. This metagrobolising personality is of a piece with his frequent assurances to readers that his stories do have a concealed dimension, as in his introduction to his favourite Outward Bound Edition, where the fictitious persona tells the reader that his cargo is 'double-and-treble figured' and that some bales bear 'private marks'.[4] Undoubtedly this refers to not only Kipling's Masonic lore (an area where I lack competence and which I mention only in passing) but also some biographical circumstances. A few of these 'private marks' therefore come into the argument where I believe that I have read them correctly and they seem relevant.

Many of Kipling's manuscripts lie under an embargo and cannot be cited, and I have therefore not used much manuscript evidence.

There are several instances known to me where it would corroborate certain readings in minor ways. In every case, though, the readings were arrived at prior to knowledge of a manuscript variant.

It will be noticed that one work is sometimes used to interpret another. This is appropriate to such a highly self-referential writer as Kipling, who at thirty had a readership which read and collected him entire; standard editions of his work started rolling from the presses before he was thirty-five. The Kipling buff was well established by 1900. Kipling could write knowing that some would read him as if he were Holy Writ, making cross-references from one collection of short stories to another.[5] Indeed, I would suggest that as his ambition of writing a Victorian-type three-decker novel receded, he came to hope that his entire *oeuvre* would shape itself into one loosely unified Book. It will also be noticed that I have been more interested in working out what Kipling is saying than in setting down which portion of his views I approve of and which I do not.

For permission to reproduce the illustrations in the plate section, I thank the trustees of Birmingham City Museums and Art Gallery.

For offering encouragement and enlightenment, I have many to thank. Cambridgeshire College of Arts and Technology (CCAT) allowed me research time to pursue this work. A number of colleagues and friends, among them Rick Allen and Ted Holt, kept on urging me to read Kipling, read draft chapters, and offered valued criticism. I have a special debt of gratitude to Kim Landers, who was a constant stimulus and clarifier, and Lisa Lewis, who generously shared her formidable knowledge of Kipling's work with me, saved me from making many silly mistakes, and sustained me with letter and talk throughout the project. I hope that her own study of Kipling will appear in the not-too-distant future.

My thanks are also due to the Kipling Society, whose London library at their 18 Northumberland Street headquarters was a welcoming resource, and who in the spring of 1988 gave me as guest speaker a platform for the argument of Chapter 4. Margaret Newsom, the Society's librarian, and George Webb, editor to its organ the *Kipling Journal*, in which parts of Chapter 5 (reprinted here by kind permission) first appeared, both rendered valuable assistance. I owe much, too, to previous scholars and critics, especially J. M. S. Tompkins and C. A. Bodelsen. Professor

Norman Page's essay 'What Happens in "Mary Postgate"?' was an *éclaircissement*, though he might not agree with the lengths to which I have taken his perceptions. Adrian Poole's 1985 address to the CCAT Literary Society on Kipling's use of upper-case began a train of thought.

Many have supplied information, made helpful suggestions and facilitated research: John Dench, Bruce Robertson and Nigel Wheale of CCAT; the National Trust, Peter Ellis and Dr Tim Wilson, who gave permission and generously gave of their time to enable me to work at the Library of Wimpole Hall; Julian Wiltshire, who did the same for the Library at Bateman's; D. H. Simpson, Librarian of the Royal Commonwealth Society; Hugh Brogan, Michael and Valerie Grosvenor-Myer, Norman Jackson and Jeremy Lawrence, who answered questions about Kipling in South Africa; my sister Professor Madeleine Mitchell, Professor Thomas Pinney, Professor Andrew Rutherford, John Shearman, Valerie and Jeffrey Meyers; the staffs of Cambridge University and Edinburgh University Libraries, who were unfailingly helpful; the *caissier* at the Hotel Regina, Paris, who courteously supplied me with details of the pre-First World War history of the hotel. Errors and shortcomings of this study are, of course, my own.

Finally, I wish to thank my patient family for their interest and support and especially two Keiths; my father, who introduced me to the *Just So Stories* back in 1943, and my husband, whose purchase of some odd volumes of the Service Edition was the crystal in the super-saturated solution and who has lived through this book along with me.

A Brief Kipling Chronology

1865   RK born in Bombay to Lockwood and Alice Kipling (30 Dec).

1868   RK's sister 'Trix' born (married John Fleming, 1889).

1871–7   RK and 'Trix' fostered with the Holloways of Lorne Lodge, Southsea – 'The House of Desolation'. Holidays with 'Uncle Ned' and 'Aunt Georgie' Burne-Jones.

1878–82   Attends United Services College, Westward Ho!, Devon. Meets Beresford ('M'Turk') and Dunsterville ('Stalky'). 'Tide of writing' begins about 1879. Reads Chaucer, Dante, Swinburne, Browning, Carlyle, Ruskin. Falls in love with Florence Garrard c. 1880.

1882   Arrives in India (Oct), becomes sub-editor on the Lahore *Civil and Military Gazette*.

1884–5   Florence breaks the engagement; RK publishes first prose tales ('The Strange Ride of Morrowbie Jukes' in Christmas 1885 family production *Quartette*).

1886   Becomes a Freemason.

1887   Transferred to the Allahabad *Pioneer*, travels extensively (*Letters of Marque* and *The City of Dreadful Night*).

1888   *Plain Tales from the Hills* and six other early collections published in India.

1889   Leaves India, arrives in London, lives in Villiers Street. Meets Wolcott Balestier, the American literary entrepreneur.

1890   Popular success; becomes a world-famous author.

1891   Book version of *The Light that Failed* published. Collaboration on *The Naulahka* with Balestier, who dies December, during RK's last visit to India.

1892–6   RK marries Balestier's sister Carrie (Jan 1892); lives at 'Naulakha', Brattleboro, Vermont. *Jungle Books*. Parents retire to Tisbury, Wiltshire.

1896–9   Return to England after lawsuit with Carrie's brother. Lives at Torquay and Rottingdean. During visit to America in 1899, six-year-old daughter Josephine dies. The Boer War breaks out. In 1899 *Stalky & Co.*, RK's fictional account of United Services College, appears; so does

	Robert Buchanan's attack, 'The Voice of the Hooligan', a watershed in RK's reputation.
1900	Sees war in South Africa (Feb–Apr). Edits Bloemfontein *Friend*.
1901	*Kim*.
1902	The Boer War ends in May. Move to Bateman's, Sussex, RK's home for the rest of his life, except for South African winters (1898–1907). *Just So Stories* published.
1904	'Mrs Bathurst' written.
1905–14	Writes *Puck* books; increasingly pessimistic about chances of avoiding war. Growing political extremism. Death of RK's parents (1910–11). War declared (Aug 1914).
1915	'Mary Postgate' written. RK's son killed.
1918–23	Post-war work for War Graves Commission; writes history of the Irish Guards. Fears cancer, but has (undiagnosed) stomach ulcer. Begins 'A Madonna of the Trenches'. Critical disfavour sets in, though sales of books among the general public remain high.
1924–32	Period of 'late Kipling': *Debits and Credits, Limits and Renewals*. Increasing attention paid to themes of shellshock and healing. Kipling Society formed (1927).
1935	Works on autobiography, *Something of Myself*.
1936	Dies (18 Jan).

1

The Significance of the Sahiba's Forefinger

> . . . but Fiction is built on fiction.
>
> (*A Book of Words*)

Among the vivid characters in Kipling's picaresque novel *Kim* (1901) is a rich, cantankerous and ultimately generous old lady called the Sahiba, who is introduced to Kim as a voice behind the embroidered curtain of a travelling bullock-cart. All that can be seen of her is a 'skinny brown finger heavy with rings'. This finger reappears later on in the book: ' "Oh, villain and shameless rogue!" The jewelled forefinger shook itself at him reprovingly' and ' "There is a talking mynah," the thrust came back with the well-remembered snap of the jewelled forefinger' (pp. 95, 97, 101, 302).

Readers of Kipling will recognise a number of his hallmarks. There is his fondness for description through a species of synedoche – making the part stand for the whole. The jewelled forefinger is a pledge of the physical existence of the Sahiba; we know thereby that she is not a voice and nothing more. It becomes a mnemonic in a book crowded with character and incident; we remember the Sahiba by it. Closely connected to this predilection is Kipling's characteristic of revelation in concealment, of forcing the reader to infer the internal from the external, of hinting at what lies behind the curtain. (Elsewhere it may be what lies behind a veil, or in a newspaper parcel, curio-cabinet, waistcoat pocket or the human heart). Next, there is the 'repetition device', to use the term coined by C. A. Bodelsen, one of the pioneers of the post-war analytical approach to Kipling's art. As with 'jewelled forefinger' above, Kipling will often use a phrase or word several times in the same story or collection. Sometimes this device is a pointer to what a French critic of Kipling called the *clou*, or central idea of a story; sometimes it provides an alternative way into it.[1]

Next, the Sahiba's forefinger bears witness to a recurrent Kipling motif: unseen female power. Kim foolishly at first thinks that

1

women hinder a man's business (p. 366). Significantly, he almost immediately falls dangerously ill. He learns that he would be unable to act at all if his body were not massaged and nourished by the Sahiba; when he spontaneously acknowledges 'Mother, I owe my life to thee' he has learned something worth knowing. Critics who say that *Kim* presents us with a man's world[2] are telling only half the story, which, taken as a whole, casts an ironic eye on male assumptions that men rule the earth. Women, in *Kim*, and elsewhere in Kipling, wield a power that is often out of proportion to their visible presence in the tale. Of no other writer is the old edict 'Cherchez la femme' more apposite.

The incident is a good example of Kipling's kind of symbolic realism. The Sahiba's cart is introduced shortly after the often-quoted description of evening falling on the Grand Trunk Road, a locus that illustrates at its best Kipling's power of sensuous evocation of place; the skinny brown finger is as real as the mango-trees, the brass tweezers or any of the other descriptive details. Yet realism shades into the mythic; the Sahiba's words are convincingly those of a 'strong-tongued' old Indian lady in the India of the 1880s, but the reader is made tactfully aware that she is also figurative. Shrouded by curtains, visible only as a finger, her presentation has intimations of the sybilline.

Reinforcing these intimations is a piece of Kiplingesque allusiveness. In 1901 among Tennyson's most admired 'beauties' were the following lines from *The Princess*:

> Jewels five-words-long
> That on the stretched forefinger of all Time
> Sparkle for ever.
>
> (II.355)

In case the reader should wonder whether the allusion in *Kim* is a conscious one, Kipling has prefaced each appearance of the 'jewelled forefinger' with a phrase exactly five words long. The Tennyson allusion reiterates the central conflict of the book, the thing which prevents it from being an undisciplined sprawl. *Kim* is a story of a youth trying to decide whether to live for this world or for the next. An orphan, he finds substitute parents in the Lama and the Sahiba. The Lama represents the claims of Eternity and the immortal soul. The Sahiba, who provides both him and the Lama with food, represents the claims of Time and the mortal body. The pull, now of one, now of the other, and the youth's attempts to reconcile the two, underlie all the colourful incidents and delight in the teeming diversity of India which constitute *Kim*'s most immediate charm. And the greater rhythm of the book is reproduced in small details. The Tennyson tag suggests to the reader early on that *Kim* has an allegorical dimension, that the Sahiba *is* in a sense Time. That the five-word phrases are far from sparkling jewels of phraseology is a pleasant joke. Kipling's embellishment is functional, and is an attempt to fulfil one of Ruskin's dicta: that 'true ornament' should be 'beautiful in its place, and nowhere else' and should 'aid the effect of every portion of the building over which it has influence' (*The Stones of Venice*, i.xxxi.4; *Works*, ix, 284). (The point of adducing Ruskin will become clearer later.)

Kipling, boy and man, was undoubtedly bookish and his art is a highly intertextual one. In his posthumously published autobiography, *Something of Myself* (1937), he pays tribute to the solace of reading during the boyhood years when he was seemingly abandoned by his parents to Mrs Holloway of Southsea (1872–7). A spare, cryptic book, *Something of Myself* is nevertheless relatively lavish with references to his early reading. Reminiscences of him during his schooldays (1878–82) at United Services College record his bookishness. His early Indian stories were written for a well-read élite who shared his easy familiarity with the classics ancient and modern. No reader fails to observe the abundance of literary allusion in his works: many of them – 'Wireless', 'My Son's Wife', 'The Dog Hervey', 'The Janeites', 'Fairy-Kist' – hinge on knowledge of a particular text. It seems hardly credible that in 1939 Ann Weygandt should have felt obliged to defend him against the charge of unlettered Philistinism. Today, a reader is more likely either to complain that Kipling is too self-indulgently allusive, that he is an irritating show-off hitching a ride on the back of his betters, or to concur with Randall Jarrell that he is a past-master at 'making literature alive to us as social fact. Literature, in Kipling's stories, is something that makes behaviour, is as much an effective part of life as religion or politics.'[3]

In the above example, the allusive repetition device simply reinforces a larger pattern which few mature readers can have utterly missed. The following has the more complex purpose of directing the reader towards meanings which the narrator(s) are not fully aware of or do not wish to make explicit. It is drawn from the strange and memorable tale that Kipling wrote about six months before his marriage: 'The Disturber of Traffic' (1891).

The narrator, fog-bound in St Cecilia's lighthouse, listens to the keeper's story of Dowse, an 'intimate friend' of his, who was in charge of a lighthouse on Flores Strait in the Java Seas. His only companion was a 'sea gypsy' called Challong, a servant with whom he sometimes had violent fights and who laughed at him. 'His skin was in little flakes and cracks all over . . . his hands were all webby-foot too' (*MI* p. 7). Dowse begins to see white 'streaks' inside his head. This is an example of what Kipling called 'the pressure line', mental images formed under conditions of stress (*BW*, pp. 101–4). Dowse's sense of himself as 'white' is disintegrating, and the disintegration is visualised as parallel white lines with gaps between. Believing that traffic through the strait is producing the streaks, he gets Challong to make bogus wreck-buoys to scare ships away, and is successful until the Admiralty Survey ship investigates. Dowse is rescued, leaving Challong behind; he is brought back to sanity of a sort through hard work and a transitional self-imposed period of proclaiming his 'crime' to the world in a purgatorial red jersey, but never completely shakes off his sense of guilt.

Morning breaks, the fog lifts; the narrator and the keeper can now 'thank the Lord for another day of clean and wholesome life', unlike Dowse. The story has been felt by critics to be 'purposely puzzling' and of a 'baffling obscurity', though it is easier to get a general sense of concealment (the fog, the oblique and unreliable narration) than to pin-point a specific area of obfuscation. Dowse has gone mad from isolation and lack of work – that is clear enough. Yet there is a character whose story is not told and whose only word may be mistranslated – Challong. He might not even exist – Craig Raine is quite certain that he is a projection of Dowse's diseased imagination.[4] His status is that of Dowse's 'shadow self'.

That characteristic nineteenth-century theme, the 'double' or 'shadow self', is treated many times by Kipling, and is often represented by a hanger-on, servant or animal companion. These companions are sometimes given names such as 'Challong' (along), 'Bimi' (by me), 'Jevins' (I came). Sometimes this relationship is symbiotic, comforting or creative, sometimes embarrassing, violent or anti-social, as here. Craig Raine has seen that Challong is a Sinbadian 'Man of the Sea', whom Dowse shakes off eventually. But Angus Wilson is also right in seeing Dowse and Challong as

variants of Prospero and Caliban. 'Challong . . . couldn't speak a
word of English except say "dam" and he said that where you and
me would say "yes"' (*MI*, p. 11) derives from Caliban's taunt 'You
taught me language and my profit on't/Is, I know how to curse',
and Shakespeare's Caliban is, like Challong, a 'strange fish'.[5]

The word 'dam' occurs many times; the last glimpse the reader
gets of Challong is of him swimming vainly in the wake of the
screw calling 'dam – dam'. As Dowse is taken to the Survey ship,
he hears a man calling over the loud hailer: 'One word he spelt
out again and again. – m-a-d, mad, – and he heard some one
behind him saying of it backwards. So he had two words, – m-a-d,
mad, d-a-m, dam; and he put they two words together as he
come on the quarter-deck, and he says to the captain very slowly,
"I be damned if I am mad"' (p. 19). 'Dam' is a *clou* of the tale. It
means 'mother' in Caliban-speak. Fenwick, the keeper, explains
that 'dam' means 'yes'; this is, however, one of Kipling's pseudo-
explanations. The reader can see more in the word, and that
Challong may be pathetically calling for his dead mother. But
Challong's mother might be, like Caliban's dam Sycorax, a
loathsome hag who tried to subject Ariel to 'earthy and abhorr'd
commands', and the cry an invocation. That Dowse has lived with
him for a whole year raises other interesting possible explanations
for his madness. Furthermore, 'dam' could be the imperative form
of a verb. Challong's 'dam – dam' could be telling Dowse to damn
his dam – that is, to curse his mother, and to curse one's mother
is to bring upon oneself the retribution of the Furies. Challong
would thus be the wicked self who tempts a man to curse his own
mother and thus separate him from the very source of life; to
recover his sanity, Dowse needs to lose him.

Here one notices the significance of there being no female
characters in the story, while at the same time femaleness surrounds
the men, who at crucial points refuse to recognise it. Fenwick says
that Dowse 'put they two words together', but the way he puts
them together is not to make, what one might expect, 'madam'
('my lady', 'my mother', 'a brothel proprietress'), but 'damned if I
am mad'. The word 'madam' has become literally unspeakable for
Dowse, having lived so long without a real female presence, which
is what has driven him to the edge of insanity. His wish to disturb
traffic resembles the disturbed Hamlet's desire to abolish marriage
because of his mother's lust. The flowery path (Flores) leads into a
strait presided over by Challong's deity, Loby Toby volcano,

gateway to hell. Dowse has become a misogynist with a fanatical mission to stop all intercourse between men and women, which is what 'traffic' stands for. When he suddenly recognises himself as 'mother-naked' on board the Survey ship, his rehabilitation can begin.[6]

Fenwick, by contrast, tends St Cecilia's light. Cecilia, patron of sacred music, is also a famous example of married chastity, having persuaded her spouse not to touch her after the manner of husbands. At dawn the men smell cows in the lighthouse pastures below, and this is part of the 'wholesome life' to which they are returned. (During the night they have been hearing a ship's siren 'bleating like an indignant calf'.) By day, below, the carnal, milky, maternal cows; by night, above, the fiercely protective white beams of magical virginity. The way in which 'above' may be related to 'below' is through the encouragement of lawful 'traffic', which prevents humans from becoming lonely islands in an estranging sea.

'The Disturber of Traffic' illustrates Kipling's allusiveness in saying the unsayable. Another technique employed is his strategic positioning of gloss and text. He locates one of the story's major themes – the self-destruction consequent on the denying and objectifying of women – in between the lines and at the margins of the story.

The short-story collection in which 'The Disturber of Traffic' occurs (*Many Inventions*) is prefaced by a poem entitled 'To the True Romance', in which a chivalrous speaker offers a prayer to a female idealism resembling Shelley's 'Intellectual Beauty' with motherliness superadded. One of her functions is to be 'A veil to draw 'twixt God His Law / And Man's infirmity'. 'The Disturber of Traffic' is the first story in the collection, and *it* is prefaced by a short poem ascribed to a pseudo-author, 'Miriam Cohen'. This ends with a prayer for

> A veil 'twixt us and Thee, dread Lord,
> A veil 'twixt us and thee:
> Lest we should hear too clear, too clear,
> And unto madness see!

This positioning means that the 'Miriam Cohen' poem follows right after 'To the True Romance', and the similarity of wording is a further hint to the reader that both sets of verses are to be directly related to 'The Disturber of Traffic'.

Who is 'Miriam Cohen'? Kipling elsewhere gives 'Miriam' as the Indian name for the Virgin and in another place stresses the Virgin's Jewishness.[7] 'Miriam Cohen', then, is an invented avatar of Mary as mediator between man and God; on the familial level, she is the angel–mother who stands between the misbehaving child and the chastising father. Similarly, the 'True Romance' is a Madonna–Muse figure, 'the curb of lust', who harmoniously controls time and tide. (The pun becomes apparent when read with reference to *tides* in 'The Disturber of Traffic'.) To abjure her is to incur the full rigour of 'God His Law'. Yet some of her praises are disturbingly ambiguous. The poet declares that it is at her decrees that mankind fashions ideas of not only Heaven but Hell also. She is an absence apprehended only in dream. Both poems idealise a female principle, while the characters in the story are chastened for failure to include it within their lives.

By presenting women in the story only under the disguises of cows, dams and lights, Kipling puts readers through a ritual of falling into an error analogous to that of the characters in the story, thus making it difficult for them to distance themselves from Dowse's mistake. This method of inducing self-identification with characters is used by many novelists, notably Jane Austen in *Emma*, but Kipling leaves the reader to write the *éclaircissement*. This 'entrapment' device is one which he uses repeatedly, and it is one of the main formal reasons for his oblique narration.

That effects such as those just discussed have not generally come to light earlier is partly due to the fact that the critical analysis of Kipling's work has not been very sizable, despite the high quality of some of it. Another, related reason may stem from the effort to define a 'good Kipling' who could be exempted from the critical disfavour that prevailed between (roughly) 1920 and 1970. The attempt, which begins with Edmund Wilson's 'The Kipling Nobody Read' (1941), detaches a novelistic Kipling canon, largely drawn from the post-1914 work. The tradition has by no means run dry. Among its most eminent representatives today are W. W. Robson, Angus Wilson and John Bayley. There are differences between the preferences of these critics and it would be wrong to say that this is the only Kipling which interests them. But the general tendency of their writing has been to privilege a Kipling who might claim a place in the same literary mansion as James, Chekhov, Conrad,

Joyce or Lawrence; one effect has been to devalue the Kipling who is working in a different or mixed genre like the romance of Hawthorne and Melville or Todorov's category, the literary fantastic.[8] Robson, for instance, wrote that Kipling's 'intent desire to have the completest possible *control* of his form and his medium can lead to impressive achievements in the realm of allegory, satiric fantasy, and fable – sometimes to the attainment of the higher reaches of symbol and myth. But it can also lead to a simplification and distortion of human character.'[9] Robson esteems Kipling most when 'his genius as a fabulist and myth-maker is felt to be shaping the story without detriment to the author's true and sensitive perceptions of actual human beings'. He locates this sensitivity in 'They', 'Mrs Bathurst', 'The Wish House', 'Mary Postgate' and 'The Gardener', which for him 'exemplify this power of the short story to suggest the *distillation* of a human life, the rendering of its essence as latent within a momentary situation'.[10]

This 'realist' Kipling is a concomitant of the placing of the True story above the Tall story, to adopt John Bayley's terms. The 'True' is the short story which derives its conventions from the nineteenth-century realist novel. It tends to shade into the novella or to give the impression of length, leisure and spaciousness, and is often written by a writer who is known primarily *as* a novelist. Plot tends to serve the demands of inwardness of characterisation or creation of mood rather than the other way round. Such are the short stories of Tolstoy, James, Lawrence and Joyce. The Tall derives its conventions from the folk or fairy tale, legend or parable. The entire story may be the expansion of a symbol. Characterisation tends to serve the demands of plot and form; it is often claimed that the form in itself is antagonistic to characterisation. In the hands of practitioners of the 'new short story' such as Babel or Borges or Tommaso Landolfi, this kind tends towards brevity, self-conscious referentiality to other literature, and preoccupation with the manipulation of conventions. If one were to apply these categories to Kipling (Bayley doesn't explicitly do so, and warns readers that they are not mutually exclusive), most would say that the bulk of his work derives from the conventions of the Tall rather than the True. Significantly, Babel and Borges admired Kipling greatly.[11]

The features which place Kipling's tales with the Tall rather than the True make him amenable to certain modern critical approaches. As Hugh Brogan put it, 'the most recent critical schools . . . have taught us how to rejoice in the cunning of narration. . . . We ought to turn to him, that most cunning of all narrators, with increased respect and with a new readiness to find out how he gets his effects.'[12] An analysis of how his most common rhetorical devices, such as paronomasia and anaphrasis, produce and reverse meaning, would be worth making, as would a critical account of certain marked stylistic traits, such as his eroticising of cars, boats, hedges, rivers and mines. However, it is on more familiar grounds that I would urge a fresh look at Kipling the allegorist, mythographer, fabulist, ritualist, satirist and artificer. Jarrell's opinion was that, though Kipling is one of 'the most effectively realistic of writers', he is 'far closer to Gogol than to a normal realist or naturalist'. I don't think that Jarrell's remark (or Brogan's) has been developed enough. It seems to be such a widely accepted truism that Kipling *suffered* from 'a constant debilitating pressure to make fable' that it has not been sufficiently considered whether the 'debilitation' may not be in some cases a strength.[13]

The result is that certain stories have been regarded as slighter, less artistically unified, boring, sentimental, pretentious or at all events *different* from what I believe them to be. Exorcisms of ferocious hatred have been read as 'pure' comic exuberance; his bitterest tales have been regarded as failed attempts to mimic the inextinguishable laughter of the cosmos. His allusiveness has been pronounced flashy decoration. Kipling, Louis Cornell has said, is a parodist who 'never fully developed the gift of assimilation. Unlike Joyce and Eliot and Pound he never learned to use the work of earlier writers in such a way as to make it his own.'[14] It would be more true to say that his example helped the first two writers to make the work of earlier ones their own, and that he had a very self-conscious relationship with his literary ancestors – that of the epigone, the less distinguished son of a distinguished father. He did not consider that he lived in a golden age of literature, nor was he encouraged to do so; that 'The Age of Giants' was dead was a journalistic cliché of the period.[15] The picture that Kipling's father drew for him of a small bespectacled schoolboy bringing up the rear behind the mighty Homer, Dante, Shakespeare, Keats, Tennyson and Browning was prophetic.[16] He had a special relationship to the second and the last, writers of the allegorical dream vision, verse tale and dramatic monologue.

In a few cases, some of his otherwise most discerning critics have helped to obfuscate his methods. One such example concerns

Kipling's names, declared by C. A. Bodelsen to be, with few exceptions, 'arbitrary labels';[17] if true, this would make him different from his contemporaries, who often gave names either quite obviously symbolic or suggestive of moral qualities and function through the association of ideas. Examples include Sue Bridehead (Hardy), Sir Willoughby Patterne (Meredith), Mrs Gracedew (James) and Kurtz (Conrad). While critics such as Marghanita Laski and Craig Raine have drawn attention to the importance of Kipling's nomenclature, it remains a remarkably unexplored area even now, and, as there is some anecdotal evidence to support Bodelsen, it needs to be argued for.

NAMES IN KIPLING

Even his most outlandish names (Pinecoffin, Masquerier) were those of real people, and their choice might simply reflect a taste for life's bizarreries. He once asked friends to supply him with unusual names for a story ('The Man Who Would Be King') and, when they came up with 'Peachy Taliaferro Wilson' and 'Dravo', he adopted them with only a few changes.[18] But he assigned the names in a way that was far from arbitrary. Peachy Taliaferro Carnehan is the survivor who brings back the tale and Dravot's head. 'Taliaferro' is imperfect Latin for 'I bear such things'. 'Dravot' suggests 'bravo', 'drive' and 'idiot', the man's pig-headed courage and demonic motivation. Kipling was following the principle that the apparent randomness of life contains design, if one can but see it, as Leonardo found ideas for compositions in the forms made by wall-mosses. Kipling at several times in his own life noticed significance in fortuitous names, such as 'Lorne Lodge' (the childhood Southsea 'House of Desolation' which he called 'Forlorn Lodge') and 'Bliss Cottage', setting of his early happy married life in Vermont.[19]

There is an interesting record of Kipling's evolution of a definitely allegorical name; in 1908 he helped Rider Haggard plot a story about Death appearing in the form of a personified Yellow Peril. The notes that survive (in Kipling's hand) show Death's name evolving from 'Taung' through 'Tarkoth', 'Murth' and 'Morgue', until it finally settles into 'Murgh', the name adopted; the process shows Kipling, in order to achieve 'economy of implication', composing portmanteau names as Lewis Carroll created portmanteau words; 'Murgh' grew from 'morgue' (both the Paris mortuary and the sorceress), but also from 'murther' with the *gh* adding a faintly Mongolian flavour via associations with Genghis Khan.[20]

Most of Kipling's names (which include those of ships and places as well as characters) fall into the following categories, with considerable overlap.

1   A substratum of names apparently intended to establish social class or nationality. Examples: Maud and Edith Copleigh (the well-bred maidens of 'False Dawn'), the Irish Mulvaney.
2   Names that may have private associations. Sir James Betton in 'The Tender Achilles' (*LR*) seems to have grown out of Sir John Bland-Sutton, Kipling's surgeon. 'Vickery' was the name of the head of Kipling's unhappy first school; one Vickery is killed off prematurely in *The Light that Failed* (p. 136) and another is disposed of in 'Mrs Bathurst'. But in the second case it may also have been chosen to suggest the character's seeming moral superiority.
3   Names alluding to other works of fiction, proverbial sayings, and the like. The Soldiers Three are called 'The Three Muske-teers' and the Cockney 'Ortheris' is a portmanteau version of Dumas's 'Athos' and 'Aramis'. It is also a homophome of 'author-is', which is a pointer that he is a persona of Kipling himself. 'Mr Wardle', the dog in 'Bubbling Well Road' (*LH*) is named after the hospitable owner of 'Dingley Dell' in *Pickwick Papers*, and, like all Kipling's pet dogs, is a warder-off of evil. 'Tedda Gabler', the silly mare in 'A Walking Delegate' (*DW*) is Kipling's dig at *Hedda Gabler*, a play he detested. 'Tillie Venner' ('Wressley of the Foreign Office', *PT*), an empty-headed flirt, is a sister under the skin to the snake-woman Elsie Venner, the eponymous heroine of Oliver Wendell Holmes's novel. ('Once upon a time there were three little sisters whose names were Elsie, Lacie and Tillie', as Lewis Carroll's Dormouse said.)

Sometimes a marker (*Mc*, *-son*) is added to suggest that the character is a successor to a literary or legendary archetype. Examples are 'McRimmon of the Blackbird Line' ('Bread upon the Waters', *DW*), McRimmon being the unscrupulous ship owner to whom the shoddily treated engineer, McPhee, transfers his loyalties. Two biblical allusions are present here – 'bowing down in the house of Rimmon' and 'the labourer is worthy of his hire' (McFee). Sometimes *-son* indicates the epigone (Nickson, Judson, Jobson). Tomlinson is a modern Tam Lin, and like his 'parent' goes to Hell and back, but, whereas Tam Lin was a true quester, Tomlinson is rejected by the devil as too feeble even for damnation.

4 Names which without being exact indicators of character or functions have a general relevance to the theme of the tale. The Freemason Brother Lemming ('In the Interests of the Brethren', *DC*) is not especially suicidal, but he has been part of the self-destructive mass stampede of the Great War. Shend ('The Dog Hervey', *D of C*) does not ruin but is ruined. Badelia Herodsfoot (*MI*) is not bad but maligned. The story is about a slaughter of the innocent and she is kicked around by a male tyrant.

5 Straightforwardly symbolic names: Dowse, Pinecoffin, Golightly, Mrs Reiver (the 'bad woman' of Simla), or those requiring little change of spelling to become so – for example, Tarrion, who 'tarries on'.

6 More complicated versions of 5, sometimes involving anagrams, homophones and macaronics. Robert Keede, the Masonic doctor–narrator of some of the later stories about disease and madness, is the man who is 'keyed' in, like a stone in an arch. His initials, 'RK', also hint that, like Ortheris, he is Kipling's second self. The tomboyish and independent Philadelphia Bucksteed ('Marklake Witches', *RF*) is unwilling to surrender the keys of her father's house to the detested housekeeper, 'old Amoore'. 'I'm never going to be married' (p. 93). 'Amoore' is of course 'Amor'; Philadelphia refuses to see that she has two suitors, and similarly screens from herself the knowledge that she is dying of a consumption. Her first name means 'brotherly love', which is all she wants from a man. She is a rebellious young filly who refuses to be 'tamed' by love and struggles to keep her independence. With 'Yardley-Orde' ('The Head of the District', *LH*) the double-barrelled name suggests that he belongs to a ruling caste but also that he kept his yard in order.

A sub-group of names indicate opposite qualities within the character. Mrs Hauksbee of Simla is both Hawk and Bee, predatory, busy, and sweet as honey. Jack Pansay ('The Phantom 'Rickshaw', *WWW*), pursued to his death by the ghost of his deserted mistress, represents in his name both the rakish jackal or 'wild dog' that he once was and the memory-crazed man be confesses himself to be. 'Pansay' derives from *pensée* (thought) and, perhaps, 'pan-say', i.e. 'tell everything'. (Why his first name is Theobald eludes me.) Dumoise, the doomed doctor of 'By Word of Mouth' (*PT*), is nicknamed 'Dormouse', a sobriquet that has obviously grown out of his name as well as his sleepy habits.

7 There is a *tendency* for certain first names to be given to characters who have a particular kind of function or cluster or related qualities. Robert (Keede) and its variant Robin are both good fellows and storytellers, benign survivors. 'Kitty' tends to be a young man's first love.

Very important is the scatter of the name Mary and its variants Maria, Maisie, Minnie and Miriam. One group of Marys is associated with the Madonna, pity, maternity and the ideal woman, as in 'Miriam Cohen' and 'Mary's Meadow' in 'Fairy-Kist'. The other group includes the virago (Maria Shemahen in 'Aunt Ellen', *LR*) and the cold-hearted virgin (Maisie in *The Light that Failed*). At least one Mary partakes of both sets of qualities: the eponymous Mary Postgate (*D of C*) combines implacable hatred with a maternal devotion to children.

INVERSION AND METAGROBOLISATION

Kipling is fascinated by situations where an extremity suddenly recoils and becomes its contrary – the fool persisting in his folly until he becomes wise, or Dante finding that the deepest point of Hell is the way out to Purgatory. Related to this are two stylistic quirks: a fondness for anaphrasis – saying, for instance, 'Bless God' when one means 'Curse God'; and for palinodic constructions – an accumulation of instances, suddenly followed by a swift clause that abolishes or inverts what has gone before with a 'which it isn't' or something of the sort. Jarrell, in what must surely be the best description of Kipling's predilection for polarities, falls himself into the style: Kipling, he wrote,

was obsessed by – wrote about, dreamed about, and stayed awake so as not to dream about – many concentration camps, of the soul as well as of the body; many tortures, hauntings, hallucinations, deliria, diseases, nightmares, practical jokes, revenges, monsters, insanities, neuroses, abysses, forlorn hopes, last chances, extremities of every kind; these and their sweet opposites.[21]

What Jarrell stops just short of saying is that Kipling fashions the heavens out of a 'metagrobolisation' of the hells. (I am not here concerned with determining whether Kipling does this consciously.) Anyone trying to track symbolic codes in Kipling quickly discovers his tendency to invert the moral and emotional meaning of his own value-system.

In his children's fiction one finds symbols, settings and narrative elements associated with playful triumph which in his adult work are freighted with pain and tragedy. For instance, one of the most popular of the *Just So Stories*, 'The Elephant's Child', is a rewriting of the disturbing 'A Matter of Fact' (*MI*), to be discussed more fully in Chapter 3. The greasy water, smell of musk, grey serpentine shapes and thrashing death-throes in the adult tale re-emerge in the children's tale transformed into a story about successfully resisting predictions of doom. The helpless serpent mate in 'A Matter of Fact' is replaced by the effective bi-coloured Python Rock Snake. Wounding produces copious blood in the first story, but in 'The Elephant's Child' Kipling excludes the idea from his child reader's visual imagination by making the young Elephant's encounter with the Crocodile's teeth produce merely soreness and bruising. Adult wanderings end in loneliness and the glimpse into the abyss. The child's curiosity, courage and simplicity lead to 'the real, the marvellous Jungle, where we may meet our friends'.[22]

Such 'metagrobolisations' can be seen within Kipling's adult fiction too. In the 'rewritten' version the wounder proves to be a healer, and that which was lost is found. This is especially true of the fiction written in the ebulliently hopeful Vermont years just after his marriage (1892–6). One of these stories, 'The Brushwood Boy' (1895), recycles the misogynistic, semi-autobiographical novel *The Light that Failed* (1890). Maisie, the destructive heroine of the latter, has black hair, grey eyes and a 'firmly-modelled' mouth. In 'The Brushwood Boy', the tale which contains Kipling's nearest approximation to a conventional romantic heroine, Miriam has black hair, grey eyes and a 'well-cut' mouth. Thereafter, Kipling systematically reverses the situation of *The Light that Failed*. Both heroes spend their young manhood abroad, but, whereas Dick is wild and promiscuous, George is a Sir Galahad. In *The Light that Failed* Dick and Maisie are orphans who, despite spending their adolescence together and having a common interest in art, prove hopelessly ill-matched. In 'The Brushwood Boy' George and Miriam have at least one supportive parent, meet only once as children, have no interests in common except, significantly, horse-riding, but are bonded to each other through shared dream experiences and innocent carnal knowledge. Whereas the heartless Maisie has a revulsion against the fleshly and shrinks with horror from the blinded hero, the child Miriam gazes with sympathetic curiosity at George's cut finger on his proudly removing his 'di-ack-lum plaster', and places a forefinger on his hand. It is this moment of knowledge in the flesh and bone rather than shared dreams or elective affinities that unites the destinies of the two children; it takes place, appropriately, during a merely mechanical operation of the spirit, a performance of the 'Pepper's Ghost' illusionist entertainment in which skeletons dance. This childhood memory is the only one which the adult lovers do not allude to when reviewing their shared experiences, and their amnesia is a pointer to its importance. The greatest intimacies are secret, and that which is not spoken of is the real thing.

Sometimes Kipling presents not 'sweet opposites' but contrasting treatments of similar subjects, and alerts his readership by their placement in the collection. Such are 'Aunt Ellen' and 'Fairy-Kist', juxtaposed in the late collection *Limits and Renewals*. The first treats its theme farcically; the second recycles it as a serious detective story. The common links are violence towards women, lorries, the name Ellen and the not-guilty man who feels the pangs of guilt. Both are about how men exorcise an irrational belief that they are being ordered by demonic forces to rid the world of 'light women'.[23]

DECEPTION AND 'THE LADY OR THE TIGER?'

At this point I should like to explore further the question of 'missing Kipling's point', which is only in part due to the predilections of critics and readers' unreadiness to take up the clues he offered. He is, as 'The Disturber of Traffic' and 'The Brushwood Boy' partly demonstrate, a layer of false trails, a maker of pseudo-apocalypses in which everything except the really crucial thing is unveiled, a treader on the dangerous edge of things where one life-filling passion lies a hair's breadth away from its opposite, a teller of parables to the blind. In finding biographical reasons for this –

Kipling's early schooling in concealing his feelings, his seeking compensation for his insecurities in privileged access to the secrets of Inner Rings – we are apt to forget that there is a well-established precedent for the conception of the artist as a concealer of knowledge. As seer or creator god, the artist is not obliged to make clear statements. As Bishop Blougram says to the hack writer Gigadibs, in the Browning poem which so impressed Kipling at school, God's naked godhead is too 'searing' to be borne:

> Some think, Creation's meant to show him forth:
> I say it's meant to hide him all it can,
> And that's what all the blessed evil's for.
> *(Bishop Bloughram's Apology,* ll.652–4)

Gigadibs and Blougram – the journalist whose role is to reveal the naked truth, and the compassionate sophist who veils it from poor humankind who cannot bear very much reality – are perpetually at war. The concept of the artist as concealer was given a forcible restatement by Ruskin, whose influence on the Pre-Raphaelites and Kipling will be treated in more detail in Chapter 2. All great art, he wrote, *intentionally* communicates by occult means. But mystification is not an end in itself: the creator is a psychologist with theories about how the mind works. He veils his truth because mystery arouses curiosity and stimulates the mind to seek for meaning. The investment of effort and the pleasure of unweaving the riddle ensure that the discovery will be indelibly printed on the imagination and memory, more so than if it had lain open on the 'surface'. Such was Bunyan's apology for writing allegory, and such was Ruskin's justification of Spenser's doing so. (The precedent was, of course, Holy Writ, where God has veiled his truths in 'Types, Shadows and Metaphors'; the most notable modern secular equivalent is *Ulysses*.) This 'withholding of their meaning is continual, and confessed, in the great poets', so 'You may not get it till you have forged the key of it in a furnace of your own heating.' One should read Greek legend as if tracing threads 'through figures on a silken damask: the same thread runs through the web, but it makes part of different figures . . . in different lights it is dark or light . . . sometimes you cannot tell black from purple, nor blue from emerald'. So the Sirens may represent either vain, fatal desire, or 'noble and saving' constant desire (Ruskin, *Works*, xix, 308–9, 315, 316).

Kipling used the same metaphor of shot silk when describing his 'double-and-treble-figured' art, both in the introduction to the Outward Bound Edition of his works and in his autobiography: 'I worked the material in three or four overlaid tints and textures, which might or might not reveal themselves according to the shifting light of sex, youth, and experience' (*SM*, p. 190). He here allies himself to Ruskin's hermeneutics – perhaps consciously; it is quite possible that the passage was familiar to him.

He also shares with Ruskin an awareness that the work of creative artists may contain a meaning 'which they themselves cannot interpret, – which it may be for ages long after them to interpret' (Ruskin, *Works*, xix, 309). In his 1926 address to the Royal Literary Society Kipling declared that what future ages may consider worth preserving of a writer's work 'may be diverted to ends of which the writer never dreamed. . . . The true nature and intention . . . of a writer's work does not lie within his own knowledge' (*BW*, pp. 283–4). This may sound like an anticipation of the concept of the 'Death of the Author', but Kipling claws back the belief that an author's intentions *are* communicable to future generations. The example he uses is that of Swift, who, he says, goes

> scourged through life between the dread of insanity and the wrath of his own soul warring with a brutal age. He exhausts mind, heart and brain in that battle: he consumes himself, and perishes in utter desolation. Out of all his agony remains one little book, his dreadful testament against his fellow-kind, which today serves as a pleasant tale for the young under the title of *Gulliver's Travels*. That, and a faint recollection of some baby-talk in some love-letters, is as much as the world has chosen to retain of Jonathan Swift, Master of Irony. Think of it! It is like tuning-down the glare of a volcano to light a child to bed!   (p. 284)

Kipling despises a 'world' that maintains a stubborn *enfantillage* and refuses to face Swift's glare; he protests against his appropriation by the nursery. (He was setting up no straw man; one still may find in the popular press *Gulliver's Travels* described as a 'children's favourite'.) Of course there is a certain amount of self-identification going on; the affinity of Kipling to Swift was noticed many years ago by Bonamy Dobrée.[24]

Despite having the benefit of hindsight (Defoe's *The Shortest Way with Dissenters* furnishing the classic instance of how irony may misfire) Kipling complicates matters for himself by tuning down his own volcano. Sometimes he can be downright disingenuous about being misread, as in his fly-leaf inscription on a copy of *Stalky & Co.*: 'It is in the nature of a moral tract – only a perverse generation insists on calling it comic and a boy's book and a lot of other things which it isn't.'[25] Yet, by filling the book with uproarious japes and cocking a snook at school stories such as *Eric or Little by Little* which *were* recognisably 'moral tracts', Kipling was ensuring, and perhaps proving to himself, that the public was 'perverse'. One is reminded of Kierkegaard's shrewd remarks on the psychology of the ironist. 'The more the ironist succeeds in deceiving and the better his falsification progresses, so much the greater is his satisfaction. But he experiences this satisfaction in solitude and his concern is precisely that no one notices his deception.'[26]

Was it one of Kipling's intentions to achieve deliberate irresolvability? The shot-silk metaphor says yes – the thread is neither dark nor bright but will appear one or the other under shifting light. And there were precedents for the 'irresolvable' story available to the late nineteenth century. One might cite the Boccacian or Chaucerian tale ending in a *demande* – the overt admission by the storyteller that the problems of moral judgement posed by the story are too complex for any one person to solve. Which of the three men – the husband, the squire or the magician – acted most generously? The *demande* has no right answers but is a test of readers and listeners, who gain in self-knowledge or reveal their characters to one another, if one supposes an ensuing public discussion.

Another precedent was the story ending in a dilemma intended to 'tease us out of thought'. One such was a favourite of Kipling's: Lewis Carroll's *Through the Looking Glass*, which poses the question, is Alice a dream in the Red King's mind, or *vice versa*? – a restatement, for children, of the old idealist–empiricist debate. Another was the once famous but now comparatively obscure 'The Lady or the Tiger?' Published in Scribner's prestigious *Century Magazine* in November 1882 when Kipling was just short of seventeen, this fable made the author, Frank Stockton, a celebrity overnight and set the magazine reading-public a-buzz. 'A "Lady or the Tiger?" literature was the result' wrote a contributor to *Century* four years later, 'while no end of it gave new life to literary and debating societies.' A modern editor writes of its contemporary impact: 'The author was besieged by thousands of letters seeking the answer to the last line of the story: "And so I leave it with all of you: which came out of the opened door – the lady or the tiger?" '[27] The build-up to this cliff-hanger was a situation in which a commoner whose crime was to love a princess had to decide his own fate by choosing to open one of two identical doors leading into an arena. One concealed a hungry tiger, the other a beautiful lady. If he opened the tiger's door he would be eaten; if the lady's, he would be married to her. The princess, having discovered which was which, had the power to save her lover by gesturing to him as he stood in the arena. But, torn between jealousy and love, which door did she indicate? The only help that Stockton gave his correspondents was 'If you decide which it was – the lady or the tiger – you find out what kind of a person you are yourself.' That Kipling knew 'The Lady or the Tiger?' is not certain, but the plot is easily transmissible by word of mouth and he need not have had access to *Century Magazine* in order to have used it as a model.[28] At any rate, we find him in his early stories hitting on a similar formula, as in 'Haunted Subalterns': 'The Devil may have been a hoax. If so, it was one of the best ever arranged. If it was not a hoax . . . but you must settle that for yourselves' (Haining, p. 82).

'Haunted Subalterns' is a rather feeble example of a group of Kipling tales which fit Todorov's theory of the 'literary fantastic'. In this genre, 'the text must oblige the reader to consider the world of the characters as a world of living persons and to hesitate between a natural and a supernatural explanation of the events described'. This hesitancy makes anxiety about the 'real' and the 'unreal' its central concern.[29] This certainly applies to 'The Disturber of Traffic', where the reader may regard Challong either as a hallucination or as a supernatural being, and, I would argue, to a number of Kipling stories not normally regarded as straddling the real–unreal boundary. At least it is still not generally recognised that in 'The Man Who Would Be King' Peachey's account of the mission can be read as a delusion which a fevered journalist's imagination has conjured up from an actual encounter, with Dravot's head having the same kind of reality as Poe's Raven and the same kind of function – to depart 'nevermore' from the narrator's consciousness. 'There the matter rests' – the tale's final sentence – contains a pun on 'matter', which is both the narrator's problem and the head which Peachey desposited on his table.

But, on further consideration, 'The Lady or the Tiger?' proves

to have an answer of sorts, one arising from the choice of genre –
the fable – and the very fact of the reader's attention being drawn
to *this* particular dilemma. The success of the story lay not just in
its clever trick ending but in its having hit a nerve, in a culture
where marriage was simultaneously regarded as a lottery and the
summum bonum. 'The criminal could not know', Stockton archly
tells us, 'whether he was to be married or devoured.' In a world
governed by chance, young men are terrified that marriage may
be devouring, the Lady a Tiger and the House of Life also that of
Death.[30]

Many of Kipling's stories are brilliant elaborations of the crude
'Lady or the Tiger?' model in which the reader's attention is
directed away from and then directed back to the real subject,
rather than deliberate exercises in total ambivalence. If we look at
the shot-silk metaphor more closely, we can see that it supposes
that there are readers who know that the 'colour' is both dark and
bright, and who can see the totality of 'figures', even though at
any given time they are forced to be looking at only one. As in
many Poe stories (for example, 'The Oblong Box' and 'Never Bet
the Devil your Head'), an unreliable narrator offers a pseudo-
explanation of a mystery. The explanation will be taken at its face
value by naïve readers, while 'knowing' readers see more.[31] The
naïve and the knowing are not, however, offered as equally valid.
The knowing assimilates the naïve. Once one has 'seen more' one
can't go back again and 'see less'. 'Friendly Brook' (*D of C*) is an
example. Was the drunken father killed by the old mother, by Jim,
by the adopted daughter Mary, or by the Brook? A close reading
reveals that all of them have connived, Jim in intention if not in
deed.

For these reasons, I think that it is often possible to determine
'what happens' in a Kipling story while balancing this against
Kipling's own awareness that a writer inevitably relinquishes
control over his creation. Hesitancy over a text's mode will affect
the state of mind produced by the reading – anxiety or excitement,
for instance – but does not necessarily make for total indeterminacy
of its events or theme. The proposition that 'The Disturber of
Traffic' is about the perils of misogyny is one which may be justified
whether the story is deemed to be a supernatural tale, allegory or
realistic psycho-drama, or whether the reader hesitates between
these alternatives.

Kipling's complicating of the 'You must settle that for yourselves' formula involved the evolution of a strategy of composition radically different from that of Stockton, who claimed that 'the story contains everything [I] ever knew about the incident'. This is totally unlike Kipling's 'blacking out' of portions of his final drafts (*SM*, pp. 207–8). The author consciously withholds something from the published version, but the 'excised stuff', Kipling wrote, 'must have been honestly written for inclusion'. This does not mean that the reader will necessarily fill the hiatus with what the author omitted, but the possibility of reclaiming the omission is always there. The resemblance between this procedure and that of Hemingway has been noticed on several occasions. In *A Moveable Feast*, Hemingway described how in the 1920s he discovered that he could omit 'anything' from a story, provided that he did so deliberately. The cutting-out 'would strengthen the story and make people feel something more than they understood'. Thus he 'omitted the real end' of his short story 'Out of Season' – 'that the old man hanged himself.' It has been plausibly conjectured that Hemingway hit on this technique through his study of Kipling.[32] In short, I consider that Kipling's stories reserve information indefinitely rather than infinitely, though it is possible that some of his stories will never be decoded by anyone and that certain figures and threads will never be seen. In *Just So Stories* the tribe preserve an alphabet necklace where P and Q are missing. 'They were lost, a long time ago, in a great war, and the tribe mended the necklace with the dried rattles of a rattlesnake, but nobody ever found P and Q. That is how the saying began, "You must mind your P's and Q's"' (*JSS*, p. 166). The missing letters are not there, yet the tribe knows what should fill the gap, so they are both retrievable and irretrievable. This little apologue furnishes Kipling's readers with an interpretative method.

'The Lady or the Tiger?' exemplifies contemporary fascination with the 'puzzle' story' and shows that there are late-nineteenth-century cultural contexts still to be made available for understanding of Kipling's art.[33] There are others, which require not so much retrieval as more attention, notably some of the sources of his symbolic realism.

2
Aunt Judy, Ruskin, Carlyle

I also know, a dark Similitude
Will on the Fancie more it self intrude,
And will stick faster in the Heart and Head,
Than things from Similies not borrowed.
(Bunyan, *Pilgrim's Progress*)

Kipling's boyhood and youth were passed during the period of
the secularisation of middle-class children's literature, previously
dominated by Evangelical 'realistic' moral tales such as those of
Mrs Sherwood. While these were still a powerful force, there were
countercurrents. What was later to harden into an early-twentieth-
century orthodoxy, the view that fairytale, folklore, legend and
myth not only could but should form the basis of early moral
education as the child re-enacted the history of mankind, was
being shaped in the 1860s and 1870s. Kipling's early reading was
so catholic that no dominant trend can be isolated, yet it was
indubitably rich in these areas – indeed, richer than most. In
addition to his imbibing the usual Grimm, Andersen, Kingsley's
The Heroes and Aesop, his favourite 'Aunt Georgie' Burne-Jones
read him *The Arabian Nights* and his honorary 'Uncle Topsy'
(William Morris) tried out on him the Icelandic saga that he
happened to be translating. At school he joined in a craze for Joel
Chandler Harris's *Uncle Remus* (*SM*, pp. 12–14).[1] The oral tradition
of Indian storytelling came to him through his ayah and he
extended his familiarity with it upon his return to India in 1882.
He was a lifelong, if miscellaneous, collector of anthologies of and
commentaries upon the mythic and folkloric.[2]

The former dominance of the 'realistic' moral tale, even when it
began to loosen, did affect the manner in which myth was
transmitted to mid-Victorian children. Evangelical habits of reading
encouraged close textual analysis, the goal of which was the
finding of meaningful patterns and moral order underlying surface
heterogeneity. Applied first of all pre-eminently to the Scriptures,
this discipline could be readily transferred to the 'reading' of nature

or art. An instance of this transference is Margaret Gatty's *Parables from Nature* (1855–71), where a detailed knowledge of botany and geology is used to illuminate the hidden purposes of a loving Creator. (Kipling's 'Uncle Ned' Burne-Jones had provided an illustration.) When at about the age of thirteen 'the full tide of writing set in' for Kipling, it was this book which he tried to imitate. He never did give up writing parables from nature.[3]

Children from the cultivated, artistic milieu into which Kipling was born were encouraged to become self-conscious interpretative critics of their reading and even their dreams, as may be seen from a mind-stretching but absurd story called 'Bryde's Riddle' by Blanche Dundas. This appeared in the 1876 annual volume of *Aunt Judy's Magazine*, edited by Margaret Gatty and, later, her daughter. In 1919 Kipling told Lady Gregory that he had 'loved *Aunt Judy's Magazine* but hated *The Sunday at Home*' as a child, which suggests that he had read more of *Aunt Judy's* than the one bound copy of 1872 which he knew 'almost by heart'. But, even if one cannot be sure that he read this particular one, it is worth quoting for its representative quality.[4]

Impetuous, bored Bryde flounces out of the schoolroom, unable to see the relevance of the story of Persephone to her life. Jumping into a convenient boat, she is swiftly wrecked. In a coma, half-drowned, she dreams of wanderings among dead things – fallen leaves, defunct harvest mice and empty nests – through a cave where she sees a plumeless peacock and a coiled-up snake lying upon dried narcissi. Then she arrives at a flowering valley, presided over by a fully feathered peacock. On being revived, she recognises the resemblance of her dream to the Persephone myth, and asks her mother to interpret further. Mother, clearly a believer in the collective unconscious, obliges. 'Why, mother, was Persephone picking a narcissus?' 'What did the snake in your dream, Bryde?' 'Sleep.' 'What upon?' 'The dried narcissus flowers.' 'It is strange, Bryde, how true to the meaning of the myth your dream was; and yet not strange either, for all the ideas were in your mind.' Mother then offers an introduction to solar mythology: 'Many clever men who have studied languages think that our pretty northern tale of "The Sleeping Beauty" is only another version of the fanciful Eastern myth . . . we may even, I daresay, find a meaning as old for "Jack the Giant Killer".' Bryde asks if the peacock 'had any value'. Mother demurs: 'You have gone to the opposite extreme now, and are determined to find a meaning in everything', but

remembers that the peacock is a symbol of the resurrection in early
Christian art. 'This leads us to a yet deeper meaning. What sleep
does winter prefigure?'[5] The message is clear: children may be
encouraged to unpick pagan myth since, wisely pursued, the
activity will lead to a greater awareness of the beauty of Christianity.

The story is also of interest because it illustrates the filtration
into children's literature of the new academic study of comparative
myth. From 1850 to 1890 this was dominated by Max Müller,
Professor of Sanskrit at Oxford. He and his disciples, the 'clever
men who have studied languages', applied philology to a theory
of the origin of myth, which they located in the worship of
cosmic forces, notably the sun. Their dominance ended with the
publication in 1891 of Frazer's *The Golden Bough*, key work of the
Cambridge-based school of mythography, which had its origins in
the work of the anthropologist E. B. Tylor. Thus Kipling's lifetime
spans a golden age of comparative mythology, which provides a
context for his own myth-making art. Though not allying himself
to any of the 'schools' of mythography, he shows himself aware
of them. There are several, rather flippant references to Max Müller
and his 'Solar Mythology' in his early work; the recurrence in his
writing of the motif of 'six months' periods (of leave of absence or
activity of some kind) indicates his absorption of the Solar Myth's
central idea. But Kipling probably found the anthropological
approach more congenial, though he never embraced whole-
heartedly Frazer's model of mankind progressing from magical
thought to scientific enlightenment, being too much of a magical
thinker himself.[6]

Kipling exemplifies rather starkly some possible effects of an
immersion in one kind of myth – the foregrounding of cyclical
time, the reification of a human nature which remains unchanged
'beneath' changing garments, emphasis on the continual inter-
penetration of the present by the past. Each generation is a
reincarnation, and the illustrious are avatars. As he wrote in his
final apologia, 'You ask: "Why inflict on us legends of your Middle
Ages?" Because in life as in literature, its sole enduring record, is
no age. Men and Things come round again, eternal as the seasons'
(*SM*, p. 223). The sentiment is hardly unique to Kipling; it may be
found in his contemporaries, and is the obverse of that mythicising
of modern life that is so marked a feature of late-nineteenth-century
and modernist art. (Ibsen's *Ghosts* is a retelling of the Curse of the
House of Atreus; Hardy's Angel Clare is a false avatar of Lord

Krishna – he does sport among the milkmaids, but his Victorian upbringing prevents him from becoming the genially divine lover that the girls desire.) Moreover, it is an underlying assumption of at least 600 years of Western culture. Chaucer's Knight put it bluntly: 'Ther is no newe gyse that it nas old.' It had a sophisticated restatement in the 1950s from 'myth critics' such as Northrop Frye, who argued that the conventions of almost all literature derive from the plot-patterns of myth.

Another effect of Evangelicanism was to shape a conception of the world that had affinities to the *mentalité* of the Middle Ages. This may seem unlikely, given the Evangelical distrust of things papistical, but the Victorian Catholic and Evangelical Protestant had common ground in their opposition to materialism. The Evangelical practice of daily meditation upon the Bible and the assiduous reading of Bible commentary and exegetical sermons preserved and foregrounded the medieval discipline of typological (or figural) interpretation of Scripture, and contributed to its nineteenth-century revival. But, as George P. Landow has shown, the mental 'set' produced by typological habits of exegesis was not confined to Evangelicals, but diffused throughout all classes and persuasions. It encouraged a propensity for seeing the whole phenomenological world as a riddle to be solved. In the nineteenth century, 'type' means 'adumbration' or 'symbol' as often as 'kind', 'class' or 'example'. The typological method of interpreting the Bible, which may be traced back to the second century AD, assumes that it is a unified text, and that the Old Testament is a detailed prophecy of the New. The type is an imperfect model, emblem or symbol of something to be realised in the future. Samson as type imperfectly 'shadows forth' or 'adumbrates' his antitype, Christ resurrected, who in turn prefigures Christ returning in glory.[7]

Strictly speaking, typology is distinguished from allegory. Typology works within a time-scale and is therefore implicitly prophetic. Representation takes place *within* categories. One person may represent another person, one situation another situation, and so on. Allegory, especially of the pictorial kind, does not require a time-scale and need not be prophetic. Representation may take place *between* categories. A person may represent an abstract idea, as does Boethius's Dame Philosophy. In practice, there is a tendency for typology imperceptibly to shift into allegory, and anyone with a typological mental 'set' will also tend to allegorise.[8] Similarly, typology is in theory opposed to cyclic myth, since the former is progressive and goal-directed, but the same mind may accommodate the mythic and the typological. Successions of types resemble the reincarnations of avatars, and mythic plots often incorporate the idea of progress – the return of the Age of Gold, for instance. During a period when Christian beliefs are in decline but the habits of mind engendered by them still operate, the distinction is even more difficult to fix. A point at which one can see typology, allegory and myth loosely merging in popular literature is Bryde's mother's question 'What sleep does winter prefigure?'

Eighteenth-century rationalism had despised typology, which was associated with obscurantist 'enthusiasm'. Its fanciful excesses (the scarlet thread of the harlot Rahab prefiguring the redeeming flow of flood from the side of Christ crucified) could impose on no reasonable man. Eventually the rationalism was to destroy belief in the Bible as a unified whole by subjecting it to historicist methods of investigation, the process known as the 'Higher' and 'Lower' criticism. However, this was a long revolution; the findings of Griesbach and Tischendorf took some time to displace the mental 'set' created by typological habits of exegesis, which were often carried intact into the secular sphere. The work of every major Victorian writer reveals the imprint of typology to some degree. Indeed, it is far from inoperative today and may be seen in the poetry of Seamus Heaney, whose bog-people prefigure the 'ritual victims' of Northern Ireland.

Secularised by Victorians, the Christian goal of the Millennium and the annihilation of Time may be replaced by the goal of biological improvement (man becoming a higher species, as in *In Memoriam*) or by the illusion of Time's annihilation in a moment of erotic rapture (Browning's 'instant made eternity'). As a narrative device in the novel or long poem, secularised typology exhibits itself in a minor episode which foreshadows the major action of the work, the 'goal'. Thus in *Middlemarch* Lydgate's admiration of a biological specimen – that 'beautiful anencephalous monster' – prefigures his falling prey to the lovely, brainless Rosamund. Even children's literature employs it, as in the fiction of Juliana Ewing, daughter of Margaret Gatty and contributor to *Aunt Judy's Magazine*. Kipling's admiration of her work is well-known,[9] and she has been credited with being an influence on his handling of child dialogue, but I do not think that it has been observed that she shares with Kipling some sophisticated narrative effects, some of which derive from the tradition of Evangelical exegesis that I have outlined above.

Her famous story *Jackanapes*, first published in the 1879 *AJM* volume, begins during the Napoleonic era with a Black Captain terrifying a little boy who is wearing a 'new nankeen skeleton suit'. It is a false alarm; the Captain is a gallant gentleman who charms the boy. But this is only a preamble to the main story. The Black Captain is killed on the battlefield; his child bride dies of shock giving birth to the Jackanapes of the title; the latter grows into a spirited young fellow, a soldier like his father, and dies in battle saving the life of a friend. The Black Captain proves to have been a harbinger of death after all; his first, emblematic appearance is to point the theme of youth making friends with mortality and learning to prefer something above its life. The particular child he plays with does not die – but in retrospect one can see that another child has been marked down. Such a reading would not have been beyond the powers of an intelligent Victorian child, schooled in the methods outlined by Bryde's mother – nor, to skip back a generation, of the nine-year-old John Ruskin, who wrote down summaries of the sermon expositions which he so frequently attended.[10]

Kipling frequently employs the tragic pun. A skeleton suit was a tightly fitting outfit worn by little boys in the early nineteenth century; in 'Without Benefit of Clergy' (*LH*, p. 159) the doomed Tota wears a 'small skull-cap'. He also is fond of the prefigurative episode. One of these we have already noted, the 'Pepper's Ghost' scene in 'The Brushwood Boy', shadows forth an event that has not yet taken place when the story closes – the wedding night of the young couple. Others, such as the Boy Niven débâcle in 'Mrs Bathurst' and the glimpse of the curios in 'A Madonna of the Trenches', will be referred to later.

PRE-RAPHAELITISM AND RUSKIN

Kipling's parents were only just off-centre of the world of the later Pre-Raphaelite artists and writers. Burne-Jones was his 'Uncle Ned' by marriage; the young Kipling spent happy Christmases at the Burne-Joneses' London house, where he met Morris and where Burne-Jones had his studio. Christina Rossetti was 'somewhere in the background' (*SM*, p. 22). If he had remained in England after leaving school, Louis Cornell argued, it is possible that he would have become a minor aesthetic poet, an imitator of Rossetti, Morris and Swinburne, a view supported by the recent publication of all Kipling's known early verse.[11]

He shares with Swinburne, D. G. Rossetti and Burne-Jones an obsession with the theme of the Fatal Woman. A notable cult book in the circle was the Wilhelm Meinhold romance *Sidonia the Sorceress*, translated by Lady Wilde in 1849; it was the subject of two Burne-Jones water colours. Kipling mentions reading it at about the age of twelve, just after his 'escape' from Mrs Holloway of Lorne Lodge, called in *Something of Myself* simply the Woman (*SM*, pp. 6, 20). However, when parallels between Kipling and Pre-Raphaelitism are drawn, it is usually the painterliness of his technique that critics have in mind. Kipling himself often implicitly encourages this parallel, throwing in for good measure that offshoot of Pre-Raphaelitism, the Arts and Crafts movement. Here is his metaphorical description of his painstaking methods:

> I worked the material in three or four overlaid tints and textures. . . . It was like working lacquer and mother o'pearl, a natural combination, into the same scheme as niello and grisaille and trying not to let the joins show. . . . I loaded the book up with allegories and allusions . . . and even slipped in a cryptogram, whose key I regret I must have utterly forgotten. (*SM*, pp. 190–1)

His deliberate cross-genericism has its counterpart in the multi-media experiments of the Pre-Raphaelites; like them he painstakingly tries to get details right; like them, he loves bright colours and precise detail. Nature is sometimes seen as a Pre-Raphaelite painting – the Yellowstone Valley and the Oodey Sagar are surrounded by 'Holman Hunt hills' (*SS*, II, 111). Their practice of embellishing the picture-frame design with some motif or quotation that extends or reinforces the meaning of the painting (most notably employed by Hunt) has its counterpart in Kipling's device of 'framing' his story with an episode which has a similar function with regard to the main action of the story.[12]

Pre-Raphaelites, both as painters and writers, looked to John Ruskin as their guru. (He was also a patron of *Aunt Judy's Magazine*.[13]) Both generations found in *Modern Painters* inspiration and justification for their brand of symbolic realism. There is a direct link between their intensely typological and allegorical paintings and Ruskin's own vision of the world as a text composed of types and symbols of eternity. But it is the second, 'Oxford' wave of the mid-1850s that concerns us here. Twenty or so years later Kipling's headmaster would regale him with stories of that heady period when 'Morris and Swinburne and Rossetti . . . were all young, and the Head was young with them, and they wrote wonderful things in college magazines.'[14]

As Ruskin became increasingly interested in the interpretation of myth after *The Cestus of Aglaia* (1865) and *The Queen of the Air* (1869), so did his disciples. One of those most under his spell was Burne-Jones, later to become perhaps the warmest and most enduring friend from all that circle, despite later divergences. He was a witness for Ruskin in the Whistler libel trial of 1878. Kipling's disparaging references to 'Impressionism' very likely have their roots in his relative's partisanship in this *cause célèbre*. Ruskin paid Burne-Jones several public compliments, singling him out in an 1883 lecture as a noble representative of the 'mythic school' of contemporary art.[15]

The first volume of *Modern Painters* (1843) had famously advised the young artist to 'go to nature in all singleness of heart . . . rejecting nothing, selecting nothing, and scorning nothing' (*Works*, III, 624). Later, *The Elements of Drawing* (1857) was to give detailed instructions for training of eye and hand through a scrupulous effort to draw natural phenomena with exactitude. But this discipline was only an apprenticeship. Ruskin disapproved strongly of the photographic rendering of minutiae for its own sake. The second (1846) volume of *Modern Painters* (the Pre-Raphaelites' Bible) applied a corrective. Detail was worthless unless the highest imaginative faculty was incarnated within it. To explain what he meant by this quality, Ruskin analysed certain pictures of Tintoretto.

Without benefit of any sort of reproduction, with nothing but his brilliant power of word-painting, Ruskin teaches the student how to 'read' the paintings that he describes. He finds significance in barely discernible detail. In *The Crucifixion* an ass is eating *withered palm leaves*, thus recalling the so-recent entry of Christ into Jerusalem, and the now-shattered hopes of his secular domination. Formal design is instinct with meaning. In *The Annunciation* a narrow line of light, the edge of a carpenter's square, directs the eye inevitably and naturally towards a white cornerstone of a crumbling palace, the key to the whole. 'The ruined house is the

Jewish dispensation; that obscurely arising in the dawning of the sky is the Christian . . . the stone which the builders refused is become the Headstone of the Corner' (*Works*, IV, 265).

Clarity and exactitude of detail mark the highest imaginative faculty, but it is also unerringly selective. It 'never stops at crusts or ashes; it ploughs them all aside and plunges into the very central fiery heart' of the subject. It 'cuts down to the root' (*Works*, IV, 250). 'The vacancy of a truly imaginative work results not from absence of ideas, or incapability of grasping and detailing them, but from the painter having told the whole pith and power of his subject and disdaining to tell more' (p. 261).

The human mind generates pictorial symbols, Ruskin believed, when it attempts to express the otherwise inexpressible. To this symbolisation he gave the (today) somewhat confusing name of the 'grotesque', but the name was not arbitrary. As adumbrated in *The Stones of Venice*, III (1853), the 'grotesque' has two aspects, the sportive and the terrible (*Works*, XI, 151), which are difficult to disentangle. For 'the mind under certain phases of excitement, *plays* with *terror*, and summons images which, if it were in another temper, would be awful, but of which, either in weariness or in irony, it refrains for the time to acknowledge the true terribleness' (p. 166). In its larger sense, and especially as developed in *Modern Painters*, III (1856), the 'grotesque' spans all products of the symbol-generating imagination from the obscene and sensational to the highest sublime. A written 'symbolical grotesque' is an emblem, concentrating a complex of ideas into an arresting image or series of images, 'shortly and at once, so that we feel it fully and see it, and never forget it', as he proceeds to demonstrate in his vivid reading of Spenser's Envy (*Works*, V, 133). And the 'symbolical grotesque' is itself one of the most vivid of Ruskin's own literary devices.

In the above selection from Ruskin's principles and practice there are features which strikingly coincide with Kipling's. 'When Earth's last picture is painted' is pure Ruskin, especially the last stanza, where Kipling playfully imagines a possible world where

> no one shall work for money, and no one shall work
>   for fame,
> But each for the joy of his working, and each, in his
>   separate star,

Shall draw the Thing as he sees It for the God of Things as
They are!

(*DV*, p. 227)

It was Ruskin who, in *The Stones of Venice*, had said that men were
degraded if they had no pleasure in their work (*Works*, VIII, 218).
And in the lecture on Burne-Jones he had offered a definition of
the essential virtue of Pre-Raphaelitism. This is 'the trying to
conceive things as they are, and thinking and feeling them quite
out. . . . Pre-Raphaelite subjects must usually be of real persons
in a solid world – not of personifications in a vaporescent one. The
persons may be spiritual, but they are individual, St George,
himself, not the vague idea of Fortitude.'[16]

Again, Kipling's career seems to replicate Ruskin's own transition
from the writer of *Modern Painters*, I, to that of *Modern Painters*, II.
Like an enthusiastic follower of Ruskin's injunction to 'go to
Nature, rejecting nothing, selecting nothing', Kipling as a young
artist-craftsman in 'My new-cut ashlar' thanks God that 'I saw
naught common on Thy Earth' (*DV*, p. 512). (The poem owes
much to Masonic imagery, but also to *The Stones of Venice*.) Later
Kipling strives for the greatest 'economy of implication'. He
describes his methods using Ruskinian metaphors of penetrating
the heart of a fire and radical pruning. He cuts out passages from
his drafts, knowing that 'a tale from which pieces have been raked
out is like a fire that has been poked. One does not know that the
operation has been performed, but every one feels the effect' (*SM*,
p. 207).

Kipling must have absorbed a number of Ruskin's ideas and
methods obliquely through the influence of the Burne-Joneses and
his headmaster, but he knew a great deal more of Ruskin directly
than appears at first sight. There are a few references to him in
Kipling's early work – a little flippant, as if the reputation of the
sage has weighed a bit too heavily upon him, yet he still uses him
as a standard, as when judging the success of the Jeypore Museum
(*SS*, I, 35). He knew something of *Sesame and Lilies*; he owned *The
Elements of Drawing* and *The Stones of Venice*.[17] But the work which
most obviously influenced him was *Fors Clavigera*, which he read
at school with Dunsterville and Beresford (the Stalky and M'Turk
of the Stalky stories).[18]

*Fors Clavigera: Letters to the Workmen and Labourers of Great
Britain*, Ruskin's discursive vehicle for an anti-capitalistic social

programme, appeared monthly until March 1878, and sporadically
from 1880 until 1884. In *Stalky & Co.* M'Turk glues up the back of
'four odd numbers' of *Fors* (pp. 43, 46).[19] It helped to shape
Kipling's style, as shown by the following sarcasm (J. S. Mill is
the butt): 'The Greatest Thinker in England means by these
beautiful words to tell you that Productive labour is labour that
produces a Useful Thing. Which, indeed, perhaps, you knew – or,
without the assistance of great thinkers, might have known, before
now' (*Works*, xxvii, 65–6).

The following three examples illustrate some correspondences
between the procedures of Kipling and the Ruskin of *Fors*. Ruskin
constantly uses the symbolical grotesque, as in Letter ii, 'The Great
Picnic'. He tells of an Irish picnic at which after 'an ample
lunch' the company offered the 'basketsful of fragments taken up
afterwards' to the attendant ragged boys 'on condition that they
should "pull each other's hair"'. Here, comments Ruskin, is capital
employed in entirely unproductive labour; he then proceeds to
apply his inverted parable of the Feeding of the Five Thousand to
the last 800 years of the history of the upper classes of Europe,
who have been one 'great Picnic party' creating strife among the
working classes (xxvii, 27–44).

The symbolical grotesque is also one of Kipling's major strategies.
(His predilection for it is, I believe, connected to his failure to
produce a major novel.) A typical early one is his sighting in the
Lahore of 1887 a beautiful 'Jezebel' whose hand, as she 'looked
out of the window', falls on the head of the chaprassi's 'blear-eyed
shrivelled mother, old and hideous as Gagool' (*KI*, p. 269); this is
Kipling's version of the medieval 'Lovely/Loathly Lady' topos.
'False Dawn' (*PT*, 1888) is an expanded symbolical grotesque about
a 'Great Pop Picnic'. The locale is a tomb; the picnic explodes into
duststorms and division between sisters after the food has been
eaten. The famous opening of 'Love o' Women' (*MI*), where the
blood of the dead man 'calling from the ground' is cracked 'lozenge-
wise by the heat' and curls up at the edges 'as if it were a dumb
tongue', is quintessential Kipling, but it is no disparagement of his
originality to say that Ruskin taught him how to write like that.
By 1936 the method has been honed to produce mysteriously
emblematic effects such as his remembered invasion of his mother's
room at dawn to quench the thirst of 'Pluto, a pet toad . . . who
lived mostly in one of my pockets' (*SM*, p. 18).

Ruskin initiates his readers into intricate mysteries, and unravels their complexities – the Cretan labyrinth (Letter xxiii; *Works*, xxvii, 397), foreign tongues. He unveils his own esoteric polyvalent method. In Letter ii he explains his choice of title: 'Fors' and 'Clavigera' each have three possible senses, so that the title means 'Strength the Club-bearer', 'Fortitude the Keybearer' and 'Fortune the Nail-bearer' (p. 29); like Kipling's, Ruskin's 'cargo' came 'double-and-treble-figured'. He unriddles (Letters lxxi and lxxii, 1876) Carpaccio's *Vision of St Ursula*. The painting is an example of how 'myth is rewritten by a great man, born in the days of a nation's strength'. After studying it closely for six years, the meaning of its 'sweetest enigma' is suddenly explained to him. He had supposed that a 'very little and bright shield' on the cornice of Princess Ursula's chamber was merely a 'minute repetition' of the escutcheon embroidered on the bed-head, and that the painter had left it blank to save himself trouble, but '(I might have known Carpaccio never would even *omit* without meaning.) And I never noticed that it was not in a line above the escutcheon, but exactly over the princess's head. It gleams with silver edges out of the dark-blue ground – the point of the mortal Arrow!' For Ruskin this completes 'without any chance of mistake', the meaning of the painting – *mors janua vitae* (*Works*, xxviii, 740–6, 760–1).

The function of the artist as rewriter of myth, the underlining of theme (in this case, foreknowledge of death) in easily disregarded or misinterpreted minutiae, the symbolism of colour, the potential of omission as a carrier of meaning, the flash of intuitive 'understanding' after years of patient looking – this is a partial description of the methods, theme and effect of a certain kind of Kipling story.[20]

UNDER CARLYLE'S PIPE

Much of the above was also available to Kipling through Carlyle; Ruskin and Carlyle each mutually reinforced the other's influence. Carlyle was Ruskin's mentor; the older man also was steeped in typology. (*Sartor Resartus* contains at least twelve examples of such terms as 'shadow forth', 'figural', 'typical' and 'adumbration'.) The effect of reading both would have been to strengthen a fondness for the symbolical grotesque, and even for certain words. Both Carlyle and Ruskin, for instance, use the word 'mother-naked', which Kipling picked up for 'The Disturber of Traffic'.[21]

The affinities of Carlyle's social philosophy with Kipling's – the gospel of Work, Obedience, faith in the Hero – are so obvious that they often go without saying. Of course there are some important divergences (the same goes for Ruskin); Carlyle tends to use 'machinery' and 'mechanism' to foreground a contrast to the 'vital' or 'spiritual', whereas a sizable portion of Kipling's work was given over to the attempt to breathe a soul into machinery; Man, as he said in one of the last letters he wrote, was unknown in the same way 'as the internal combustion engine, every detail of which is explicable *except* the nature of the Spark that causes the mixture to explode'.[22] Still less did he share Carlyle's admiration for Prussia, which may be one reason for the scarcity of overt reference to him. He did not write Carlylese, though some passages from *Letters to the Family* are strongly reminiscent of *Heroes and Hero Worship*, and the catch-phrase used by Herr Breitmann – 'Too much Ego in your cosmos' – could be a pseudo-utterance of Carlyle's Professor Teufelsdrockh himself (*LT*, pp. 135–7; *LH*, p. 300; see also *LF*, p. 61).

Kipling as a boy used to visit a house where a maiden lady wrote novels underneath a pipe that Carlyle had once smoked. He acquired a set of Carlyle's works, probably during the Vermont period, and also owned Carlyle and Emerson's *Correspondence*. The text that influenced him most was *Sartor Resartus*, which he read at about the same time as *Fors Clavigera*;[23] this speaks the early Romantic Carlyle who is still in touch with his painful youth, the Carlyle who is bursting to transmit to a British public the lessons he had learned from Goethe and German idealism, the prophet who had not yet hardened into the admirer of Frederick the Great and anti-democrat. *Sartor Resartus* will never become again what it was in the closing decades of the nineteenth century, the Bible of autodidacts. But it is probably less of a Great Unread now than twenty years ago. It is possible even today to empathise with the excitement that gripped the youth of the last century upon encountering Carlyle's spiritual autobiography and the philosophy of life that he retrieved from despair, not to mention the self-congratulation upon tackling a text that had the reputation for being a milestone of eccentric obscurity. The flurry caused some years ago by Robert Persig's cult book *Zen and the Art of Motorcycle Maintenance* was a feeble shadow in comparison.

The tripartite *Sartor Resartus*'s central figure is a man with two sides to his head, the German Professor Diogenes Teufelsdrockh

('God-born Devil's dung' or 'Heavenly asafoetida' – a purge[24]) and whose scattered papers the narrator claims to be editing. After the mock-digressive manner of Swift's *A Tale of a Tub*, Teufelsdrockh's early struggles and disappointment in love (a disguised account of Carlyle's experiences) unfold. He descends into a personal hell where the Universe is wholly evil and is prey to a 'continual indefinite pining fear'. One day, in the 'dirty little *Rue Saint-Thomas de l'Enfer*' he summons up the mental fight to defy the abyss, drawing from this experience a positive life-view. Man's unhappiness derives from the combination of his egoism with his capacity for greatness. This leads him to suppose that he has a right to be happy in this world. Once he glimpses that there is 'a HIGHER than love of happiness' he may learn to 'love the Earth while it injures'. But this glimpse must be reinforced by conduct, which alone can remove doubt and the fatal tendency to pine after the ideal instead of finding it in the actual. Teufelsdrockh thence expounds his creed of the duty of Action (*Sartor* ii.vii, ix).

Part iii shows the Professor's mental activity investing the dunghill of the world with spirituality; he develops the 'Clothes Philosophy', which gives the book its title ('The tailor patched') and which he had adumbrated in the chapter 'Prospective' of part i. There he had stated his idealist solution to the matter–spirit problem and *his* theory of language:

> All visible things are emblems; that thou seest . . . strictly taken, is not there at all. Matter exists only spiritually, and to represent some Idea, and *body* it forth. Hence Clothes, as despicable as we think them, are so unspeakably significant . . . all Emblematic things are properly Clothes, thought-woven or hand-woven. . . . Nay, if you consider it what is Man himself, and his whole terrestrial Life, but an emblem; a Clothing or visible Garment for that divine ME of his, cast hither, like a light-particle down from Heaven? Thus is he said also to be clothed with a Body.
>
> Language is called the Garment of Thought; however, it should rather be, Language is the Flesh-Garment, the Body, of Thought. I said that Imagination wove this Flesh-Garment; and does she not? Metaphors are her stuff: examine Language; what, if you expect some few primitive elements (of natural sound), what is it all but Metaphors. . . . ? (i.xi, p. 43)

The pith of part iii is to be found in the chapters 'Symbols' and

'Natural Supernaturalism'. There Teufelsdrockh expounds the 'benificent efficacies of Concealment . . . SILENCE AND SECRECY'. By 'Silence' Carlyle meant the precondition without which the mind and creative imagination would be distracted and dissipated. 'Secrecy' hides from man's consciousness the fact that virtue originates in the mire of human veins; if admitted to consciousness, the ensuing self-contempt would inhibit all virtuous effort:

> Neither shalt thou prate even to thy own heart of 'those secrets known to all'. Is not Shame the soil of all Virtue, of all good manners, and good morals? Like other plants, Virtue will not grow unless its root be hidden, buried from the eye of the sun. Let the sun shine on it, nay, do but look at it privily thyself, the root withers, and no flower will glad thee. O my Friends, when we view the fair clustering flowers that over-wreathe, for example, the Marriage-bower, and encircle man's life with the fragrance and hues of Heaven, what hand will not smite the foul plunderer that grubs them up by the roots, and, with grinning grunting satisfaction, shows us the dung they flourish in! (iii.iii, p. 134)

To preserve Silence and Secrecy while making communication possible arises the 'Agency of Symbols'. But symbols have a higher purpose: they enable commonplaces to be imprinted more forcibly than by bald statement and, finally grant release from space and time, which are but Thought-Forms; man is living in an everlasting Now could he but apprehend this.

> In a Symbol there is concealment and yet revelation: here, therefore, by Silence and by Speech acting together, comes a double significance . . . in many a painted Device, or simple Seal-emblem, the commonest Truth stands-out to us proclaimed with quite new emphasis. . . . In the Symbol proper . . . there is ever . . . some embodiment and revelation of the Infinite. (Ibid.)

Carlyle's above illustration enacts his own argument; symbols of marriage bowers, dung and rooting hogs themselves reveal and conceal attitudes to human sexuality and tell yet do not tell 'the secrets known to all'.

To the revelation of the infinite in the finite Carlyle gave the name of 'Natural Supernaturalism', and the concept will no doubt be familiar to most readers. What Carlyle's early readers found so puzzling is the form in which it is presented. The editor frequently interposes himself as a counter-voice. Ostensibly the Professor's admirer and apologist, he often mocks him and admits his garrulity, nebulousness and sentimentality. When Teufelsdrockh offers his final revelation, the editor introduces it in a way that leaves room for a scepticism about his status as a seer and visionary. The tactic is supposed to protect the Professor against hostile critics by drawing their fire, but this is a double-edged weapon, and at many points one cannot be sure how seriously the editor takes the Professor. All the Professor's claims to have attained the truth are undercut by the editor's 'Beware, O Teufelsdrockh, of spiritual pride!' (I.ii, p. 61)

There is in many Kipling stories a similar dichotomy between a hero who makes a journey to 'the end of the passage' and a narrator who interposes deflatingly. This is particularly marked in *Plain Tales from the Hills*. But sometimes the narrator reminds one of Teufelsdrockh, and never more than when he laughs. Much is made of the one occasion on which Teufelsdrockh laughed, prompted by Jean-Paul Richter's 'Proposal for a *Cast-Metal King'*. The Professor

> burst forth like the neighing of all Tattersall's, – tears streaming down his cheeks, pipe held aloft, foot clutched into the air, – loud, long-continuing, uncontrollable; a laugh not of the face and diaphragm only, but of the whole man from head to heel. The present Editor, who laughed indeed, yet with measure, began to fear all was not right: however, Teufelsdrockh composed himself. (*Sartor*, I.iv, p. 20)

The resemblance between this and the exaggerated, hysterical and ultimately unexplained mirth of some of Kipling's narrators ('My Sunday at Home', 'The Puzzler', 'The Vortex') is patent. It is the mirth that has bitter springs. Teufelsdrockh's laugh is a *horse-laugh*, that is, one of derision; inasmuch as one can work out what has prompted the Professor's glee, it is scorn for the human race. The editor fears that he is mad. One is not, of course, to assume that all uncontrollable laughter in Kipling is an alternative to a scream of agony. Especially in his children's stories it is genial and forgiving. But if the reader fails to be as convulsed with merriment as the narrator, this may be because Teufelsdrockh's pipe is being held aloft over the latter's head. That pain may be misinterpreted as amusement is an idea that appears in Kipling as early as a strange little 1887 *jeu d'esprit*. It affects to have discovered that Lewis Carroll's 'Jabberwocky' conceals a tale of jealousy and betrayal. 'Word by word and line by line came to the surface, as a dead man's face rises through dark water, the original poem. Lo! Under the cap and bells of Folly, lay the drawn face of human woe' (*KI*, pp. 256–7). More grimly, in the 1926 'The Eye of Allah', a monk explains that the ancient belief that he who eats buttercup juice will die laughing is based upon mistaking agony for hilarity: 'for the juice of that herb, I know by experiment, burns, blisters, and wries the mouth. I know also the rictus, or pseudo-laughter on the face of such as have perished by the strong poisons of herbs allied to this ranunculus. Certainly that spasm resembles laughter' (*DC*, p. 381).

Many phrases in *Sartor Resartus* stimulated Kipling's imagination, a few of which may be mentioned here. From Carlyle derives the image, which Kipling uses in 'Mrs Bathurst' and elsewhere, of 'consuming one's own smoke', meaning to bottle up one's emotions (II.vi, p. 92). The germ of the idea of 'The Colonel's Lady and Judy O'Grady' being 'sisters under the skin' is found in Carlyle's hint that were clothes to be abolished it would be found that 'Carmen and Kings' and 'Joan and My Lady' possess the same 'viscera, tissues, livers, lights and other Life-tackle' (I.x, p. 38). Teufelsdrockh places papers relating to his life in six bags, each called after the name of a sign of the Zodiac (I.xi, p. 46). Kipling represents phases of life as *bags* in 'Baa Baa Black Sheep' (*WWW*), where they are conflated with the 'three bags full' of the nursery rhyme.

Kipling also makes considerable use of Carlyle's clothes metaphor. Of course such phrases as 'the loom of language' and 'the dress of thought' – the word 'text' itself – are among the most ancient of metaphors and are available to all. That said, there is an unusually high incidence of imagery of cloth, nakedness, patches, shreds and rags in Kipling. Tompkins noticed Kipling's elaborate 'use of the image of woven stuff' – webs shot and embroidered, stuffs that show well 'only in the dark places where they were made', bales with private markings – to describe his art in his introduction to the Outward Bound Edition of 1897.[25] One suspects that even the word 'yarn', which Kipling applied in private letters to his work with seeming self-deprecation, had a serious meaning.[26]

Carlyle, too, places private markings on his 'bales' ('the dirty little *Rue Saint-Thomas de l'Enfer*') and may have shown Kipling how to do the same.

Both Carlyle and Kipling excel in depicting suicidal states of mind. Both draw on a common stock of imagery in the Bible, Dante, Milton and the Wandering Jew legend. Nevertheless, the emphasis in both on images of dung to express world-disgust, and of Gehenna, volcano or vortex to express mental agony, is very marked. Kipling drew on Carlyle's image of madness as a 'mysterious-terrific altogether *infernal* boiling-up of the Nether Chaotic Deep' in 'Bubbling Well Road' (*LH*), his story of a journey towards insanity, where the narrator refuses to look into the black well that gives the story its title. Teufelsdrockh 'feels himself not guilty but suffering all the pains of guilt' (*Sartor*, II.viii, p. 97); the figure haunted Kipling, and appears in his work as Morrowbie Jukes and as Wollin in 'Fairy-Kist'.

Kipling has been criticised (notably by Angus Wilson) for the evasion of introspection, of further questioning of the sources of the despair and anxiety and guilt that enmesh so many of his best characters;[27] there is, I think, more questioning than Wilson gives Kipling credit for, but in any case Kipling's method is a calculated one, and is based on certain assumptions about human behaviour for which he found a rationale in Carlyle and which had consequences for his literary methods. First of all, Carlyle and Kipling both start off with an awareness of the limits of introspection; for Carlyle the Greek 'Know thyself' is an impossible command and must be translated into 'this partially possible one, *Know what thou canst work at*' (II.vii, p. 101). For Kipling, the journey into the psyche uncovers so many unworthy motives and ugly propensities that the end is self-hatred and accidie, yet their existence is undeniable. Hence, in his work, the use of silence and symbol to conceal and reveal 'those secrets known to all'. For assuredly they will be revealed, one way or another, and they externalise themselves as symbolic corpses, cannibals, dunghills, demonic women, little grey shadows, warring tribesmen, wild beasts.

Most striking of all are the similarities between Carlyle's silence, secrecy and symbolism and Kipling's practice. For Kipling (as for Carlyle), symbolism is an intermediary between the material and the abstract, and provided for him what he called the Fourth Dimension, a realisation of the infinite in the here and now through language. The artist's function is both to provide such an experience and to find new symbols so that the old verities may be proclaimed 'with quite new emphasis'. Of course the *uncontrollable* symbol-generating imagination yields its own kind of horror, as in the *Plain Tales* story 'In the House of Suddhoo' (the Seal-Cutter is a Carlylean maker of 'simple Seal-emblems' gone perverse); the spiritualising of the world may animate the *caput mortuum* only to fill it with demons.

There are moments in Kipling's fiction where one sees him fighting Ruskin and Carlyle's natural supernaturalism, as in a famous passage from *Kim*. The sick youth recovers his health, experiencing a liberating disburdening from his consciousness of a weight of metaphor and metaphysical meaning which has clogged up his perception of the world. The world suddenly becomes just itself, not to be looked at and interpreted but to be acted in. 'Roads were meant to be walked on, houses to be lived in, cattle to be driven, fields to be tilled, and men and women to be talked to' (pp. 403–4). But Kim, though reanimated by, cannot rest in, this Edenic three-dimensional world for long, which becomes naked only to be clothed again in clean array.

Having been prepared by Pre-Raphaelitism, biblical exegesis, Ruskin and Carlyle to 'look more closely' into things, it is not surprising that Kipling should have written his stories to be read as they read Nature, paintings, myth and the Scriptures. I am not saying that this is the only way to read them – merely that it is a profitable and appropriate way to do so. The next chapter takes five stories – usually read as tall tales, imperialist propaganda and pure farce – and attempts to show that they become rather more interesting if approached in the above manner.

3

Pigs, Serpents, Cannibals, Bats and Bees

Tout est vérité – tout est mensonge
(Charles Nodier)

Each of the five tales discussed in this chapter 'hooks on', to use Tompkins's term, to one or more of the tales which form the staple of the argument in Chapters 4–7. To give just a few instances: 'Pig' is a 'metagrobolisation' of the hunting-of-the-beast-in-man theme to be found in Swinburne's *Atalanta in Calydon*; 'A Matter of Fact', like 'Mary Postgate', calls into question the status of 'fact' and is about the 'awful orderliness of England'; 'A Deal in Cotton' contains a creator–destroyer Madonna figure, of which 'Mary Postgate' and 'A Madonna of the Trenches' supply darker variants, and shares with 'Mrs Bathurst' an African heart-of-darkness locale; 'The Village that Voted the Earth was Flat' contains the dual Peri–Hecate and 'Village of the Dead' motifs, which both figure in 'The Strange Ride of Morrowbie Jukes'; and 'The Vortex' is, like 'Mrs Bathurst', a revelation of the inferno that lies underneath the pleasant landscape of normal existence.

'PIG' (1887, *PT*)

'Pig', which was written during the latter part of Kipling's period (1882–7) as a journalist on the Lahore *Civil and Military Gazette*, is generally discussed as a skit on bureaucracy and a lightweight example of a favourite Kipling theme, the elaborate hoax used as a means of revenge. It attracts notice as a harbinger of later stories such as 'The Village that Voted the Earth Was Flat' and 'Dayspring Mishandled', but is not rated among the best of the *Plain Tales from the Hills*, into which it was later collected.

Pinecoffin, an Assistant Commissioner, sells Nafferton a horse 'with a twist in his temper . . . by whom Nafferton was nearly

41

slain'. Pinecoffin laughs, but Nafferton, an 'earnest' man, swears revenge and gets it by pretending to have a plan for feeding the army in India on pork. Pinecoffin is forced by the Government to supply Nafferton with endless information about pigs, until he is exhausted by the paperwork and baulks at more. Upon this he receives a rebuke from the Department of Castigation, which will 'stick like a burr' to him for the rest of his service. Nafferton then calls it quits, reveals his strategy to the whimpering Pinecoffin, smiles 'ever so sweetly', and asks him to dinner.

'Pig' seems a good example of Kipling's provision of superior newspaper 'filler'. Yet it possesses a memorable intensity. Cornell observed that 'it is difficult to watch Nafferton gulling his victim without a growing sense of uneasiness'.[1] What *is* driving the story and saving it from being merely anecdotal?

Kipling gives the reader some indications that 'Pig' is a weightier affair than may appear on the surface. He prefaces it with a poetic 'fragment', the last four lines of which run,

> But for pleasure and profit together,
>   Allow me the hunting of Man, –
> The chase of the Human, the search for the Soul
>   To its ruin, – the hunting of Man.

He draws attention to the peculiar names of his characters: 'You can see from their names that Nafferton had the race-advantage of Pinecoffin', the former being a Northerner as hard as the Strid, while Pinecoffin was 'a South Devon man . . . as soft as a Dartmoor bog'. 'All the Pinecoffins come of a landholding breed, and so the land only took back her own again' (pp. 222, 223).

'Pig' is a harbinger of the tales ('On the Gate', 'Uncovenanted Mercies') which adopt for framework the Smaragdine Tablet's 'That which is above is like unto that which is below.'[2] It is a parable of the deadly war waged between flesh and spirit, and the apparently unmotivated intensity we respond to is the result of its conflict being one about which late Victorians really cared. Kipling skilfully employs a number of traditional symbols. Pinecoffin represents the body, the casket of the soul.[3] 'Devonian Red Sandstone' is a geological term; South Devon is a red-earth area, and red earth is both the meaning of the name 'Adam' and the stuff from which he was compounded. The unruly horse that nearly kills Nafferton is, as it has been from Plato onward, blind impulse or carnal lust; it is the 'official stalking-horse', a stalking-horse being one that has been trained to allow a fowler to hide behind it so as to take the game more easily. Given the prevalence in Kipling's writing during this period of the association between treacherous horses and bad or wronged women, a sexual temptation is hinted at.[4] 'Nafferton' is the name of a Yorkshire town, but also suggests the non-affirming, impermissive conscience.

The soul punishes the body for its near ruin by setting it the task of discovering the nature of Man; the quest lands Pinecoffin in a 'hideous tangle'. He discovers that Man is a swine. He produces a monograph on 'Products of the Pig'. 'This led him, under Nafferton's tender handling, straight to the Cawnpore factories, the trade in hog-skin for saddles – and thence to the tanners. Pinecoffin wrote that pomegranate-seed was the best cure for hog-skin' (p. 228). 'The Cawnpore factories' is Kipling's sardonic reference to the massacres at Cawnpore during the 1857 Mutiny, when over 200 women and children were hacked to death and their bodies thrown down a well, an atrocity which drew savage reprisals from the British. The immediate cause of the Mutiny was the outrage of devout Muslims at having to bite cartridges greased with pig's fat. 'Pig' was first published about a month short of the thirtieth anniversary. It is Kipling's 'Remember Cawnpore!'[5]

What must be remembered is not only the treachery of the Indians but also the excesses of the British response. Pinecoffin's investigations teach him to wish for death, 'the best cure for hog-skin' – it was the eating of six pomegranate seeds that kept Persephone in the underworld. He learns to loathe his flesh ('He realised that he had wrapped himself up in the Pigskin without need'), despise himself and to long for deliverance. When he reopens face-to-face communications with Nafferton, he is acknowledging the need to live on good terms with his soul, which he had previously denied, but he begins by reproaches: 'It's too bad of you – on my soul it is!' (p. 230).

Nafferton demurs, as well he might, for, being Pinecoffin's soul, he knows better. 'Have you ever been stuck with a horse?', he asks. 'What I resent is the chaff that follows, especially from the boy who stuck me.' 'Chaff' is laughter, but it also means 'rubbish'; in Psalm 1 the ungodly are 'like the chaff which the wind driveth away'. The ruin of the soul will be followed by the reduction of the boy's body to 'chaff'. The soul resents being dragged down by the sensuality of thoughtless youth and chastens the body for the sake of their mutual health. To emphasise this parabolic quality helps to explain why the reader's sympathies are marshalled on the side of Pinecoffin, whose complaint is not unlike that of Marvell's Body in his 'Dialogue between the Soul and the Body': 'O, who shall me deliver whole, / From bonds of this tyrannic soul . . .?' Like 'The Disturber of Traffic', 'Pig' expresses the fear of the divided self lapsing into brutishness. It exhibits Kipling's recourse to grotesque humour in the face of the frightening.[6]

The 'Plain Tales' are no more plain than *The Secret Agent* is 'A Simple Story'. 'Pig' has a number of stylistic devices which anticipate Kipling's later work and exhibit the truth of Robson's observation, 'Of no author is it more true than for him "in my end is my beginning".'[7] First, 'The chaff that follows' shows him grimly playing on the literal and metaphorical meanings of a phrase; 'the land only took back her own' is another example. Many instances can be furnished from his later work, of which that given by Bodelsen from 'A Madonna of the Trenches' – 'I'm dyin' to see him' – is the best known. Others include 'A gentleman has taken a bottle of poison' ('My Sunday at Home'), 'We back-to-the-landers' ('Mrs Bathurst') and 'as a man flies' ('The Edge of Evening'). Secondly, 'Pig' shows Kipling exploiting the ambiguity of upper-case and the facetious sobriquet in 'Our Government' and 'The Department of Castigation', something which he also does in 'The Village that Voted the Earth was Flat', 'The Vortex' and 'Mary Postgate'. Thirdly, we find here a propensity to make a double statement by means of the reciprocity of analogy. 'Pig' is a comment on the nature of bureaucracy and the nature of the conscience. The poem 'The Liner she's a Lady' (*DV*, p. 158) is about the dependency of Britain's prosperity upon humble 'little cargo boats' and about the dependency of the virtue of 'nice women' upon prostitution.

'A MATTER OF FACT' (1892) (*MI*)

On board the ship *Rathmines* one of Kipling's 'knowing' journalist narrators and two fellow professionals witness the death-throes of a huge sea-serpent which has been injured in an underwater volcanic eruption. On arrival in England the American journalist finds that no British newspaper will accept his sensational scoop, supposing it to be one of the narrator's 'infernal yarns'. Overwhelmed by the *vis inertiae* of the British character, he loses the will to cable the American papers. The narrator triumphantly declares that *he* will publish the story, but as fiction, 'a lie'. The story one has just read is that lie.

In contrast to 'Pig', 'A Matter of Fact' has been widely noticed and admired for its terrific description of the cataclysm and the blind, toothless monster battering its wounds with its white head while its anguished mate swims vainly around. But the 'framing episode' has been criticised for irrelevance. Kipling is said not to have found an adequate vehicle for his powerful central image and has filled the gap with some cheap anti-American satire, rounding it off with a clever but shallow paradox. The title both asserts and denies its own fictional status. The episode is described with the verisimilitude, including technical detail, that Kipling used in order to refer to the 'real world'. But the reader knows all the time that Kipling is writing within the conventions of the tall story and that no such serpent really exists. The 'frame' seems to be making explicit at tedious length the author's intention of compelling belief in the incredible and playing tricks with his readership.

Now, there is some intrusive anti-Americanism, but the frame is far from inartistic. The story's last words are, 'And a lie it has become, for Truth is a naked lady, and if by accident she is drawn up from the bottom of the sea, it behoves a gentleman either to give her a print petticoat or to turn his face to the wall and vow that he did not see' (p. 181). If we do Kipling the justice of trying to take this seriously, it must mean that the words on the page – the 'print petticoat' – are a veil for some naked truth which is being covered up for the sake of decency, and that the story is in a sense true. The sense in which it is true is the area of the 'Fourth Dimension'. We are invited to ponder on what the awful death-scene might symbolise.

One clue is afforded by the reaction of the boatswain, 'Frithiof the Dane', upon the appearance of the serpent: 'Frithiof drew in his breath and held it till the red letters of the ship's name, woven across his jersey, straggled and opened out as though they had been type badly set' (p. 173). The detail – apparently put there merely as a reminder that the narrator is a dyed-in-the-wool journalist – is also an emblem. The reader is invited to ponder the significance of the expanding red letters *Rathmines* written over a man's heart.

The volcano brings to the surface the 'untouched deep water of the sea . . . the chill, still water that kills all life and smells of desolation and emptiness'. This produces a clinging fog, through which are heard an 'appalling' steam siren and the threshing of a Castle liner. Or at least so the men interpret a glimpsed object looking 'as though it were grey and red' and which is followed by the siren of another vessel, colour unspecified (pp. 169–70). The two supposed steamers are prefigurations of the two serpents, one of which is a threshing and bellowing 'grey and red Thing', the other of which (colour unspecified) also bellows. As we are also told 'The Thing was so helpless, and, save for his mate, so alone', the association of the serpents with the steamers is intended to reinforce a parallel with the human condition of loneliness, via suggestions of 'ships that pass in the night' – or, in this case, the fog. But the dying sea-serpent more specifically symbolises the wounded 'elemental man'; his appearance, covered with grey ooze and blood as he surfaces a second time, has the force of an enormously magnified symbol of masculinity, like the red-daubed stone lingams with which Kipling was so impressed on his journey to Chitor (*SS*, i, 94, 95, 100).[8] What then of the second serpent? 'The two Things met – the one untouched and the other in its death-throe – male and female, we said, the female coming to the male.' That 'we said' is a characteristic Kipling marker that a perception may be unreliable. The second serpent is called 'she' throughout but could be of either sex.

The theme of the story is conflict between the instinct to bellow aloud the pain of one's private loss of friend or lover (which the British code inhibits) and the duty to bear it with silent dignity (which American lack of reticence does not respect). The narrator comments, 'No human eye should have beheld him; it was monstrous and indecent to exhibit him there in trade waters' – which is one reason why he and Zuyland, the other journalist, decide not to submit their stories. (This is another unexplained area where the reader has to make deductions.) Another reason is the 'green and awful orderliness of England', a society which connives at the covering-up of emotion both because of a regard for privacy and because the unleashing of such instinctual, 'animal', 'unmanly' grief would be profoundly shocking to the British public. The conflict is resolved through expressing the extreme of painful bereavement through art, in the guise of the 'infernal yarn' – which anyone who has had the experience will recognise as fact. As

Carlyle wrote, 'Facts are engraved hierograms for which the fewest have the key' (*Sartor*, II.x, p. 123).[9]

'A DEAL IN COTTON', 1903–4 (*AR*)

One of Kipling's most underrated stories is the rarely discussed 'A Deal in Cotton'. It is usually treated as a crass piece of imperialist propaganda about the wonderful work our men are doing in Africa, a nostalgic recycling of old characters (the Stricklands, Stalky, the Infant), with Kipling's Daemon of inspiration conspicuously absent. But as so often in Kipling there is an ironic interplay between the apparent control that the white men exercise over the emergence of the narrative and the features that go unregarded by them; what has fired his imagination is the glimpse of the nether chaotic deep.

The Stricklands arrive as guests at one of those country houses found so often in Kipling after his settling in England in 1902. Adam, their son, is sick unto death with fever, on six months' leave from the 'Centro-Euro-Afro-Protectorate', where he is Assistant District Commissioner, 'leaning heavily' on the shoulder of his 'quite European' Punjabi 'body-servant', while his mother, the adorable Agnes, anxiously watches over him. Adam has piloted a cotton-growing industry in his district, in a belt of black soil, using cannibal labour. He recounts how he acquired the money to finance the project through fining a slave-dealer who trespassed on his territory, offering some of the cannibals for sale. After his early retirement to bed, the Indian servant is induced to tell the whole truth. At the time when he was worried about raising the capital, Adam had unknowingly saved the life of Ibn Makarrah (the former chief enemy of the Protectorate, now its ally) when the latter had been found, apparently poisoned, disguised as an old Hajji. Adam subsequently fell sick, and the unsuccess of the cotton scheme preyed on his mind. The Hajji, who now owed him a debt of gratitude, could have given him the money, but knew Adam to be incapable of taking what would have looked like a bribe. So the servant and the Hajji concocted a scheme by which Adam could lawfully fine the latter £200. The Hajji poses as the slave-dealer; in his fever-crazed state, Adam is deceived and never realises that the acquisition of the money is a put-up job of dubious legality.

Why is the tale so convoluted if it is just propaganda about civilising savage peoples, half-devil and half-child? The interesting thing is that Adam is still sick, and there is no assurance that he will recover. Moreover, although he is under stress beforehand, fever strikes only after the Hajji appears. In some way the presence of the Hajji is bound up with the illness; the oddness is compounded by the mysteriousness with which he appears and the strangeness of the name given to him ('That One'). Adam's boss is given a similarly resonant name ('the Man with Stone Eyes'). Both are referred to as Great Ones, and the reader realises gradually that the story is a morality and that they are types of Satan and God, a realisation helped by That One's exclamation, 'Be quick with my trial. I am not Job' (p. 191). The implication is that it is Adam who has been allotted that role, and that he is being tested, as Job was tested by God's deliverance of him into the hand of Satan. But, unlike Job, Adam has unwittingly made friends with the Devil, who has in return adopted him as a son.

In this framework, what is the role of the absent mother, who has retired to play 'Once in Royal David's City' on the organ in the next room upon the first mention of cannibals? She is given the last tune, and the closing words of the tale could be taken to indicate that the son will be saved by her tender care. 'Presently she passed us on her way to the music-room humming the *Magnificat*' (p. 196). So she is a Mary-figure. But then the Magnificat is Mary's triumphant thanksgiving to God for her exaltation as mother of the Saviour. The meek Mary's greatness is contingent upon her son's crucifixion as well as upon the Incarnation. The flowers that Agnes Strickland orders for the table are marigolds, Mary's flower. But, as the old India hands in the story all know, they also mean death.

The applicability to the situation that Adam faces is complex. When he first goes to his district the cannibals offer him 'four pounds of woman's breasts . . . skewered up in a plantain leaf' (p. 179). Horrified, he wishes to exterminate all the brutes, but the only way of doing this, his District Commissioner tells him, is to let himself be killed by the cannibals, so that reprisals can then be taken for the death of a white man. In other words, he can stop outrage being offered to motherhood (represented by the breast) only by self-sacrifice and ensuing slaughter, and it is at this point that the signs of mental strain begin to show. To turn breast-devourers into useful cotton-growers offers one way out of the impasse. But this he can do only by lies, which are carefully screened from him by his shadow self, his black *body*-servant, and we are not told whether his workers have stopped their practices. Moreover, evil *must* exist in order for him to do good. If there were no slave-dealers for him to fine, he could not have got his first injection of capital. Now that he is in England, he seeks to launder the money by persuading his father's friends to invest. His mother, whose name, 'Agnes Strickland', is significantly the same as that of the once-famous Victorian author of *The Queens of England*, hands him over to the servant: 'You'll take your arsenic, and Imam Din'll take you up to bed, and I'll come and tuck you in' (p. 186). She urges on him a poison that is also a medicine and acts in consort with the shadow self. She adores him, of course, but she is also making him well that he may go back into the heart of darkness to defend her interest. The black soil which is converted into white cotton is black indeed, but what hand will not smite the foul plunderer who grubs up the plants? As Imam Din says of the Great Ones, 'They profit by silence. . . .'

The story also takes up Carlyle's clothing-metaphor. Cotton is the raw stuff of which clothes are made, and thus the young man is involved in a venture that draws a literal veil over nakedness and is also a garment of thought, a symbol that mediates between the concrete and abstract, and which both conceals and reveals the interdependence of good and evil. The tale is a commentary upon Carlyle's dictum that virtue can grow only in secrecy and shame. One has not only to sup with the Devil, but to be ignorant of so doing. But it is equally true that there is a price to be paid both for the supper and for the concealment from oneself. No wonder Adam is sick. He is an entangled hero, not guilty yet feeling the pains of guilt, like the narrator of 'In the House of Suddhoo'; but unlike him he represses conscious awareness of the forces that are controlling him.

'THE VILLAGE THAT VOTED THE EARTH WAS FLAT', 1913–14 (*D of C*)

This story divides readers. A magistrate and MP, Sir Thomas Ingell, has trapped the journalist narrator and his two friends into a speeding-offence. Enlisting the help of Bat Masquerier, an impresario, one of the trio rigs an election by which Ingell's village votes that the earth is flat, and publicises the event. Ingell is

ridiculed on the stage; the music-hall darling of the moment, Miss
Vidal Benzaguen, sets all England singing a catchy song called
'The Earth is Flat' and dancing a sort of conga called 'The Gubby'.
Eventually the madness reaches Parliament, disrupting all business
and forcing an adjournment.

Some regard it as Kipling's funniest revenge hoax, a licensed
feast of fools with Kipling giving his Demon of Irresponsibility a
holiday. Tompkins relates it to the Gilbert and Sullivan of *Iolanthe*,
because that, too, ends in a metamorphosis of the House of
Commons. But she also regards it as a disquieting tale: it 'grew
out of a conviction, at once zestful and misgiving, of the enormous
power of the modern Press and the other publicizing industries
and arts, especially the Music Hall, that were linked with it'. Philip
Mason finds something distasteful in the monstrous scale and
laborious ingenuity. For Tompkins it is a deliberately ambivalent
story; for Mason a farce that Kipling has been unable to control.
There has been, however, at least one reader who denied that it
was intended to be funny at all. B. S. Browne, a frequent and often
perceptive writer to the *Kipling Journal* during the 1930s and 1940s,
called it 'a somewhat grim study of how modern methods of
publicity can be used to drive a man out of public life'.[10] I think
Browne is nearest to the mark; it is an 'entrapment' story – less a
Feast of Fools than a diabolic Wild Hunt. If the reader finds it
funny, that is perhaps because Kipling wrote it as Swiftian satire
and parable for the blind, then sat back to see whether a perverse
generation would tune down his volcano.

Readers assume that the narrator must be sympathetic, because
he is a journalist and lover of the music hall, like the young Kipling.
Actually he is an inversion of the young Kipling, a representative
of the irresponsible power of the press, which Kipling called 'the
harlot's prerogative throughout the ages'[11] and Teufelsdrockh
called 'Satan's Invisible World Displayed' (*Sartor*, I,vi; p. 27). And
the music hall is no longer the Gatti's that Kipling loved; we are in
the rag-time era now.

The journalist narrator is a literary demirep, whose motivation
is pleasure and power rather than money. His antics incur the
rebuke 'Publish and be damned!' – the words of Wellington to the
blackmailing Regency courtesan Harriet Wilson. In his conceit at
his own cleverness he fails to see that he and his friends have
made a diabolic pact with the impresario and unleashed a flood of
evil. Bat Masquerier is a large flaxen-haired man (Kipling gives

him Teutonic features) who is called the 'Personal Devil', the letter
R of whose name on the posters is finished off with a 'long wedge-
shaped flourish', like a tail. He is a bat out of Hell, leading a
masque, a harlequinade, and Harlequin was originally the infernal
Wild Huntsman.[12] The journalists' japes create a diversion from
the urgent problems to which Parliament should be addressing
itself – Ulster, the arraignment of the guilty ministers in the Marconi
scandals, the German menace. The story depicts the English
sinking giggling into the sea, lemmings enacting an anti-fertility
ritual. It registers Kipling's frustration at the tactics of Cecil
Chesterton's *Eye Witness* and his despair of the electoral system
during the pre-war years of the strange death of Liberal England.
To *vote* the earth flat is to use democracy in the service of the curse
of Lear, who called on thunder to strike flat the thick rotundity of
the world.[13]

Whereas in *Stalky & Co.* the Head is there to step in when the
revenge hoax gets out of hand, as in 'The Impressionists', here
there is no authority in the land. The unco' guid Sir Thomas Ingell
(angel) tempts motorists into speeding and then traps them. Here
Kipling introduces one of his ruling ideas – that excessive control
gives lawlessness its opportunity. The Rector and the Doctor (who
vote against the earth's flatness) are too naïve to give a lead, and
are easily discredited. Woodhouse, the newspaper proprietor who
has given publicity to the joke in order to pep up his ailing
newspaper, is by the end beginning to have an inkling of the
infamy of his role, but is by then unable to put the genie back in
the bottle. Only the Speaker of the House has authority, and his
powers are limited to the paradoxical imposition of silence.

To argue in detail for this reading of 'The Village' would take
one into a lengthy examination of English political events in 1913.[14]
I will therefore take one facet, hoping that readers may be induced
to go back to the story and do the rest for themselves. This is the
treatment of the music-hall star, which has a relevance to the Fatal
Woman theme mentioned in the last chapter.

'Dal Benzaguen is ostensibly an adorable young thing, who is
trying to emulate Nellie Farren, the star Kipling admired. But, as
a character says to the narrator, 'The art of the music-hall's changed
since your day.' Nellie, like 'Ellen', a name meaning 'light', is, the
story stresses, dead.[15] She has been replaced by false light,
meretricious glamour, which a magnetic stage presence, exploiting
the public's willingness to be duped, palms off as the real thing,

and if we don't read Kipling very carefully we are duped too.

'Dal is 'worshipped' by 'the youth of that year' and belongs to the Trefoil, which is, with the Jocunda, one of the music halls promoted by Bat Masquerier. Both have names associated in some way with Dark Ladies; the 'Jocunda' (Gioconda) is another name for the Mona Lisa, who is well-known for being older than the rocks amid which she sits, and 'Trefoil' has suggestions of both Diana Trivia (the goddess of the Three Ways whose triple nature includes that of Hecate) and the emblem of Ireland. She is starring as Morgiana in a 'fluid and electric review' called *Morgiana and Drexel*. The peculiar name of the review is a reference to Drexel, Morgan and Co. Drexel, a scion of the Philadelphia banking family, was famous for an unsuccessful 'back to the land' scheme,[16] and this, as in 'Pig', has a punning consonance with the general theme of 'seeking death'. But Morgiana is the slave-girl in 'Ali Baba' who stabs the robber chief while doing the seductive dagger dance. The question is, who is 'Dal's master? Undoubtedly at first Masquerier, who says, 'I *made* 'Dal Benzaguen' (my italics), and whose relationship with her is a kind of Svengali–Trilby one. By the end of the story, though, 'Dal seems to have assumed a kind of independent power. She is also a peri or a sorceress – as much a Fairy Morgue as a Morgiana.

'Dal's act follows the 'Gubby' dance; this begins as a 'sinuous and silent procession . . . it danced the dance which bit all humanity in the leg for half a year, and it wound up with the lock-step finale that mowed the house down in swathes, sobbing and aching'. The theatre scene then changes to 'Morgiana's Manicure Palace'. 'Lock-step' is a drill-term referring to close marching in a line, each man toe to heel. The silent procession *is* a snake. After the mass death from this snake in the grass comes the descent into the underworld. 'Manicure' is 'man I cure'. Like the pomegranate seed in 'Pig', death seductively offers rest from all ills. The Palace is the abode of the Queen of the Night, 'Dal, 'an electric star in her dark hair, the diamonds flashing in her three-inch heels':

> The star on her forehead went out, and a soft light bathed her as she took – slowly, slowly to the croon of adoring strings – the eighteen paces forward. We saw her first as a queen alone; next as a queen for the first time conscious of her subjects, and at the end, when her hands fluttered, as a woman delighted, awed not a little, but transfigured and illuminated with sheer

compelling affection and goodwill. I caught the broken mutter of welcome – the coo which is more than tornadoes of applause. It died and rose and died again lovingly.   (p. 188)

'Dal is a sort of a Rossettian Astarte Syriaca, and like her has the qualities of both love-goddess and moon-goddess.[17] She first excites the audience with her electric star – the emblem of Venus – and then, having aroused passion, the star fades and is replaced with a moony glow. Masquerier comments that her power over the audience is due to her artistic instinct in quenching the star; in other words, Venus is most dangerous when she appears serene and chaste. She is presented as the hypnotised audience sees her, through the medium of theatrical illusion ('We saw her first *as* a queen', etc.). The apparently unequivocal rhapsody about her star quality is mediated through an unreliable narrator in ambiguous terms.

Announcing that she has just come from 'The Village that Voted the Earth was Flat', the name of which (Huckley) may be derived from '"Argile", on account of its much clay' (p. 171),[18] she leads the audience in the big show-stopper, the chorus of which runs '*Earth* was flat – *Earth* was flat'. The stress falls heavily on the word 'Earth', as Kipling reminds readers by no fewer than twelve subsequent repetitions; the populace is under the impression that it is singing a satirical version of 'Nuts in May', but it is chanting a literal *dirige* to the grave and unconsciously voicing a death-wish. Finally the MPs sing it, 'first, because they wanted to, and secondly – which is the terror of that song – because they could not stop' (p. 211). When the House adjourns, some of the members are 'nearly on all fours', which is what Circean temptresses do to men. The earth compels. We are dying, Egypt, dying.

'THE VORTEX', 1914 (*D of C*)

Randall Jarrell disarmingly summarised the plot of this tale in the single sentence 'The railway station and crossroads of an English village are immobilised by four cartons of bees', and said, 'One enjoys Kipling's farce for its charm and landscape, and is indifferent to its point.'[19] Others have seen it as an amusing political fantasy. Here, seemingly, is Kipling treating Empire in a playful way, saying that there is no bore like an imperialist bore, praising with faint damns British amateurism, and working in his great interest in bee-keeping.

The story reintroduces a character first encountered in 'The Puzzler' (*AR*), 'the Hon. A. M. Penfentenyou, once Minister of Woods and Waysides in De Thouar's first administration; later, Premier in all but name of one of Our great and growing dominions; and now, as always, the idol of his own Province, which is two and one-half the size of England' (*D of C*, p. 381). Dressed in a white waistcoat, black frock-coat and top-hat, he announces 'ambassadorially' that 'We have come to have a Voice in Your Councils. By the way, the Voice is coming down on the evening train with my Agent-General.' When the narrator asks for the name of the Voice, Penfentenyou replies, 'We call him all sorts of names, but I think you'd better call him Mr Lingnam.' Mr Lingnam, he adds, talks so much about imperialism as to cure nearly anyone of it. The narrator takes his visitors on a motor tour into the peaceful English countryside, where the misadventure with the bees, caused by the pompous Mr Lingnam's inability to master English left-hand driving-habits, wakes the latter up to the power of the unexpected to disrupt grand ideas. At the end of the day the badly stung Lingnam–Voice is still talking federation, but has drawn a lesson from the day's events. Before, he had deplored militarism, but now advocates 'Permanently Mobilised Communities' ready to strike at the first 'buzz' of war irrespective of 'the merits of any *casus belli*'.

Federation of the British Empire was a hardy perennial during the thirty years before the First World War, and was topical again after the Imperial Conference of 1911. Kipling passionately believed in it, but considered that the Empire should be held together by ties of loyalty and love, leaving each Dominion free to leave.[20] De Thouar, it has been argued, was loosely suggested by the former Canadian premier Sir Wilfred Laurier (whom Kipling despised), with Penfentenyou as an imaginary French-Canadian politician. Laurier at the Imperial Conferences of 1902 and 1907 voiced Canada's fear of being engulfed in a 'vortex of militarism', and this had become a famous catch-phrase.[21]

The Canadian identification works up to a point. Mr Lingnam repeats Laurier's 'vortex of militarism' phrase and is confused about which side of the road to drive on. But then it breaks down. Mr Lingnam is in favour of federating the Empire and setting up a Pan-Imperial Council, but Canada was not. He also proposes that each Dominion should shoulder the burden of the defence of the Empire, instead of leaving the expense to Britain. This was not Canadian policy, which was for developing Canada's own independent defence force, as distinct from subscribing to an imperial one. The only Dominion that supported an imperial defence force was New Zealand, whose Premier, Sir Joseph Ward, had mooted it at the 1911 Conference. But this cannot make Mr Lingnam a New Zealander either. To deplore the 'vortex of militarism' while simultaneously supporting imperial federation was not a position held by any Dominion during this period. A further puzzle lies in Penfentenyou's disagreement with his own spokesman; why has Mr Lingnam been appointed the Voice if he is not only stupid but also out of accord with his premier-in-all-but-name?

Some light begins to dawn upon finding out that in 1913 the only province of the Empire which was two and a half times the size of England was the Presidency of Bombay in British India, in which Kipling was born,[22] and upon noticing that 'De Thouar' is a pretty transparent anagram of both 'Our Death' and 'Thou Dear'. Who, then, or what, is the black-and-white garbed Pentenfenyou, De Thouar's former minister? His name has a note of menace, like the refrain of a child's counting-out rhyme ending in 'Out goes you!' Is he not, then, what Kipling called the 'Personal Devil' or the 'Black Thought', a sort of anti-guardian-angel whose visitation prompts a momentary vision of the world as one of the hells? The narrator calls him his friend ironically; 'friend' in Kipling often means 'fiend'.[23] He has been assigned him at birth and been visited by him over the years, and Mephistopheles is, after all, a gentleman, who seduces with fair words and false smiles. (That Penfentenyou is just such a charming wheeler-dealer is stressed in both 'The Vortex' and 'The Puzzler'.) The Agent-General is De Thouar's and Penfentenyou's factotum, which makes him a variant of the Angel Azrael, who appears several times in Kipling's work.[24] At one point he squeezes the narrator's hand affectionately, saying, 'We have just found out that we are brothers.' In context, this means that they are both fans of Stevenson and Osbourne's *The Wrong Box*, a story whose jocular treatment of death is relevant to 'The Vortex'. But they are also both artists; Kipling, like Azrael, has the power to kill off his characters. Mr Lingnam is self-deluding Elemental Man (as he is called at one point); his name is an anagram of 'manling' and is very nearly 'lingam'. Of course Kipling intended that the contemporary reader should think of Canada, but Canada is only a front. Mr Lingnam is the voice of British India trying to have a say in the Conference of the powers and parroting Laurier's catch-phrases.

The adventure in Penfentenyou's car gives the narrator a mild foretaste of England's green and pleasant land as inferno. As the car crosses the symbolic bridge into the village, the narrator's perceiving mind enters the 'Fourth Dimension', where past, present and future are almost perceived as 'One Awful Whole'. Lingnam nearly kills a boy riding a bicycle, onto which has been piled four bonnet-boxes loaded with bees. The sheer unlikelihood that a bicycle could take such a load or that bees would be transported in this way are markers that Kipling has moved out of the realistic mode. As the bees 'sweep forward cone-wise like shrapnel', the Foresters, who are holding a fête in the village, 'shouted like Sodom and Gomorrah'. Shut up in the railway station waiting-rooms to avoid being stung, the 'prisoners . . . cried out a great deal'. The narrator says, 'I argued that they were dying of the heat' and shouts out to Penfentenyou that the scene looks like Hell. Penfentenyou – such a hypocrite, considering that he comes from the place – feigns shock at this profanity and accuses the narrator of extremism.[25]

The association between Hell and bees is found in Milton and Pope, authors well-known to Kipling.[26] The bees in 'The Vortex' are she-devils. They belong to a 'silver-haired lady', are called collectively 'Deborah' after the formidable Old Testament judge, whose name means 'a bee', and are, of course, 'bees in the bonnet' of crazy females, such as Kipling's *bêtes noires*, the suffragettes.

Mrs Bellamy, the silver-haired owner of the bees, seems at first to be a benign 'wise woman', like the ancestor of the Bee-Boy in 'Dymchurch Flit' (*RF*). She is called Bellamy (Belle Amie – beautiful friend) and appears to be an enemy of Penfentenyou, refusing to let him bribe his way into her house. But, when he snatches up a little girl and tucks her under his coat, 'the woman's countenance blanched, the front door opened, Penfentenyou and the child pressed through' (p. 391). She has evidently admitted Penfentenyou in order to protect the child, but once he is inside the house he seems to seduce her into complicity. Her house becomes a Swinburnian one of death and birth, and she emerges as a quarrelsome scold. She and Penfentenyou contrive to dress Lingnam in her dead husband's clothes, at which point he undergoes a personality change, destroying the bee-boy's bicycle and threatening to kill her.

Has Mrs Bellamy been a friend or not? She has forced Mr Lingnam to recognise conflict as an inescapable part of life. Kipling was certain that the only way in which Germany could be deterred from an attempt at world-domination was to have a fully armed and defended Empire, and that those who deplored the 'vortex of militarism' were inviting the Day of the Storm-Cone (the unmentioned vortex) and Armageddon. His sardonic point seems to be that the monstrous regiment, in rousing men from sentimental apathy and nebulous talk, will indirectly mobilise the forces of the Empire against the Hun menace. But, if they ensure that Britain does not go naked into Armageddon, they are advancing the date. Lingnam's new readiness to go to war 'at first buzz', irrespective of the rightness of the cause, is the mark of the fools in Horace who, in trying to avoid one vice, rush into its opposite.[27] 'I don't want to hear any more of your damned, detached mugwumping excuses for the other fellow', he snaps, refusing to acknowledge his error. Penfentenyou congratulates him on his new-found extremism: 'Now you are beginning to see things. I hope you won't backslide when the swellings go down' (p. 402), on which sinister pun the story ends. Penfentenyou, the narrator has told us, is acting on behalf of an unscrupulous Province, and sees a chance of enlarging it by encouraging Mr Lingnam's irrational behaviour.

Kipling's preface poems and epigraphs are sometimes counter-statements. A poem may be the song of innocence to its accompanying tale's song of experience, for instance. But sometimes it is a guide as to how to read the tale, as with 'The True Romance'. The preface poem to 'The Vortex' ('The Fabulists') declares that, 'When all the world would have a matter hid / For Truth is seldom friend to any crowd', writers are forced to have recourse to fable, 'jesting at that which none will name aloud'. Even 'when diligent Sloth demandeth Freedom's death' in 'that certain hour before the fall', truth-tellers are forced to keep their readership amused: 'Unless they please they are not heard at all'. They work so that 'men taking pleasure may take heed', but, though they please, they are unheeded.

'The Vortex' was published in a grim month: August 1914. The great Anarch is about to let the curtain fall. It is a jest written by a despairing modern Momus, who, powerless to mend the bad times, decides that it is better to laugh than to cry. The cap-and-bells knows that his eleventh-hour warning will fall on deaf ears and that some problems have no solutions. Perhaps readers would now like to try 'The Puzzler'.

Of the tales discussed at any length so far, all except 'Pig' and 'A Matter of Fact' are concerned in one way or another with female power, which as much as work or the Nether Chaotic Deep is one of Kipling's major themes. As previously stated in the Introduction, this study is not offering an adequate account of Kipling's treatment of gender, but, as powerful females are prominent in the central stories discussed in each of the next four chapters, some prefatory remarks on this topic come appropriately at this point.

The view that his notorious line 'The Female of the Species is more deadly than the Male' sums up his attitude to women is still strong, though it has been modified in more recent years by the critical notice paid to late stories such as 'The Gardener' and 'The Wish House', where women are the central consciousness. But Angus Wilson was swimming against critical opinion in 1977 when he claimed that 'Kipling's early work . . . is largely marked by his extraordinary understanding of the unfairness of women's lives, with his sympathy and liking for them.'[28] Even so, he had to admit that *The Light that Failed* was a disappointing regression.

To place these two views together is to see that they are complementary. Men in Kipling give way to misogyny because they cannot take any longer the burden of their bad record towards women and (in chivalrous souls) the strain of maintaining an excessive, compensatory worshipfulness. No one rendered more acutely than Kipling the neuroses of a patriarchal society that feels inwardly bad about being patriarchal; when woman is more deadly than the male it is *because* her wrongs at his hands have been flagrant and appalling. Therefore she is revengeful – inevitably so.

The view is the same as that expressed by Byron in *Don Juan*, II.cxcix–cc:

> their revenge is as the tiger's spring,
> Deadly, and quick, and crushing; yet as real
> Torture is theirs – what they inflict they feel.
>
> They are right; for man to man so oft unjust,
> Is always so to women. . . .

A good deal of Kipling's work can be regarded as an expatiation on this passage.[29] Seducers and philanderers are usually punished, sometimes by the *wili*-like phantom images of the women they have wronged. The victim becomes demonic and powerful after death. The victim woman also often has a powerful ally–agent within her own sex such as a mother, niece or aunt; the revenge of the powerful sisterhood is savage but just.[30]

When men suffer gratuitously because of women it is often because they are paying for enormities committed by others. This is the real moral of 'The Man Who Would Be King'. Cornell, ignoring the importance of the woman's biting Dravot and thus revealing him to be merely human, sees it as the tragedy of a man who defies the God of things-as-they-are, and 'attempts to impose upon modern reality the dreams that properly belong to poetry, history and legend'.[31] Actually Dravot's fall comes about because of his ignorance of poetry, history and legend, which could have told him that he was behaving dangerously in taking a wife from a community which sacrifices women to sate the lust of gods, for the woman has nothing to lose, and something to gain, by testing his divinity. Peachey was right to warn him off dealings with women, not because women are intrinsically evil and clogs on the realisation of men's dreams, but because they have a long score to settle. Moreover, Dravot, though incredulous of the idea that, *qua* god, he might kill a woman, intends to have a queen only for the winter months, and has just talked of the Kafiristani girls as though they were so much meat: 'We can take the pick of them. Boil 'em once or twice in hot water and they'll come out like chicken and ham.' Of course that's just a manner of speaking, but in Kipling *idle words are dangerous*.[32]

Peachey is stupid too: he refuses to see that, willy-nilly, he has already had dealings with women. He tries to finance the expedition by getting hush-money from a native rajah who has filled 'his father's widow' with red pepper and slippered her to death as she hung from a beam. Instead of exposing the rajah as a professional journalist should, Peachey intends to take the money and suppress the evidence. He entrusts the narrator with a mission 'for the sake of my Mother as well as your own' (that is, the Masonic Mother Lodge), but the brutal death of a literal mother, the 'father's widow', who, one may assume, had declined to commit suttee, is to him merely the means by which he may become a king. There is a cruel likeness between Peachey's own fate (crucifixion and eventual death from sunstroke) and that of the dead ranee/mother. The effect of this is to blur the differences between the barbaric natives and the civilised white men, who also metaphorically sacrifice women to achieve their god-like ambitions. Dravot and Peachey are tragic heroes, as Cornell says, because their obsessive singlemindness both focuses their questing energy and leads them into fatal complicity with women-enslavers and mother-haters.

Sometimes Kipling treats the theme comically. In 'The Post that Fitted' (*DV*, p. 11) the impecunious Sleary devises an ingenious but heartless cheat. He proposes to Minnie Boffkins. When her father finds a lucrative post for him, he simulates epileptic fits so that she will break the engagement. The clever chap then marries his sweetheart. But in the very last verse Minnie's mother suddenly pops up like a wandless bad fairy:

> Year by year, in pious patience, vengeful Mrs Boffkins sits
> Waiting for the Sleary babies to develop Sleary's fits.

Since the fits were produced by Pears soap, there is no possibility of a *hereditary* curse. And yet . . . : it is an ominously open ending. There may yet be a pay-off for Mrs Boffkins's piety and patience. We now turn to a different Mrs B, the most famous in the Kipling canon.

4
Kipling and Dante (I): 'Mrs Bathurst'

*'Setting that aside, so to say, 'ave you ever found
these little things make much difference?
Because I haven't.'*
('Mrs Bathurst')

'Mrs Bathurst', written in early 1904, just after 'A Deal in Cotton', when Kipling was spending his winters in South Africa, was published later that year in the collection *Traffics and Discoveries* (1904).[1] Its setting and theme of the journey into the interior from which one emerges with unspeakable knowledge has caused it to be compared with Conrad's *Heart of Darkness*. At the same time, it has acquired the mystique of being like Henry James's 'The Figure in the Carpet' – a great uncrackable, 'the hardest of all the stories'. 'The reader turns on the brilliantly contrived treadmill of speculation, an endless spool which no critic has yet succeeded in halting', as Richard Holmes puts it. Few critics of his adult fiction have been able to resist the challenge, and there is a sizable 'What happens in "Mrs Bathurst"?' literature, to which I am about to add. Those who resist the challenge do so on the grounds that the story is over-compressed to the point of unintelligibility or even downright pretentious. For Angus Wilson the problem of its meaning 'will remain unanswered' because it 'probably never had much meaning'.[2]

Four men – Hooper, a railway inspector; Pyecroft, a naval petty officer; Pritchard, a sergeant of Marines; and the narrator – meet and drink in a railway-siding near Simon's Bay, Cape Province, shortly after the Boer War. After reminiscing about a certain Boy Niven, who once lured 'seven or eight' young seamen into walking around a barren island in the Vancouver archipelago, and Moon, who deserted his sloop *Astrild*, conversation turns to the disappearance of a naval warrant officer, 'Click' Vickery. Pyecroft reports that 'Click' had been attending Phyllis's travelling circus in Capetown: every night he compulsively watched a film showing a Mrs Bathurst alighting from the Plymouth–London train. She is his ex-mistress or bigamous wife (we gather), the proprietress of a seaside hotel in New Zealand, an unforgettable woman, a feeder of lame ducks and a trampler on scorpions, the sort whose effect on a man 'struck' with her is that he 'goes crazy – or just saves himself'. With the departure of the circus imminent, Vickery has become increasingly deranged, but his captain, after a long private inter-view, has given him (exceptionally) a solo assignment to dispatch some Navy ammunition at Bloemfontein. After completing the task Vickery has vanished. Hooper then discloses that about a month before, at M'Bindwe, a railway-siding in the teak jungle past Bulawayo, he spotted the bodies of two tramps. They had been burnt to charcoal by a lightning-bolt, but Vickery was identifiable by his tattoo – the letters 'M. V.' with a 'foul anchor' – which showed up as white, and by his false teeth, which Hooper has retained. Pritchard is very upset by this revelation. Covering his face for a moment 'like a child shutting out an ugliness', he murmurs, 'And to think of her at Hauraki . . . with 'er 'air-ribbon on my beer. . . . Oh, my Gawd! . . .' 'Thank Gawd he's dead!' says Pyecroft.

What is the relevance of the Boy Niven episode? What did Vickery say to the captain? Is Vickery punished or saved? What are the men shuddering at in the end? Above all (and in the end most questions about the mystery of 'Mrs Bathurst' come down to this), who is Vickery's companion in the teak forest?

That these questions are insoluble is a proposition to which Kipling himself gave some licence. A Miss Tulse, who seems to have asked, 'What had Vickery done?' shortly after the book's publication, received the reply, 'No man but Vickery knows what Vickery had done. He may have represented himself as a single man and so have won her widowed heart. Whatever it was it was *The Thing Too Much* which a man mustn't do.'[3] It isn't likely, however, that Kipling would have offered readers a helping hand. His introduction to the Outward Bound Edition contains a refusal to provide interpretation: 'It is not needed to show strangers our charts, for these be of man's making and each must prick his own for himself.' When Capel Hall sent him a 'solution' his reply was merely that it was very interesting.[4] In Miss Tulse's case I think he was being thoroughly disingenuous, answering her question *au pied de la lettre*, instead of directing her to the question she should have asked. It is indeed true that no man within the fictional world of the story can *know* what Vickery has done; none of them was witness either to a seduction of Mrs Bathurst or to his death. What can be deduced, however, is the understanding that the men have arrived at by the very end, the story that they have constructed between themselves. Or, to be more precise, the story that the reporter–narrator has edited. To understand that is to understand the mystery of 'Mrs Bathurst'. In fact the mystery is not what Vickery 'really' has done, but what the narrator thinks the men think, what kind of shared understanding he believes has flashed between them in the last few paragraphs of the tale. The mode of the story allows one to speculate that the narrator and the men have got it wrong and that the facts in the case were really quite different, but there is no way of getting at *them* or outside the narrator's possibly distorted consciousness.

Actually, the scrutiny that 'Mrs Bathurst' has received over the last sixty years has considerably advanced understanding of what kind of story it is. It is recognised that no detail is gratuitous. 'The story is as precise as a Swiss watch. Everything fits, but the reader has to wind it up', wrote Craig Raine.[5] The Niven and *Astrild* episodes are no longer seen as irrelevances, but are seen as underlinings of the theme of desertion and dereliction of duty. 'The margins of the story are thus littered with flotsam and jetsam, those who have cut loose from the brotherhood so crucial to the other stories and must wander the face of the earth without belonging anywhere' as Hermione Lee wrote in a fine description of the tale's emotional effect.[6] It is often noticed that the early cinematograph, with its flickering, repetitive, grey, ghost-like images, functions as a metaphor for the way the story develops and should be read. Kipling was among the first, if indeed he was not the first, to realise that the new medium changed the consciousness, especially in the sphere of the erotic, and that the experience of seeing the object of desire, magnified and impalpable, could add a new intensity to frustrated fantasising and give a modern application to Keats's 'I eternally see her figure eternally vanishing'.[7]

Much of what we now understand about the story is owed to three critics, J. M. S. Tompkins, C. A. Bodelsen and Elliot L. Gilbert, who came up with different readings, but who were nevertheless agreed in their approach.[8] The reader must infer the unknown from the known. Gilbert wrote that the whole narrative may . . . be considered an extended example of aposiopesis', the 'device of classical rhetoric which seeks, on every level, to withhold the ultimate secret'. Kipling's use of the unfinished sentence as in '"Two?" Pyecroft said. "I don't envy that other man if – "' exemplifies his overall strategy. The close reader can 'reconstruct the end of the sentence and so . . . participate . . . in the creation of the story.'[9] The cue to do so is given by one of the narrative voices, Pyecroft: 'I used to think seein' and hearin' was the only way to ascertainin' facts, but as we get older we get more accommodatin'' (*TD*, p. 353).

Bodelsen wrote 'The story *must* have a definite meaning, and it must be possible to get at it, if only one picks up the right trail.' Though Gilbert would accommodate this 'definite meaning' within an overarching concern with 'man's eternal quest for knowledge and control and his permanent inability to achieve either',[10] they agreed that Mrs Bathurst has been deserted – and Kipling's reply to Miss Tulse hints as much. Both critics saw a pointer to the 'right trail' in Kipling's epigraph to the story, an enigmatic pastiche Jacobean dramatic 'fragment' entitled 'From Lyden's *Irenius*'. The narrative (such as it is) concerns a poor groom who is to be hanged, cursing Fortune and women's love, damned to death by a woman who 'knew not that she did it, or would have died ere she had done it. For she loved him' (p. 338). Gilbert and Bodelsen both took this to mirror Mrs Bathurst's behaviour in some way, but diverged thereafter.

Gilbert believed that Mrs Bathurst has destroyed Vickery, but unwittingly; her image, fixed on film by sheer accident, pursues him to his death, while she remains oblivious of her devastating powers. Had she known that they would have this effect, she would have sooner laid down her life. Thus Pritchard's shock registers his appalled recognition that even the most innocent of females is the blind agent of a 'terrible power totally beyond [her] understanding and control'.[11]

Bodelsen at first thought that Mrs Bathurst was an avenging fury, but later decided that she had saved Vickery's soul. He attached great significance to the whiteness of Vickery's 'foul anchor' tattoo, which to him suggested the purification of falsity by fire. Elements of a mother-figure in her presentation made her a likely redeemer, who pardoned the man responsible for her death.

It is necessary for his reading that Mrs Bathurst should be dead when Vickery watches her on film. He adduced some strong arguments which Gilbert did not engage with. Since 'we have been pointedly told that Vickery's wife has recently died in childbed and that he has only a short time to wait before he is pensioned off, . . . there would be nothing to prevent him from marrying Mrs Bathurst, *if she were still alive*. . . . There would be no need for him to torture himself by seeing her picture every night.'[12] He inferred that she had followed Vickery to England; he had rejected her, or perhaps revealed that he had a lawful wife, whereupon she had killed herself or died of grief. Vickery's wife had died only after he left England for South Africa, and he must have been maintaining marital relations with her since she was pregnant. This would account for his enigmatic confession to Pyecroft: 'Remember, that I am *not* a murderer, because my lawful wife died in childbed six weeks after I came out. That much at least I am clear of' (p. 362). For Bodelsen this indicated that Vickery had an 'unlawful' wife, whom he did not actually kill, but for whose death he feels responsible. (Vickery tells Pyecroft when the latter asks 'I wonder what she is doin' in England?' that 'She's lookin' for me'.)[13]

While the reading that I am going to put forward does not absolutely hinge on the assumption that she is dead – it would still work if Vickery thought that she was lost to him for ever and that he would never find her again – it does work more neatly if we accept Bodelsen's reasoning. He could have strengthened it by taking more account of the mythic dimension of the story, a dimension already well-recognised. Gilbert perceived that the Mars–Venus myth lay behind the story, and saw significance in this sentence from '*Irenius*': 'Not an astrologer, but would ha' sworn he'd foreseen it at the last versary of Venus, when Vulcan caught her with Mars in the house of stinking Capricorn.' This indicated for Gilbert the passionate nature of the relationship of Mrs Bathurst and Vickery; he pointed out that Vulcan was the artificer of lightning-bolts.[14] He could have added that both South Africa and New Zealand are under Capricorn and that the white letters 'M.V.' of Vickery's tattoo could stand for Mars and Venus.[15] To J. M. S. Tompkins the South African setting suggested a Greek coast and hence a suitable place for the appearance of Aphrodite. Bodelsen, agreeing, commented that the introduction of Greeks who sell the narrator beer is 'one of those discreet verbal pointers that Kipling was later on to use so much as a means to direct the reader towards the right associations'.[16] Another, hitherto unrecognised, is 'Phyllis's circus'.

The myth of Phyllis and Demophoön was one with resonances for Kipling's family. Burne-Jones's painting of the subject (1870) offended the Old English Water-Colour Society because of its frankness, and he resigned because of the committee's prudery. The story had a private meaning for him and was bound up with his unhappy liaison with a beautiful Greek sculptress, Maria Zambaco.[17]

Phyllis, a Thracian queen, hanged herself after the desertion of her lover, Demophoön, the seafaring stranger prince, who in some versions of the legend is smitten with remorse. Phyllis is a narrative voice in Ovid's *Heroides*. There the wrong done to a *trusting hostess* is emphasised; there are verbal resemblances between the description of the seashore where Phyllis at first contemplates drowning herself and the symbolic 'False Bay' where the story opens.[18] In Chaucer's *The Legend of Good Women* (Kipling's knowledge of Chaucer will receive attention later), Phyllis writes to Demophoön, 'My body mote ye se, withinne a while, / Ryght in the haven of Athenes fletynge, / Withoute sepulture and buryinge' (ll. 2251–3). Substitute 'Capetown' for 'Athenes', interpret 'fletynge' (floating) as 'gliding in space' rather than 'lying on the water', and one has Vickery's experience at the film. The circus in 'Mrs Bathurst' is Phyllis's because it conveys the message of a modern Phyllis to Vickery from beyond the grave.[19]

The groom in the epigraph is *hanged*, a pointer to the significance of *hanging* within the tale, where it figures overtly as the condign punishment for mutiny. It is also suggested covertly at several points. When describing Mrs Bathurst as she was in Auckland, Pyecroft says 'an' she always wore black silk, and 'er neck –'. He is interrupted by Pritchard, who proceeds to describe her trustfulness (*TD*, pp. 349–50). This, I think, is one of Kipling's significant aposiopeses. On the realistic level the reader can finish Pyecroft's sentence with ''ad a gold watch an' chain round it'. Pritchard's story is about her taking her watch and chain off her neck and lending it to a bosun who had come without his 'ticker'. Once, however, the reader has seen Mrs Bathurst as re-enacting Phyllis's story, the attention drawn to her neck by the aposiopesis will recall the fate of Phyllis when her trust was betrayed, and the watch-chain will be seen as anticipatory of a noose.[20]

Another telling detail is contained in Pritchard's description of another of Mrs Bathurst's memorable actions; he alludes to it in his horrified climax: 'And to think of her at Hauraki . . . with 'er 'air ribbon on my beer.' On Pritchard's first departure from Auckland, Mrs Bathurst had cut off her ribbon with 'that old dolphin cigar-cutter on the bar – remember it, Pye?' and tied it so as to identify the last four bottles of his 'particular' brand. Five years after he returns to find that she immediately remembers him, calls for his beer, and draws the corks saying 'I do 'ope you 'aven't changed your mind about your particulars.' The telling detail is that the ribbons are tied 'in a bow round each of their *necks*' (pp. 350–1, my italics).

The 'dolphin cigar-cutter' is another detail placed to alert us to the non-naturalistic quality of this episode. The dolphin in Greek myth conveys sailors safely to land, and is a lucky charm appropriate in a hotel kept by a hostess whose special care is of wandering sailors. The beer is similarly treated. Beer-bottles function as an emblem of women themselves, considered as objects to be 'consumed', and the keeping of a 'particular' beer for a man is a pledge of her fidelity; reciprocally, there is a parallel drawn between fidelity to a particular woman and fidelity to a particular beer. The symbol of woman-as-bottle is not private to Kipling – it is a part of a generally understood turn-of-the-century picture-code, and found, for instance, in *Jude the Obscure* and Manet's *Bar aux Folies Bergère*, where the woman is as available as the beer she sells. (Interestingly, both 'Mrs Bathurst' and Manet's painting feature a bottle of Bass and a group of four bottles, though in the case of the painting they are of champagne.) The most famous case is the Coca-Cola bottle, the design of which was reputedly inspired by the hour-glass shape induced by corseting.

Mrs Bathurst is respected by the sailors because she does not actually go to bed with the Navy – 'she wasn't *that*'. But they adore her because, symbolically, she offers herself to all yet 'keeps herself' for each, no 'Dol Common' but 'Dol Particular'. She embodies a nineteenth-century male fantasy – the genuine Madonna–whore: liberal, yet still innocent, maternal and faithful, not hardened and venal. Her lending of her 'ticker' shows her heart to be of the purest gold – 'ticker' was also current slang for the heart; she has qualities of the 'Mother o' mine' who rescues even those damned of body and soul, and is especially cherished by promiscuous men such as Pritchard and Pyecroft. The bosun has to catch the 'last boat'; there are overtones here of the woman whose love redeems a dying man from eternal perdition. Like Mrs Hauksbee, she is given an oxymoronic name. She is both the bath of bliss (or the bar) which refreshes thirsting man, and the thirst that rages in her absence.

More crucial, however, than the 'Is Mrs Bathurst dead?' problem, is the question of Vickery's companion. Who is the tramp? Since the story first started being discussed in the 1930s, readers have been divided into those who immediately assumed that it was Mrs Bathurst, the lightning-bolt standing for the fierce, lawless passion that has consumed them both, and those who as immediately assumed that it was a totally new character, a male drifter who just happened to be around. In Alan Sandison's opinion this is a blemish on an otherwise fine story: Kipling cheated in not allowing Hooper to say whether the figure was a man or Mrs Bathurst, 'for he was there and he saw them'.[21]

Those who want the tramp to be Mrs Bathurst say that it would not have been typical of Kipling to introduce a completely new and functionless character into such a tightly constructed story. (This receives some external support from the advice he gave Charles Warren Stoddard.[22]) Gilbert's reply was that the tramp had a function – to make the point that Vickery has committed passive suicide. When the lightning strikes, he stands up to attract it. Unless one had another figure by way of contrast (the dead tramp is squatting down), the point would not have been made. If so, this is a very clumsy device, and puzzling. What has the poor tramp done that he should be made to share Vickery's fate? Nothing, apparently, except to stray into Kipling's mind when stuck for a plot-mechanism. Gilbert, however, had a more powerful string to his bow, and one to which he was more committed. If the tramp had no function, the very gratuitousness of his appearance would be underlining the story's wider theme – man's search for meaning in a chaotic universe.[23] Unfortunately, the first bowstring gets in the way of the second. If the appearance of the tramp is supposed to be emblematic of the chaotic and random workings of the universe, then he really ought to have no discernible function at all. In any case, Kipling could surely have contrived a more arbitrary, less appropriate-seeming death for Vickery – one freer of associations with divine vengeance, the fires of passion or spontaneous combustion resulting from suppressed emotion (among the last words Pyecroft says to him are 'Consume your own smoke'). More importantly, any reading which is certain that the second corpse is not the dead Mrs Bathurst must reckon with features which have led readers to suppose that it is.

Chief among these is the use Kipling makes of the ballad 'The Honeysuckle and the Bee', which is sung by some picnickers immediately after Pritchard's 'Oh my Gawd!':

> On a summer afternoon, when the honeysuckle blooms,
>   And all Nature seems at rest,
> Underneath the bower, 'mid the perfume of the flower
>   Sat a maiden with the one she loves the best.

'This is clearly meant as an ironic curtain for the tale', Bodelsen commented, 'where the "bower" was a tropical wilderness, and the maiden and her lover two charred corpses'.[24] Bodelsen also saw in the positioning of the lovers in the song a correspondence with those of the corpses. 'One of 'em [Vickery] was standin' up by the dead-end of the siding an' the other was squatting down lookin' up at 'im, you see', which to Bodelsen suggested looking up with the assurance that he was forgiven. The phrase is certainly significant; Hooper repeats it, changing the wording slightly: 'like his mate squatting down an' watchin' him, both of 'em all wet in the rain'. The added words 'his mate' are also important. 'It is easily overlooked that [they] may at a pinch be applied to a woman, though the inspector no doubt thinks they are men', commented Bodelsen.[25] There are additional verbal links, not spotted by Bodelsen, between the bower and the wilderness. The 'Bee' corresponds to Mrs Bathurst, who is several times called 'Mrs B'. The name of the siding, M'Bindwe, suggests by aposiopesis the word 'bindweed'; the honeysuckle arbour, the traditional emblem of wedded love, is contrasted to 'bindweed', or convolvulus, also a twining plant, but scentless, predatory and emblematic of lawless passion. Holman Hunt uses it in *The Awakening Conscience* to symbolise the sterility of the kept mistress's love-nest; in Kipling's early poem 'Discovery' it is emblematic of the aftermath of 'dead love' (*EV*, p. 144).

Bodelsen also thought that Victor Prout's illustrations to the magazine version of the story were conclusive, claiming that the picture supposed to be of Hooper finding the bodies showed an unquestionably feminine figure. Kipling would never have allowed it through, he argued, if it was untrue to the intentions of his story. Unfortunately the available evidence points to Kipling having no control over magazine illustrations, and there is one known case of an illustrator ludicrously misreading his text.[26] Moreover, the charred tramp looks rather more masculine than feminine and the hands do not match those of Mrs Bathurst behind the bar. In my opinion this is a red herring, but two illustrations are reproduced in the plate section of this book that readers may judge for themselves.

However, Bodelsen saw that the tramp's corpse could not be that of Mrs Bathurst. How had she got there? Was she in men's clothes, and, if so, why? But in any case his argument required that she was dead. Yet he found it impossible to ignore the pointers that in some sense the tramp *was* Mrs Bathurst, and came up with the following ingenious shifts. One was that on the naturalistic level the dead tramp was indeed a chance-met male companion, but that at the moment of death he supernaturally 'became' Mrs Bathurst. Her soul had entered his body, so that Vickery and she could be together for all eternity. Bodelsen produced a naturalistic alternative: 'Vickery had a hallucination by which he believes that the tramp is Mrs Bathurst's ghost.'[27] Either way, Vickery died with the assurance that he had been saved at the last moment.

One wonders why it was necessary in order that the souls of Mrs Bathurst and Vickery should be reunited in the afterlife that her disembodied spirit should have to descend into a body again, even for a split second – the 'moment of death'.[28] Or why Vickery should imagine that the tramp was Mrs Bathurst's *ghost*. Since the tramp was material enough, it is more plausible that he would have imagined that his companion was Mrs Bathurst's *reincarnation*. All things considered, Bodelsen's explanation does not hold together. Nevertheless, the very difficulties that his theory presents lead to what I consider to be the answer.

Vickery leaves Cape Town 'happyish' and saying to Pyecroft, 'Phyllis's Circus will be performing at Worcester to-morrow night. So I shall see 'er yet once again' (*TD* p. 361). This shows that he intends to follow the circus for as long as he can. The film show goes on an 'up-country' tour – Hooper has seen it when he was there (p. 353) – so it has gone north by way of the Southern Africa railway system. This explains why Vickery has gone as far as Bulawayo, the last big town on the railway line and a likely place for the circus to have turned round and headed back south. But when Vickery dies he is destitute, living on hand-outs from the railway folk. Clearly, there came a point where he ran out of money and could no longer afford even the 'tickey' (threepence) which readers have been told was the cheapest entrance fee. They have also been warned that 'deprived of 'is stimulant' – that is, unable to see the film – he is likely to commit a violent crime. Pyecroft is afraid that 'he might react on me, so to say, with a hatchet' (p. 360).

When Vickery runs out of money, then, he is in the very state which makes Pyecroft fearful for his own safety. But the attitude of the corpses shows that he has not murdered his companion. There is, however, another violent act which someone in his position might commit, especially if, deprived of the film (''is stimulus'), he had filled the void with his own fantasies and come to mistake his 'mate' for his dead mistress restored to life. This is sodomy, which in 1904 was a crime. Vickery and his companion standing in the 'dead end' of the siding would then have both participated and hence both incurred the biblical punishment – destruction by fire from heaven, the fate of Sodom and Gomorrah and of those who 'go after strange flesh' (see Genesis 19:24; Jude 7). Vickery, then, has been struck not by accident nor even by Aphrodite but by the Wrath of God.

One objection is that, while this offers a plausible answer to the mystification surrounding the second tramp – the explanation is one from which Kipling's reading public would have flinched – it is no more plausible than others to date, and does not arise out of the demands of the story. On the contrary: social context, setting, imagery, literary allusion, repeated words, puns, framing episodes, characters – *all* join together to point the reader towards this conclusion.

To take social context first: the main action of the story can be dated fairly accurately, as Bodelsen pointed out. The Boer War is recently over, as the Navy still has ammunition. The circus comes to Capetown in Christmas week, stays a week and thus leaves early in the New Year. This establishes the time as the turn of the year 1902–3. Vickery has left his ship for four months when the men meet in the railway carriage, which takes us to the end of April 1903; his body has been discovered when Hooper was up-country – that is, about a month before – and he could not have been dead for very long. His death occurred, then, about the last week of March 1903.

It was in February 1903 that the first act of a once-celebrated military tragedy began to unroll. Major-General Sir Hector Macdonald, hero of Omdurman and pride of Scotland, returned to London from Ceylon to clear his name of charges involving (according to one version) homosexual behaviour with Ceylonese boys in a railway carriage. After an *in camera* hearing, the War Office ordered him back to Ceylon to face a court-martial; Lord Roberts, who had played a key role in the decision, wrote later that he had hoped that Macdonald would disappear to some remote area.

What happened was that Macdonald shot himself in a Paris hotel on 25 March 1903. His death caused consternation, especially in his native Scotland, and was rapidly telegraphed all over the world, reports tending to stress the advisability of not probing his death. The *Cape Times*, for instance, gave the case considerable publicity between 25 and 28 March 1903, using the coded language of the day, of which this extract from the obituary of 27 March is a fair sample: ' "Fighting Mac" has been driven by some dreadful mystery to turn the weapon he used so often to such purpose against the enemies of England against himself. The cause of the tragedy is unknown and it is well that it should remain so.' (The *Cape Times*, the leading local newspaper, would have been the one that Kipling read when sojourning in South Africa. The editor, Maitland Park, was an old associate of his on the Allahabad *Pioneer* and owed his editorship to him.)[29]

Macdonald held an exceptional place in the history of the British Army. A private who had risen by courage and ability 'to all but the highest military rank', he came from the Tommy Atkins class with which Kipling instinctively sympathised, and had served the Empire in the countries with which Kipling was most emotionally involved. Promoted by Lord Roberts (a personal friend of Kipling) after the 1879 Afghan War, he was nicknamed 'Fighting Mac' after the model of Roberts's 'Fighting Bobs'. During the Sudan campaign the name of his batman was Pritchard. He was one of Roberts's stalwarts during the taking of Bloemfontein in 1900; one of his subsequent exploits was the recapture of a large store of British ammunition pillaged from the railway at Brandfort, just north of the city. The strain of a workaholic career began to show around this time; his transference to Ceylon was rumoured to be the War Office's tactful way of removing someone who would be 'difficult' in a post-war situation requiring extreme delicacy. The coincidence of the dates of the two deaths is striking, as is that of the following features: an ammunition store on the Bloemfontein railway line, a secret hearing and a sudden, explosive death as an alternative to a court-martial. The association of boys with railway carriages and a 'hotel' is a feature common to both Macdonald's tragedy and 'Mrs Bathurst', as will be seen later. Macdonald had a passionate belief in the necessity for a conscript army, and before going to Ceylon had gone on a punishing, proselytising lecture tour of the Antipodes.[30] This passion he shared with 'Bobs' and Kipling, who had written 'The Army of a Dream' in support of it. More political tract than story, one of Kipling's most wooden imaginings, he nevertheless was to write to a friend in 1905 that *Traffics and Discoveries* had been put together solely for the purpose of carrying that tale.[31] Thus he identified as the focus of the book a piece of propaganda which happened to be perpetuating the 'work' of Macdonald beyond the grave. (For further comment on the Macdonald case, see Appendix I.)

The men in the story have met together during the aftermath of Macdonald's death and the recriminations surrounding his huggermugger funeral. These may therefore be supposed to be, like the Boer War settlement, part of their mental furniture. 'Mrs Bathurst' resembles Joyce's 'Ivy Day in the Committee Room' in that both use an absence to suggest the presence of a real historical figure – Parnell in the case of the latter. But in 'Mrs Bathurst' the historical figure has been distanced and metagrobolised – transformed into a type of the man who has been tried too far.

Next the setting: the Southern Hemisphere, 'under stinking Capricorn' in the words of the epigraph; to someone brought up in the Northern Hemisphere, literally 'the world upside-down', where December is summer and June is winter. Astrological sign of the lustful Goat, in Teufelsdrockh's life the 'Bag *Capricorn*, and those near it' exhibited 'confusion a little worse confounded' (*Sartor*, i.xi; p. 47). It functions in the story as a symbol of *inversion*, a term at the time made newly current by Havelock Ellis's *Studies in the Psychology of Sex* (1897). Interestingly, one critical monograph describes 'Mrs Bathurst' as 'an experiment in inverse (it is more than indirect) narration'.[32]

Of all South African cities, Capetown is designated as particularly 'unnatural'. 'Why, even Durban's more like Nature', says Pritchard. 'Not bein' a devotee of Indian *peeris*, as our Doctor said to the Pusser, I can't exactly say', is Pyecroft's dry retort, his answer showing that the 'unnaturalness' of Capetown consists in its lack of women (*TD*, p. 354). To Pritchard, Durban is tolerable because of the availability of Indian prostitutes, even with the attendant risk of venereal disease. (This is the point of Pyecroft's ascribing the remark to the ship's *doctor*, leaving the reader to imagine the purser's question.[33]

Kipling wrote that in his mind the idea of the British Empire shaped itself as a picture of 'a semi-circle of buildings and temples projecting into a sea – of dreams' (*SM*, p. 91). The landscape of the story is the inverse of this – a concavity instead of a convexity, a barren crescent of beach, no shelter except for a broken-down railway van, jocularly called 'the old hotel'. In Simon's Bay the narrator 'got food and drink from the Greeks who sell all things at a price' (*TD*, p. 339). The phrase is one that Kipling used in a Rhodes dinner speech of 1924, in which he warned his listeners that the gods 'who sell all things at a price . . . continue to be just Gods and should you hold back even a fraction of the sum asked for your heart's desire, they will say nothing, but they will furnish you with a substitute that will deceive even you until it is too late' (*BW*, pp. 262–3). Here, I think, Kipling was allegorising his own story (the subject of his speech was the realisation of a vision of Empire). Indeed, 'Mrs Bathurst' itself has latent within it a political allegory about the frustration of Rhodes's African dream, the drawing-out of which lies outside the scope of this book. The salient point for this argument, however, is the idea of Nemesis common to both situations. A ruinous and deceptive *imitation* is the inevitable result of a less than total dedication to a true love.

The early 'framing' episode also contains a curious passage in which the narrator describes a state of near-lapse under the combined influence of sun and beer into 'magical slumber'. His original goal, the ship *Peridot* ('fairy's dower') being *not* there, he has accepted Hooper's invitation to the railway 'hotel':

> The hills of False Bay were just dissolving into those of fairyland when I heard footsteps on the sand outside and the clink of our couplings.
> 'Stop that!' snapped Hooper.   (*TD*, p. 340)

Hooper thinks that it is some 'dirty little Malay boys', but it is Pyecroft and Pritchard – one of the frequently recurring instances of the erroneous in the story, as Craig Raine pointed out.[34] It is not clear that Hooper's brusquerie *did* jolt the narrator out of his trance. Unlike 'The Army of a Dream', where the entire story is a reverie from which the narrator surfaces at the end, Kipling has deliberately blurred the status of the narrative in 'Mrs Bathurst'. Is what follows a vision or a waking dream? Has the narrator awoken from a false fairyland to a nightmare truth?

When we turn to the imagery, we notice the incidence of the *vicious circle*. Vickery goes to Phyllis's *circus* with its endlessly circling reeel of film. In addition Vickery and Pyecroft for five nights visit the Capetown bars and the Gardens in an unvarying 'desperate round'. Boy Niven keeps the deluded seamen 'walkin' in circles' around the island. Taken with the story's visionary qualities and Vickery's suggestion that he is carrying his own torment within himself ('I'm *it*'), another area of literary allusion is invoked: Dante's *Inferno*.

To think of Hell – on earth or in the mind – *without* thinking of Dante, was extremely difficult for a literate nineteenth-century Englishman, so accessible did *The Divine Comedy* become through numerous editions of Cary's translation. For someone whose favourite uncle knew Dante Gabriel Rossetti and whose sister called herself Beatrice it was impossible. *Aunt Judy* strongly approved of him: 'Dante served in the cavalry and acquitted himself very well, thus proving that a man may be a good soldier and yet write fine poetry.'[35] After Shakespeare and Scott, he was one of the authors most frequently quoted by Ruskin; Letter xxiii of *Fors* ('The Labyrinth') has a detailed description of his map of Hell (*Works*, xxvii, 410–13). In short, it was inevitable that around 1879 Kipling should have discovered, as he put it in a deceptively off-hand way, that 'there had been a man called Dante who living in a small Italian town at general issue with his neighbours, had invented for most of them lively torments in a nine-ringed Hell'. He began on an Inferno of his own 'in the Hiawatha metre'. The *Inferno*, then, was, with *Parables from Nature* one of his first models when the 'tide of writing' set in (*SM*, pp. 34–5). Chapter 5 will discuss his knowledge of Dante in more detail; at this point, the reader is asked to take it on trust that he had an extremely detailed acquaintance with certain parts of the *Inferno* in the Cary version, of which he owned two copies in his maturity.[36]

But which episode of the *Inferno*? Here, again, the clue lies in a recurrent image – that of *sand*. The story takes place in 'a bay of drifted sand'. The plank platform is 'half buried in sand'. 'Moulded dunes' roll inland. 'A circle of dry hills whose feet were set in sands of silver' locks the party in 'against a seven-coloured sea'. The wind (a strong south-easter) 'dusted sand into our tickey beer'.

The narrator is lulled by the 'drift of fine grains'. Pritchard on entering the railway carriage 'dusted the sand nervously from his fingers'. The singing picnickers are 'sunburned, wet, and sandy'. Elsewhere sand is implied. The *Astrild* spends half her commission 'rompin'' up the beach like a she-turtle, an' the other half hatching turtles' eggs on the top o' numerous reefs' – turtle eggs being incubated in sand.

This establishes the corresponding Dantean locale as that of canto xiv (Cary translation):

> It is a plain of dry and hot sand, where three kinds of violence are punished; namely, against God, against Nature, and against Art; and those who have thus sinned are tormented by flakes of fire, which are eternally showering down upon them. Among the violent against God is found Capaneus, whose blasphemies they hear. Next, turning from the left along the forest of self-slayers, and having journeyed a little onwards, they meet with a streamlet of blood that issues from the forest and traverses the sandy plain.[37]

Canto xv's headnote adds that this streamlet is embanked by 'mounds'.

As the honeysuckle bower is a 'fairyland' version of the teak wilderness, so the sandy coast, with its carefree picnickers and fishermen, little river, dunes and constantly drifting warm sand, is a landscape the delusive brilliance of which masks an infernal inner reality – hosts of lost souls, a rill of blood, mounds, and continual flakes of fire. Moreover, the chief actors in these cantos have counterparts in Kipling's story. The narrator is of course Dante, whose function it is to have the vision, listen, and ask leading questions. Hooper, railway inspector and circumnavigator of the terrain, is Virgil.

Pritchard and Pyecroft combine the roles of the 'violent against God' and the 'violent against Art', being profane infringers of literary decorum. Kipling, I think, was here sardonically alluding to his own reputation as 'The Voice of the Hooligan', Robert Buchanan's 1899 jeer which he never really lived down. Buchanan lambasted Kipling for his imperialism, his indecency and his choosing as narrative consciousnesses brutal and, especially, *blaspheming* characters. Hence, for Kipling, those who do violence against God and Art are the same.[38] Pritchard is Dante's Capaneus, chief of the 'violent against God'. Capaneus, a blaspheming 'huge spirit', led the 'Seven against Thebes'. Pritchard, likewise, was the leader – 'pulled bow in the gig' (*TD*, p. 343) – of a disastrous expedition involving seven: Boy Niven's trek around the island. (We are told variously that he deceived 'seven or eight' and 'eight', but in fact only seven individuals are named.) Pritchard's size is stressed; he is a 'monster', a 'giant' and a blasphemer. 'The Sergeant called all the powers of darkness to witness his bewilderment' (p. 348). He takes the name of the Lord in vain: 'Good Lord Alive an' Watchin!'; 'Oh my Gawd!' Pyecroft, a milder blasphemer, was also on the Boy Niven trek. He does not correspond to anyone in particular in Dante, nor does Kipling offer an exact parallel to the episode of the violent against Art, which is much briefer than the others.[39] But the colours and animal imagery of the emblems worn around the necks of Ubbriachi and Scrovigni find conflated echoes in Pritchard and Pyecroft. Ubbriachi's is a goose (white on a red ground), while Scrovigni's is a 'fat and azure swine'; he speaks 'like an ox / That licks his nostrils'. Pritchard, a redcoat, is called a 'fat marine' and a 'silly ox' by Pyecroft (p. 349). Pyecroft, the blue jacket, is accused of having a 'beastial mind' (p. 355).

There remain the 'violent against Nature'. In that episode the outstanding character is the superior Brunetto Latini, 'by one . . . sin polluted'.[40] Vickery is, we are told twice, a 'superior man', which is 'what we'd call a long, black-'aired, genteelly speakin', 'alf-bred beggar on the lower deck' (pp. 347, 353). 'Brunetto' has suggested 'black 'aired', and 'Latini' ''alf-bred', by way of 'the Latin races'. ''Alf-bred' ostensibly means here 'underbred, not a real gentleman', but it can also mean 'of mixed race', 'of intermediate colour, neither black nor white'. Vickery's last recorded words, 'The rest is silence', have a verbal parallel in Latini's answer when Dante asks him about the rest of his 'tribe': 'To know of some is well . . . . But of the rest silence may best beseem'.[41] If Vickery is of the tribe of the Latini, then 'beggar', translated back into 'bugger', recovers its literal meaning. It would be a strange rereading of Kipling to do this to all his 'beggars' but that it is true of this story, if no other, is a proposition that I am now going to consider.

As the word 'sand' is implied by the *Astrild* episode, so the word 'beggars' is implied by the situation of the tramps, who subsist on the charity of the railway staff. 'Beggar' is used three times in 'Mrs Bathurst': once about Vickery, the second time about Moon, who was also on the Boy Niven expedition. Moon 'always showed signs o' bein' a Mormonastic beggar' (p. 345), and deserts the sloop *Astrild* during a South Sea 'cruise'. The ship's name is an ominous one, suggesting 'ill-starred', and recalling Estrild, the German princess who was taken as a second wife by King Locrine of Britain, an act of disloyalty which plunged the kingdom into disorder and bloodshed.[42] What is implied is that Moon is a polygamist who has been found out by his women. Knowing the punishment that awaits him on his return, he has tried to escape while he can.

To understand fully what Kipling implies by a reference to Mormonism (it isn't, of course, necessary to suppose that Pyecroft has it in mind) one should go to his account of a visit to Salt Lake City in 1889; while grudgingly admiring the organisation that had made the desert productive, he disapproved thoroughly of the Mormon practice of polygamy, which he saw as perverting Free-masonry in order to oppress women, reversing the 'centuries of training' which had taught them 'that it is right to control the undivided heart of one man'. Looking down on the 'City of the Saints as it lay in its circle of forbidding hills', he speculated on the resultant 'mass of human misery, the loves frustrated, the gentle hearts broken, and the strong souls twisted from the law of life to a fiercer following of the law of death'.

> How must it have been in the old days when the footsore emigrants broke through into the circle and knew that they were cut off from hope of return or sight of friends – were handed over to the power of the friends that called themselves priests of the Most High? 'But for the grace of God there goes Richard Baxter,' as the eminent divine once said. It seemed good that fate did not order me to be a brick in the up-building of the Mormon Church, that has so aptly established herself by the borders of a lake bitter, salt, and hopeless. (*SS*, II, 128–9)

This passage contains the seeds of 'Mrs Bathurst': a foreshadowing of the landscape of 'False Bay', the hopeless circle, the loss of friends, their replacement by other, sinister 'friends' (Vickery's biograph show is called 'Home and Friends'). So far this has some bearing on Vickery's 'two wives', if not much on the Circle of the Sodomites. But Kipling's word is a portmanteau one, formed on Lewis Carroll principles, and combines 'Mormon' and 'Monastic'. Moon may have 'Just saved himself' by a retreat into strict celibacy, but Kipling did use 'monastic' to mean homosexual on one other occasion. By putting them together, Pyecroft is implying that polygamist and monk (or homosexual) are two sides of the same coin.[43]

The cruise of the *Astrild* is imaged in terms of futile attempts to imitate acts which can be literally performed only by a living female, pregnancies which give birth to reptiles. The sloop 'spent half her commission rompin' up the beach like a she-turtle, an' the other half hatching turtles' eggs on the top o' numerous reefs' (*TD*, p. 345). That is Pyecroft's circumlocution for saying that the *Astrild* had frequently run aground because of an inefficient navigating officer (another of the numerous images in the story of going astray, being misled, losing one's bearings). For a ship *literally* to hatch eggs would be a feat out of Nature; that the ship spends so much time stranded on reefs indicates long periods in which the men are imprisoned with no women and no *work*. The *Astrild* is in terrible shape on its return, and, as in the Boy Niven episode, an innocent party is blamed. Pritchard comments at the end of the *Astrild* story – it is not clear *à propos* of what – 'They *do* do strange things at sea.' No one, in fact, knows what has gone on aboard the ship, except that there has been an attempt at a cover-up.

The third 'beggar' is Boy Niven. ''E said he was born at the back o' Vancouver Island, and *all* the time the beggar was a balmy Barnado Orphan!'

The Boy Niven episode has been recognised as prefiguring the central tale of betrayal of trust. It is, however, even more integral than has been supposed. Niven has promised the sailors farms, but their dream of fruitful land yields to sterile actuality – court-martialling and prison. The episode is notable for its use of erotic metaphor to describe the orphan's deceit. He has 'lured' them; the sailors and Marines are 'very young an' very curious', 'lovin' an' trustful to a degree'. They are literally *seduced* – led astray – by him. His making the crew 'walk in single file for fear o' bears' contains a buried pun: in military science, the changing of ranks into files is technically known as *inversion*. At their court-martial they are *broken-hearted* at Niven's accusation that they had misled *him* (pp. 343–4). That Niven is an ex-Barnado orphan is also relevant. He never had a real home and mother, nor has he found a compensation for early deprivation in comradeship and loyalty to the Navy. He is thus a *potential* Son of Belial, as are most orphans in Kipling.

Boy Niven, then, is associated with deceptive innocence and sending people off course; Kipling signals that a suggestion of sexual deviance clings to him, and there has been at least one reader who has responded to the signal.[44] It is therefore somewhat disturbing to find that Pyecroft has lately heard of him as the 'signal Boatswain in the Channel Fleet, I believe' (p. 344). There is no reason for the inclusion of this detail unless the reader is being warned that he might still be up to his old tricks. But whom could he lead astray?

Or, rather, whom might Pyecroft (who is inclined to believe in extra-sensory perception) have in mind? Pyecroft particularly remembers the *clicking* of Vickery's false teeth, which has earned him his nickname. 'I'm not so fond o' navigatin' about Cape Town with a South-Easter blowin' these days. I can hear those teeth click, so to say' (pp. 362–3). Pyecroft is recalling the occasion on which Vickery had said that Mrs Bathurst was looking for him. ''E was clickin' his four false teeth like a Marconi ticker. "Yes! lookin' for me," he said, an' he went on very softly an' as you might say affectionately' (p. 359). The detail of the Marconi ticker provides the clue. Vickery's teeth are, to adopt Pyecroft's lingo, 'so to speak' signalling to the spirit of Mrs Bathurst, using the medium of the Hertzian waves – that is, the waves of the 'ticker', the heart (*Herz* in German). The wind, a South-Easter, is also playing its part. In relation to Capetown it blows from the direction of Auckland, and is blowing towards England, the place of Mrs Bathurst's death.

That the magnetic attraction of passion works in a way analogous to the wireless telegraph is a speculation entertained by the narrator of 'Wireless', another *Traffics and Discoveries* story. A lovesick tubercular apothecary's assistant is 'possessed' by the spirit of Keats and writes garbled Keatsian verse unconsciously employing metaphorical 'Hertzian waves' while a wireless 'ham' tries to reach Poole. It reflects Kipling's excitement over the Channel Fleet's 1898 experiments with the Marconigraph and Marconi's December 1901 transatlantic messages; Kipling placed 'Wireless' before 'Mrs Bathurst', probably in order to educate readers to read the later, subtler story. Indeed, the Marconigraph is as much a model for the form of 'Mrs Bathurst' as the early newsreel; the reader must make sense of incomplete coded messages, which bypass 'wires' – the linear narrative line – and arrive through a buzz of distracting interference.

Niven, the boatswain, then, in the world where such things can happen, is in a position to act as a dishonest broker between Vickery and the spirit of Mrs Bathurst. That Niven is tempting Vickery from afar, when he is at his most lonely and guilty, having lost both women, is indicated by Vickery's agony – the Gardens of Capetown suggest Gethsemane – and his 'desperate round' recalls the earlier Canadian episode. He is gripped by feelings which he admits he is unable to explain. Could he have mistakenly summoned Niven? Or, in other words, would it be reasonable for the men to think that Niven is the second tramp, and that in actuality, not in some supernatural or fantastic way?

Kipling has left time for Niven to arrive 'up country' and meet Vickery. Between Vickery's departure for Bloemfontein and the finding of the bodies is an interval of about eleven weeks, which allows for a sea voyage from England to Capetown (about seventeen days) and a journey by rail and foot to Rhodesia. Niven could easily have overtaken Vickery (who had to go to Bloemfontein and was further delayed by his pursuit of the film), and attached himself to the latter at, say, Bulawayo. We don't know much about Niven, but almost every detail given contributes to a hypothesis as to how he might have ended up in the jungle, whereas there is an entire absence of such detail in Mrs Bathurst's case. He is 'balmy' and gets 'ideas' from reading books. He is physically tough and has tramped through backwoods and has an obsession with 'free land'. Such a character might easily take it into his head (without any supernatural persuasion) in 1902–3 to go to the new country of Rhodesia hoping to make his fortune. 'We get heaps of tramps up there since the war', says Hooper (p. 363). He has a reputation for deserting ship and for cunning and could have enrolled as a crew member of a tramp steamer or stowed away on both ship and trains. That people do use the railways for bad purposes is an idea inherent in Hooper's explanation of his 'Stop that!' as the narrator drifts into 'fairyland'. 'It's those dirty little Malay boys, you see; they're always playing with the trucks . . . . ' 'Don't be hard on 'em. The railway's a general refuge in Africa', says the narrator. ''Tis – up-country at any rate', replies Hooper. This links the *dirty* boys, who are thought to be disturbing the 'couplings', with the two tramps for whom the railway is a refuge, and if one tramp has the nickname 'Boy' there is an even closer verbal link.[45]

Kipling has also supplied a naturalistic explanation of Vickery's behaviour; he is under great stress, drinking heavily and in a fit state to imagine himself hearing voices and feeling his consciousness invaded by evil powers. He is evidently terrified of remaining on the ship and going to the remote Tristan da Cunha, and requests an interview with the captain. His words to Pyecroft, 'I'm *it*', I have previously glossed as 'I am my own hell', but like 'Fors Clavigera' they have several possible meanings, all of which are appropriate: 'I'm as good as dead', 'I am singled out for damnation' and 'I'm neither he nor she.' The reader is to understand that Vickery has decided to confess his predicament to the captain. This would explain why the latter had on his 'court-martial face' yet, extraordinarily, was willing to allow him to leave the ship. He was giving him a chance to pull himself together by giving him a job of work to do, but also a chance to disappear for ever, and thus get rid of a disruptive influence with the minimum of fuss. His description has been circulated[46] so that it will not appear that the captain has wanted him to get lost. If he is found, he can be court-martialled and dismissed anyway. Vickery goes off 'happy-ish' because he can still see Mrs Bathurst. But his behaviour is such as to intensify to the highest pitch a confusion of self-contempt and sexual desire. When the money runs out and he can no longer see the film, there is a huge vacancy. It is in such a 'swept and garnished' state that a man is most likely to be possessed by the unclean spirit returning with the seven other spirits more wicked than himself (Matthew 12:44–5).

For Niven has a supernatural function too. If Mrs Bathurst is Vickery's good angel, he is his devil. His name – Niven means 'little saint' – must be read inversely. His initials give the clue to his real character. He is, Pyecroft tells us, 'Mr L. L. Niven' (p. 344). Pyecroft, a Cockney like Pritchard, sometimes drops his aitches; the choice of Cockney narrators allows Kipling to blur the distinction between 'L. L.' and 'Hell, Hell.'

Returning to the Vancouver episode, one notices the suggestions of the diabolic in Niven's behaviour. 'Remember, Pye, when 'e 'opped about in that bog full o' ferns an' said 'e could smell the smoke of 'is uncle's farm? An' *all* the time it was a dirty little outlyin' uninhabited island.' (One notes the reiteration of the words 'dirty little'.) 'Hopping' can refer to an idiot boy's gleeful motions, but also to the leaps forward taken from a squatting position by a toad or frog, and, given that he is hopping about in a *bog*, his resemblance to a toad, a familiar shape of the Devil, becomes patent. That the Vancouver archipelago area is an (extinct) volcanic one might explain why he is sniffing *smoke*, and suggests a link with Vulcan (Milton's Mulciber) and the hellish landscape containing volcanoes, bogs and dens (Niven warns against bears) through which march the 'adventurous bands' of rebel angels in *Paradise Lost* (1.615–25). Who is this 'uncle' who, Boy Niven says, is compelled by the 'law of the land' to give everyone a farm? Is it that Empire-builder who has 'room, not like these narrow limits, to receive [the] numerous offspring' of Earth? (*PL*, IV, 384–5). Niven survives the murderous revenge of his dupes after their release from prison because he is 'unusually tough' ('If that thou be'st a devil, I cannot kill thee' – *Othello*, v.ii.2).[47]

If we now return to the episode of the tramps' discovery, the resemblances between the second tramp and Boy Niven become inescapable.[48] Bodelsen's reading of the 'squatting' figure as an attitude of adoration never was very convincing; it suggests, rather, a crouching toad. And, when one recalls that the situation of the two tramps parodies that of the embowered lovers, another Miltonic allusion surfaces. It is to the episode in *Paradise Lost* where Ithuriel and Zephon look for Satan in the Garden of Eden:

> these to the bower direct
> In search of whom they sought; him there they found
> Squat like a toad, close at the ear of Eve;
> Assaying by his devilish art to reach
> The organs of her fancy, and with them forge
> Illusions as he list . . . .
>
> (IV.798–803)

The second tramp is fixed at the moment of death in the likeness of a *tempter*; he collapses into a black soggy mess at Hooper's touch. This echoes Satan's assuming his true shape at the touch of Ithuriel's spear even as 'the smutty grain' of gunpowder ignites, 'for no falsehood can endure / Touch of celestial temper' (IV.811–12). It is 'Ithuriel's Hour', the name Kipling later gave to the moment which shows 'everyone exactly and truthfully what he [is]' (*LST*, p. 158).

Vickery, then, has succumbed to the dirty Boy's temptation, and reached his nadir. The attitudes of the two in death are profoundly ambiguous. One can see the second tramp as provoking Vickery to become habituated to vice, Vickery rising above the temptation and preferring to die rationally, like a man.[49] Or his stance means that he dies defying the 'Good Lord Alive and Watchin'' at the behest of a 'wife' who, like Job's, has said, 'Dost thou still retain thine integrity? Curse God, and die.'[50] According to the letter of the law he has delivered himself to Hell; the white tattoo with its 'foul anchor' proclaims him the 'mate' of Niven. 'M. V.' can mean not only 'Mars–Venus' but also 'Mars–Vulcan'.

The appalling thought that occurs to the men at the end is that this is Mrs Bathurst's revenge, and that her spirit has actually sent Niven to ruin Vickery. As Lewis pointed out, 'We are shown [Mrs Bathurst] "feeding a lame duck" when she lends a watch to a sailor; but we never see her "set 'er foot' on a scorpion" – unless Vickery is meant.'[51] And her mode of 'setting her foot' on the faithless Vickery is a conversion of a literal act of mercy into a metaphor, where it becomes an act of revenge. (This is analogous to life being transformed into the biograph.) Both the anonymous sailor and Niven are bosuns, one good, one bad. Both have 'come ashore without 'is ticker' – Niven is *heartless*, and it would be the 'last boat' for him too. The watch (ticker) which stands for the heart (ticker) in the first case becomes the Marconi ticker which transfers her spirit's 'Hertzian waves', now converted to hate. 'So close must any life-filling passion lie to its opposite', as Kipling said in the throwaway line which could serve as a comment on his entire work (*SM*, p. 16).

The phrase 'She that damned him to death knew not that she did it, or would have died ere she did it' now takes on a new meaning: 'She would not have damned him to death when she was alive, but being dead she could well have done so.' Applied to Mrs Bathurst it means that she becomes in death what she was not in life. Alive she was 'blindish' – a slave to love;[52] dead, she is a Fury, her blindishness that of a bat, a Bat-hurst, an infernal grove, instead of a Ba-thurst.

Such a thought does not have the status of a final revelation about the true nature of women. It is a projection of the men's minds. For each sees himself as an exploiter of women and *therefore*, by the moral logic of the story, a potential sodomite. Mrs Bathurst has tied the ribbons around four bottles of beer, proleptically, one for each man in the 'hotel'. (This answers a question sometimes asked about the bottles: why *four*?) The emblem has itself become bisexual. At the beginning of the story the beer-bottle with a ribbon represented the generous victim woman. By the end, it has become a self-confronting emblem of each man's guilty self, a manling standing condemned to be hanged at the bar of the tribunal of women.

Now that the jigsaw is complete, the men momentarily have the opportunity of mutually admitting this shared knowledge, but pass it up because silence is the best guarantee of virtue. Hooper is an imperfect Ithuriel; as the story progresses he has become increasingly identified with Vickery; there are hints that he is a man who has 'just save[d] himself'; he, at least, has a mother. 'What walks!' he exclaims as Pyecroft describes his 'desperate round' with Vickery. 'Oh my soul, what walks!' as if reliving an experience he has had (*TD*, p. 359). He keeps Vickery's teeth in his waistcoat pocket, which symbolises a refusal to speak and thus pluck Click's secret (and his own) from out of his bosom. 'He was a *friend* of you two gentleman, you see' are his last words (my italics); it was when he said, 'It's those dirty little Malay boys, you see', that Pyecroft and Pritchard appeared. The point is, I think, that, by mistaking the self-confessedly promiscuous pair for 'dirty boys', Hooper has made the narrator aware not of what they are but of what they might be – Pritchard the Marine is what Kipling once called 'a kind of a giddy harumfrodite – soldier an' sailor too!' (*DV*, p. 433): a joke, as long as it remains a metaphor. Pyecroft – 'Pye' for short – is a black and white bird, the magpie; the name suggests that he holds within himself potential for extremes of good and evil. He comes off a ship called *The Hierophant*, but declines to be one. This is one 'dark and bloody mystery' which he will not expound; he urges that the subject be dropped for ever: 'I'm inclined to finish the beer and thank Gawd he's dead!' And the narrator? We are told little about him except that he too quenches his thirst with the excellent Bass and drinks to the health of the 'large-minded' maid who gave it.

Remarks on homosexuality in Kipling's letters and *obiter dicta* almost always occur in a context of zeal to protect youth against 'beastliness'.[53] Yet in some of his fiction, while still fervently disapproving, he permits himself to express a larger-minded empathy which one doesn't see outside it, unless one partially excepts his reported opinion of *The Well of Loneliness*. Predictably, he was against publication, but his grounds, as summarised by Hugh Walpole, are interesting: 'Too much of the abnormal in all of us to play about with. Hates opening up reserves.'[54] The narrator's first-spoken and never-rescinded words, referring to the 'dirty little Malay boys', are 'Don't be hard on 'em', and this may be taken as part of the complex 'moral' of the story. Along with the other embargoes on asking awkward questions ('Don't ask whether the woman is to blame', 'Don't ask what Vickery has done') goes suppression of the voice of the late-Victorian blasphemer who dares to speculate that the 'Lord Alive and Watchin'' might be bad, not good; might be Swinburne's 'Supreme Evil' who 'makes desire and slays desire with shame', or Omar Khayyám's 'Thou' who has encompassed man with pitfall and with gin.[55] Such a God is in league with the Devil; Jupiter employs Vulcan as his maker of lightning-bolts. Kipling does not allow the question to be officially asked because, not being sure of God's existence himself, he suspects that 'blaming God' is a way of denying human free will and responsibility; the blasphemer is a madman, and must either be killed off or be brought to his right mind. But inasmuch as his imagination is dominated by notions of fate and predestination ('There but for the grace of God goes Richard Baxter'), his empathy extends to the man who has been tried too far by the sorry scheme of things entire, and who has pressured himself to live up to the standard of official virtue. It is on the seventy-two mile stretch of railway line (representing the life of threescore and ten odd years lived on the straight and narrow) that, Hooper says, the greatest number of derailments occur.

Kipling has laid pitfall and gin for readers too. For anyone assuming that the tramp was Mrs Bathurst has made an error in the Fourth Dimension of language analogous to Vickery's – mistaking a man for a woman.

5

Kipling and Dante (II): Home and Friends

> *In Doubt which is Self Contradiction.*
> *A dark Hermaphrodite I stood.*
> (Blake, 'The Keys of the Gate',
> in Gilchrist's *Life*)

Gender confusion, treated sometimes as the dangerous edge of things, sometimes as offering freedom from stereotypes, is an important theme in Kipling, and reflects confusions within his culture. Tension was inherent in a society which strove to maintain polarised definitions of true manliness and womanliness at the same time as the behaviour upon which these are based was changing rapidly. George Meredith's lecture 'The Idea of Comedy' (1877) argues that it is comedy's task to reveal the essential similarity between man and woman and break down distinctions of sex on the intellectual plane. Women in the second half of the nineteenth century go to university, mountaineer, bicycle, smoke. Alcott's Jo March introduces the tomboy as a role-model, while the idea of the gentle man/gentleman is restated. Juliana Ewing in *Jackanapes*, following Tennyson, tells her young readers and their mamas and papas that the sexes should partake of each other's qualities, with some telling reservations:

> A young maid is all the better for learning some robuster virtues than maidenliness. . . . As on the other hand, Jackanapes (who had a boy's full share of the little beast and the young monkey in his natural composition) was none the worse, at his tender years, for learning some maidenliness – so far as maidenliness means decency, pity, unselfishness and pretty behaviour.[1]

These conflicting signals have their counterpart in the exalting of male friendship as an exhibition of the noblest and tenderest in human nature, 'passing the love of woman', while coupling this exaltation with warnings that its physical expression could lead to the vilest behaviour. In the second half of the nineteenth century, anxiety over the blurring of distinctions of gender increases as homosexual behaviour becomes the object of scientific study, and the concept of a homosexual 'species' emerges; this builds on and supersedes the earlier phrenological notion of a 'bump of adhesiveness' which governed the predisposition to form attachments to persons, including 'excessively fond' ones.[2] By 1885, the year Kipling's short-story writing got under way, homophobia produces the Labouchère clause which was to send Oscar Wilde to prison.

In the literary world the tensions are especially acute because of the nineteenth-century attraction to the idea that the poet's nature is 'inclusively woman'; that 'great poets are bisexual' – Shakespeare being, of course, the great exemplar. Yet, when a male poet threatened to exemplify this ideal, he could be criticised, as Tennyson was in 1869, for not being 'even fairly manly very often'. (The 1870s fuss over the 'Fleshly School of Poetry' centred partly on its carrying the principle of 'double-naturedness' too far.)[3] One of Kipling's near-contemporaries, William Sharp – he of the prophecy that Kipling would die mad before the age of thirty[4] – acted out the double-naturedness and wrote secretly under a female pseudonym, 'Fiona Macleod'. He dressed in women's clothes when being Fiona, who had a fey, Celtic personality. Another manifestation of such contradictions may be seen in the reputation of Walt Whitman, a writer popularised by W. M. Rossetti and Swinburne and admired by the young Kipling.[5] His message of 'the beautiful and sane affection of man for man' was regarded with suspicion, but defended because it came along with a healthy call to explore the great outdoors and could be read in a purely mystical sense.[6]

However, this general background does not in itself validate the foregoing reading of 'Mrs Bathurst', which is vulnerable on two counts. First, Kipling wrote that the 'key' sentence about the duck and the scorpion was overheard ten years after his first visit to Auckland. 'Then – precisely as the removal of the key-log in a timber-jam starts the whole pile – those words gave me the key to the face and voice at Auckland, and a tale called "Mrs Bathurst" slid into my mind, smoothly and orderly as floating timber on a bank-high river' (*SM*, p. 101). Since the Auckland visit took place in 1891, the words could mean that the entire story was in his mind in 1901; if that were so, there would not be any room for

Hector Macdonald. Secondly, though it would not entirely dispose of the argument, it would weaken it somewhat if the *motif* of 'mistaking a man for a woman' were to be found nowhere else in his work, or if 'Mrs Bathurst' were unique in its use of a Dantean framework. For all his claim that he refused to repeat himself, if an important theme, author or set of circumstances occurs in one Kipling story it will almost certainly turn up again somewhere else in his *oeuvre*.

The first difficulty raised is quickly dealt with: Kipling wrote that the story began to move smoothly into his mind in 1901, but he did not write it until early in 1904.[7] As we have seen, the narrative is mostly set in 1903. So new logs joined the batch of timber as it smoothly progressed towards its destination.

The second – whether 'Mrs Bathurst' is unique in its theme and use of allusion – requires a more complicated and extended treatment. We don't find the above elements in combination anywhere else. But we do find them separately. And some time after 1914 he wrote an epigrammatic 'version' of Horace's 'Cynara' Ode (iv.i), where Horace confesses to middle-aged desire for a young man. Kipling makes Horace say, 'I'm learning, as most men of sin do / That when Love flies out at the door / Perversion comes in at the window' – which is the essential plot of 'Mrs Bathurst'.[8]

The fear of 'mistaking a man for a woman' appears in 'His Wedded Wife' (*PT*) published in the *Civil and Military Gazette* about five months before 'Pig'; like the latter it has undercurrents beneath the farcical surface, and has been treated as one of Kipling's simple revenge anecdotes. In addition, it shares with 'Mrs Bathurst' the following elements: wife-desertion, diabolical possession and an incriminating tattoo.

Henry Augustus Ramsay Faizanne is ragged by the Senior Subaltern of his high-caste regiment 'The Shikarris' under the name of 'The Worm' because he has no visible talents to compensate for his being 'an exceedingly pretty boy, without a hair on his face, and with a waist like a girl's' (*PT*, p. 155). He obstinately keeps writing to his mother and sisters. The regiment determines to 'soften' him up, by which Kipling of course means 'harden'.

When the Senior Subaltern, an engaged man, borrows his trap for a non-existent lady but uses it himself, the Worm finally turns, and lays him a wager that 'I [will] work a sell on you that you'll remember for the rest of your days, and the Regiment after you when you're dead or broke' (p. 157). One night two months later, at the start of the hot weather, when the Senior Subaltern is praising his fiancée to the officers and their wives, a women suddenly appears. She is looking for the Senior Subaltern, whom she accuses of desertion. His indignant denials that he ever had a wife are not believed by the company, though they feel sorry for him, because, it is implied, every man fears, irrationally, that he might be guilty of bigamy. Indeed, *four* men 'jumped up as if they had been shot' when she first appears asking for her husband.

It is a very obtuse reader who has not guessed that the woman is the Worm in disguise, and the trick is soon revealed, to the great relief of all. The story seems to be no more than a fairly predictable smoking-room *jeu* at the expense of women. The underlying assumption of the narrator would seem to be that, since all men share a terror of making a mistake in choosing a wife and being thereafter trapped into a loveless marriage, chaps should stick together and do nothing that might bring youthful indiscretions into the open. This seems to be the explanation for the company's verdict on the Worm's acting after he had revealed himself: 'It leaned as near to a nasty tragedy as anything this side of a joke can' (p. 161).

But there are some easily overlooked remarks in this brief story which point to a more deeply concealed disturbance among the company. The narrator is even more disapproving of the 'sell' than the others: 'Personally, I think it was in bad taste; besides being dangerous. There is no sort of use in playing with fire, even for fun' (p. 162). On three occasions he describes the disguised Worm in terms that stress his sexual attractiveness. The woman is 'very lovely with black hair and great eyes full of tears . . . tall with a fine figure'. (She is also dressed in grey, a colour which Kipling associated with dangerous women.) 'Under the lights . . . we saw how beautiful the woman was.' 'We, noting how lovely she was and what a criminal he looked, esteemed him a beast of the worst kind' (pp. 158, 159, 160). The Worm explains his histrionic talent by saying that he used to act at Home with his sisters. 'But no acting with girls could account for the Worm's display that night', the narrator comments mysteriously. The surface explanation is that The Worm's convincing performance was fuelled by revenge. But the narrator's refusal to elaborate on his cryptic remark points to another possibility: that he suspects that The Worm is able to act the part of a deserted 'wife' because he has experienced desertion in real life, and real anguish lies behind his performance.

He could have, like the young Rudyard, have felt abandoned by his mother, or he could have been thrown over by some girl – or boy; it does not matter. What his experience has given him is a 'womanish' insight into the vulnerability of his fellow Shikarris. 'Finally, the woman wound up by saying that the Senior Subaltern carred a double F.M. in tattoo on his left shoulder. We all knew that . . .' (p. 160). They all know this figuratively as well as literally. What the 'woman' has revealed is the androgyne in every man; 'F.M.', represents the first two syllables of 'effeminate', as well as 'female' and 'male'; that it is *double* suggests that he needs two mates.

The Shikarris' nickname for Faizanne, 'The Worm', expresses their contempt for him as the weakest of creatures, but a worm is also a feeder on corpses – thus having the last laugh on men – and a serpent. His seductiveness and talent for disguise and the detail of his 'dusty' shoes suggest that, momentarily, the old story of the Devil's disguising himself as a woman and has been updated, and the Undying Worm has appeared among the Shikarris. 'Home' and 'sisters' are Hell and the Furies. The 'sell' that has been worked on the Shikarris is, but for one letter, a spell. Almost, but not quite – this is a comedy and the unclean thought must be *dispelled*. 'The Worm' is made president of the regiment's dramatic club, where he proves to be 'a good Worm; and the "Shikarris" are proud of him' (p. 162); ever after he is known as 'Mrs Senior Subaltern'. So he has become the Senior Subaltern's second wife after all, but safely, within the context of amateur theatricals. In much the same way, the Lincoln Imp has become one of the best-loved curiosities of English ecclesiastical architecture. The real moral of the story is that to try to eradicate 'feminine' traits from a man and to mock his tender affections is a dangerous thing to do.

As for Dante, I have already mentioned his pervasive presence in nineteenth-century writing, Kipling's attempt to imitate him at school and his ownership of the Cary translation. I am also virtually certain that he knew Gustave Doré's famous illustrations to the *Inferno*, and that Doré, rather than Dante himself, lies behind some of the details in Kipling's infernal yarns. There are scattered, admiring references to Doré throughout his work. They are almost invariably connected to the idea of a 'City of Dreadful Night', though the only Doré book that I find him mentioning by name is Balzac's *Contes drolatiques*.[9] Kipling's own black-and-white drawing shows traces of Doré's influence. The illustration for 'The Sing-song of Old Man Kangaroo' in *Just So Stories* is, in my opinion, a witty parody of Doré's *Inferno*. Kipling has extracted elements from the gloomy Paola and Francesca and Satan plates in order to compose a cheerful myth of the progress which may result from running round in a circle in the desert. (See plate section.)

However, the reading of 'Mrs Bathurst' depends on an assumption that Kipling did not merely know Dante, but identified himself in some way with the poet who was born exactly 600 years before him. That an avatar or type of Dante is one of Kipling's favourite masks is a view that at least one critic seems to have been edging towards in the last twenty years. Elliot Gilbert, in an acute essay, 'Silence and Survival in Rudyard Kipling's Art and Life', seems to want to say so when discussing the difficulties of 'placing' Kipling in any century.

> People who are born, as Kipling was, in a year numbered sixty-five are so placed chronologically as to have their biblically allotted three-score and ten year life exactly bisected by the turn of the century, and to be often a little uncertain, therefore, about which of the two centuries they ought to identify with. . . . Literary people are likely to have their own experience coloured by this fact, as, most famously, was Dante's, and in particular to think of the two halves of their lives as being – and perhaps even to act so as to cause them to be – radically discontinuous.[10]

Kipling could hardly have missed the fact that the midpoint of Dante's life and the turn of the century coincided, as it forms the substance of Cary's very first footnote.[11]

He has been recognised as 'Dantean' when his subject is 'Cities of Dreadful Night'. Louis Cornell thus described his early travel-writing: 'Seeing himself as a modern Dante with spectacles and a notebook, he wandered through sordid urban Infernos in Lahore, Calcutta, Hong Kong, San Francisco, and London'; and quotes from the beginning of 'Deeper and Deeper Still', Kipling's account of the underworld of Calcutta:

> And where next? . . . 'To the lowest sink of all', say the Police after the manner of Virgil when he took the Italian with the indigestion to look at the frozen sinners . . . they cease not from leading till they come to the last circle of the Inferno – a long, long winding, quiet road.[12]

'To the lowest sink of all' shows Kipling quoting Cary from memory; the translation (which comes from canto XIV, examined in the last chapter) has 'to the lowest depth of all'.[13] It is perhaps the most detailed, overt reference to Dante's Hell to be found in Kipling, but there are others. McIntosh Jellaludin, another of Kipling's fallen angels, promises the narrator 'the material of a new Inferno' that should make his 'greater than Dante' (*PT*, p. 330). In 'The Last of the Stories' (1888) the Devil invites the narrator to 'play Dante to my Virgil', but warns, 'I can't guarantee a nine-circle inferno.'[14]

Dante is often present even when not named. His circles lie behind the representations that Kipling constructed of the world as one of the hells, using what he could see with his own eyes – racetracks, burning ghats, brick kilns, railway systems, tarred roads, trenches. (I don't meant that he is the sole literary model, of course.) The hellish, dust-storm-swept electro-erotic atmosphere of 'False Dawn' (*PT*) derives from the Paolo and Francesca episode (canto V).[15] The Dantean wood, visualised again through Doré's illustrations, appears in 'The Tree of Justice' where Dan complains that 'this tale is getting like the woods . . . darker and twistier every minute' (*RF*, p. 323). This is the last story of *Rewards and Fairies*; Dan is about to become a Dante and say farewell to childhood. The tales have been a preparation for the moment when he, too, will have to enter the wood, the Big Miz-Maze of error.[16]

When inspiration fails Kipling, he retreats to the Dantean framework, as if to a magic formula that might summon his Daemon. A feeble story called 'A Naval Mutiny', written (1930) in Bermuda during an outbreak of psittacosis in the West Indies,[17] has as its leading figure a Mr Winter Vergil, 'the biggest liar in the Service' – all poets are liars. He explains that his hand is bandaged because of trying to subdue seventy-two mutinous pet parrots – 'more like the works of vulshures' (*LR*, p. 186). Much is made of the parrots' resembling women. The germ of the story is the episode of the grove of the harpies (canto XIII).[18]

The story in which Dante is the most abstruse presence – or absence – is 'The Eye of Allah' (1924), set in a thirteenth-century monastery. Kipling imagines what might have happened if the microscope had been invested by Arab scientists and introduced into England. John Otho, an artist monk, brings one back from Spain, and derives from the microbes which it reveals models for the astonishing painted devils with which he illuminates his manuscript of St Luke. The painting is accomplished some time between Mayday of that year and 'around Midsummer', at which point the microscope is shown to other senior clergy. The sight of the microbes in a drop of putrid water appears to them as a new view of Hell. The Abbot realises that the instrument could be used to eliminate disease. But the Church will burn them as heretics, for they will be judged to have looked into Hell without her permission. The invention is premature. 'This birth, my sons, is untimely. It will be but the mother of more death, more torture, more division, and greater darkness in this dark age' (*DC*, p. 394). He therefore smashes the microscope to smithereens.

'The Eye of Allah' contains references to historical events which allow a time-scale to be worked out. (Whenever Kipling does this it is worth inquiring for a possible reason.) The first to work it out was L. A. F. Lewis, who noticed that the time-span of the story is about two years. It opens when Cardinal Falcodi is still papal legate, and closes 'around Midsummer' of a year when Falcodi is Pope.[19] His elevation seems recent, for Friar Bacon calls him 'Falcodi . . . our English-hearted Foulkes made Pope' (p. 391), as if he has not yet got used to calling him by his papal title. This points to the first year of his papacy (1265). John Otho, then, would have accomplished his painted vision of devils, which he has said has been 'waiting these months to – ah God! be born' (p. 372) under the sign of Gemini of the year 1265, which is the period during which Dante was born as well. John Otho, then, is a forerunner to someone mightier than he. The Abbott does not order the destruction of his great work, which will stand as a record of what was seen under the microscope. And, even as it is accomplished, his antitype is being born, one who will later write that he 'found the original of my hell in the world which we inhabit',[20] and who is to create an image of evil so powerful that it will imprint itself on the European consciousness for 600 years. Scientific knowledge may be impeded by censorship, but the artist's magnifying vision cannot be aborted.

The above examples show that we must not expect to find evidences of Dante blatantly signalled in Kipling's work. This should be borne in mind when considering 'The Impressionists' from *Stalky & Co.*, that 'moral tract'. Dante is there in a general way, the school of *Stalky* being a sort of reverse Inferno, where 'young devils' are trained before being let out into the world to do good, but we can also see, more specifically, Kipling's use of the seventh circle.

Incensed by being split up by the unpopular master Prout – his charge is specifically that they crib from each other – Stalky, M'Turk and Beetle spread the rumour that there is a rash of usury in Prout's house. Prout falls for the trick, orders an inquisition, but uncovers no more than the *'natural* and inevitable system of small loans that prevails among small boys' (p. 114, my italics). The inquisition breeds 'a fine air of plot and intrigue':

> M'Turk and Stalky invented many absurd and idle phrases – catch-words that swept through the house as fire through stubble. It was a rare jest, and the only practical outcome of the Usury Commission, that one boy should say to a friend, with awful gravity, 'Do you think there's much of it going on in the house?' The other would reply, 'Well, one can't be too careful, you know.' (p. 115)

Prout overhears a junior boy begging Beetle (Kipling's *alter ego*) not to finish a story he was telling: 'It's too beastly.' (This 'beastly' story turns out to be merely a version of Margaret Oliphant's *A Beleaguered City*.) He accuses the bewildered Beetle of 'pandering to the baser side of youthful imagination', which will lead to 'soul-corrupting consequences' (*SC*, p. 120). His reaction is so violent that their friend, the Padre, feels impelled to satisfy himself that they have not been 'perverting the juniors'. And the Head, while admitting that he is committing a 'flagrant injustice', gives them a caning for having 'bothered' him. 'The Head had seen all that was hidden from the house-master' (p. 127). As the boys compare the weals on their shoulder-blades in the washroom, Prout calls down the stairs suspiciously, 'What are you doing there?' and is told that they are washing off the blood.

Part of the story's black humour is missed unless the reader realises that Stalky & Co. *have* unwittingly created an unhealthily furtive atmosphere in pursuing their private revenge, but it is Prout who should be beaten, not they. The idle catchphrases that they put around assume a life of their own detached from context, as words are prone to do in Kipling; they suggest to Prout's imagination that he should really be seeking to extirpate that horror of Victorian housemasters – 'beastliness'. This will readily be seen if one substitutes 'sodomy' for 'usury' throughout the story and takes note of how Prout fails to differentiate between the coded sense of 'beastly' and its casual schoolboy slang use. The Head's task is to stop the rumour-mongering while keeping the threesome ignorant (and thus genuinely innocent) of what they are really suspected of.

Following Dante, usury and sodomy are treated as virtually interchangeable. In Thomist ethics they are bracketed together as crimes against Nature's kindly law; Virgil explains to Dante that this is why usurers, sodomites and blasphemers are placed together in the third compartment of the seventh circle: 'And thence the inmost round marks with its seal/Sodom, and Cahors, and all such as speak/Contemptuously of the Godhead in their hearts' (canto xi).[21] The *clou* of the story is contrast between the 'natural' and generous behaviour of the boys, who lend each other money and help one another with homework, and what the unsavoury mind of Prout makes of these acts. What to Stalky & Co. is sharing and the propagation of knowledge, to Prout is 'unboylike', 'abnormal' and 'unsound'.[22]

'The Impressionists' originates in an incident at United Services College just before Kipling left. A housemaster called Pugh, the original of Prout, had transferred him away from his friends as a suspected bad influence, but Kipling did not find out why until four years later. 'Rabidly furious' he then wrote to his old classics master, saying that, although at the time 'not innocent in some respects, as the fish girls of Appledore could have testified', and aware that Pugh thought him a liar, he had had no inkling of 'much worse', though 'by the light of later knowledge I see very clearly what that moral but absolutely tactless Malthusian must have suspected'. Kipling admitted to a desire for revenge on Pugh, who 'must be a very Stead in his morals and virtuous knowledge of impurity and bestiality'. He threatened to put him into his novel and 'to finish the revenge I shall marry him to a woman who shall give him something else to think about!'[23] A somewhat revealing choice of punishment. The novel (*Mother Maturin*) never materialised, but Kipling did get back at Pugh, as we have seen. The incident is treated again in the much later tale 'The United Idolators'.[24] Even in 1935, recalling his schooldays, the injustice still rankled (*SM*, p. 23).

But the most Dantean of Kipling's stories, apart from 'Mrs Bathurst', is 'The Strange Ride of Morrowbie Jukes' (*WWW*), that nightmarish tale of entrapment in a 'Village of the Dead'. Kipling began writing it on 8 December 1884, and continued working on it for at least three months. It was published at Christmas 1885 in a family compilation called *Quartette*. About a month after his last diary entry regarding the making of 'The Strange Ride', he visited Peshawar, which he called 'The City of Evil Countenances'. 'You shall see a scene worthy almost of a place in the *Inferno*', he wrote, and proceeded to catalogue the horrors: 'lineaments stamped with every brute passion known to man. . . . Women, of course, are invisible in the streets, but here and there instead some nameless and shameless boy in girl's clothes with long braided hair and jewellry – the centre of a crowd of admirers.'[25]

This shows that Dante was in his mind during this period; the story and the report have some resemblances, the most striking being an atmosphere or moral evil and stench in which a white man moves through a crowd of contemptuous human animals. The interesting thing is that Peshawar could not have inspired the story; if anything, it was the other way round: Kipling saw the city through the story which he had just been writing.[26]

It is a much-admired tale, but the ending – Jukes's sudden rescue from the trap – has been criticised as 'inartistic and improbable'.[27] It is as if Kipling, having got his hero into an impasse, could not think how to finish the story and so resorted to the sort of tactic used by the apocryphal strip-cartoonist when faced with a similar problem: 'With one bound Bob was free!' I would disagree: on the contrary, the structure of the story makes the ending the only satisfying one possible.

One reason why the artistic propriety of the ending has not been perceived might be that the tale is almost universally read as a study in the fear of the white ruling class of being overwhelmed by the subject races, a view which seems to me indubitable, but one-dimensional. The exclusively 'colonial malaise' reading depends on one's screening out certain elements, or relegating them to the status of plot machinery – the dog-shooting episode at the beginning, for instance. Nor does that reading account for the climactic effect of Jukes's discovery of the dead body of a fellow sahib in the pit. It overemphasises Kipling's political maturity (the story is very much a young man's fantasy to my mind) and underestimates the story's artistic coherence.

Kipling, in the 'frame' which he added for the final version, begins with an assurance that 'there is no invention about this tale' – the usual signal that a very tall story indeed is to follow – but which is also a double bluff. The story will turn out to be in some sense 'A Matter of Fact'. Because, says the narrator, it is well known that there is a wonderful city in the middle of the desert in which retired money-lenders drive about in expensive barouches 'and buy beautiful girls, and decorate their palaces with gold and ivory and Minton tiles and mother o'pearl' (*WWW*, p. 170) there is no reason why Jukes's 'Village of the Dead' should not exist. In other words, the nightmare is evolved from the materialistic fairyland. Usury, the enslavement of women for man's pleasure, and conspicuous consumption (mother o'pearl replacing mother o'mine), create a universe of death. And, as Ruskin had written in *Unto This Last*, 'There is no wealth but life.'[28]

Jukes's narrative of his adventure then follows. The fussy and precise details (the inventory, a count of exactly how much money he has in his pockets) are wonderfully played off against the phantasmagoric horror of the setting. A sensible Civil Engineer, he gets an attack of fever while working in the desert. Plagued by the howling of pye-dogs, he shoots one and in a sort of delirium determines on a mad plan to ride off and kill the ring-leader. His horse falls into a deep sandy crater (an anticipation of the sterile crescent-shaped concavity used again in 'Mrs Bathurst') occupied by half-starved Hindus who have been thrown there after reviving on their funeral pyres. The inhabitants of this village live in fetid burrows and survive by catching crows. They mock the now powerless sahib. Jules meets a former acquaintance, Gunga Dass, once a proud Brahmin and telegraph master, who maliciously tells him that there is no escape, and that he will become as degraded as they. (The crater is open at one end, but the exit is guarded by quicksand and a gun-boat.) Jukes rides frantically and vainly against the crater walls, blaspheming.

After a hideous night, during which Jukes's horse is killed and eaten, Jukes learns from Dass that he has had a predecessor, a sahib who was said to have been shot by a gun-boat bullet. He demands to see his body, which Gunga Dass brings out from a burrow in a mummified condition. Jukes takes an inventory of his possessions and then discovers, by examination of his corpse, that it is Dass who has shot him. He discovers in the binding of the sahib's notebook a slip of paper on which are written some puzzling words. Dass tells Jukes that they are directions to the exit route, which, he says, the sahib had discovered before his murder. Jukes and Dass plan to escape together that night, but Dass drops the paper, knocks Jukes unconscious and disappears. When Jukes recovers consciousness, he is rescued by his loyal dog-boy,

Dunnoo, who has tracked him to his prison. The *Quartette* version has a final paragraph, in which Jukes voices a hope that someone will identify the sahib.

The Dantean framework supplies one possible answer to that question. The first person to notice this framework was Evelyne Hanquart,[29] who pointed out that, besides drawing on Dante for its general atmosphere of horror, the tale contains specific allusions to the leopard, the centaurs and the harpies, as well as to the sepulchres of the heretics in the city of Dis; Gunga Dass she identified as a parody of Virgil. She stopped just short of noting the origin of Kipling's sand-trap in Dante's third compartment of the seventh circle and of the sahib in Brunetto Latini.

Dante and Jukes are each irresistibly drawn towards a representative of their own kind, damned or dead. Dante, startled to find Latini in Hell, insists on walking with him; his smirched visage cannot disguise his superiority to the other lost souls. The sahib, of whom Jukes urgently demands information from the cringing and treacherous Dass, is literally superior – 'above middle height' (*WWW*, p. 193). Latini commends to Dante his *magnum opus*, 'il mio Tesoro'. This is the subject of a lengthy note in Cary, which turns into a detailed description of another production by Latini, the *Tesoretto*.[30] The latter is an unfinished allegory in which the poet wanders into a wood, then through a savage desert. (Cary quotes eighteen lines about the desert wanderings, and supplies a translation.) The poet ventures into further strange lands, learns from Ovid how to conquer the passions, and seems on the point of achieving wisdom when the poem breaks off. From this note Kipling would have learned that Brunetto in the *Tesoretto* mentions 'with great horror' the sin for which Dante condemns him in the *Inferno*, and that the poem supplied Dante with his idea of opening his poem with being lost in a wood.

Jukes inherits the sahib's writings, which include a supposed route out of the pit of sand. (Whether the directions are a genuine or false treasure will be discussed later.) To Dante, Brunetto seems like the winning contender for the prize of the green mantle of Verona.[31] Jukes's sahib is actually dressed in green – 'an olive-green hunting-suit'. Finally, and this is the nearest thing to a giveaway in this terrain of false trails, the monogram on the sahib's ring is 'either "B.K." or "B.L."', a curious detail on the realistic level, as the letter *K* is not normally confused with an *L*.[32]

Brunetto's sin is the clue to the real identity of the Village of the

Dead, but there are others, notably from the Bible. Gunga Dass is said to be fond of English puns, so one looks for examples. One occurs when he answers Jukes's question about how the villagers spend their time. He replies that Jukes may see for himself and that 'this place is like your European Heaven; there is neither marrying or giving in marriage' (*WWW*, p. 182) Dass has sardonically perceived that the same words may define both Hell and Heaven. There is no marriage in Heaven because everyone has transcended the body and love even as the angels. There is no marriage in this Hell because no one has transcended the body and there is an imbalance of the sexes which ensures a perpetual atmosphere of sexual violence and raging frustration. The inhabitants of the pit number sixty-five, made up of about forty men, twenty women and one child 'who could not have been more than five years old'. Kipling may have been thinking of Doré's plate 38 here, which shows about sixty-five figures inhabiting the third compartment, though there are fewer than twenty women (see plate section). The child is, of course, Kipling's own addition, a little lost black sheep.

The diary of 'B.K.'/'B.L.' contains references to 'a Mrs L. Singleton, abbreviated several times to "Lot Single"'. This jotting recalls Lot and his wife, who were spared the destruction of Sodom. Lot became single when his wife turned into a pillar of salt (Genesis 19). The village, then, is a City of the Plain, and the faecal imagery prominent in the story is a metaphor for that city's abominations, which included fornication as well as 'going after strange flesh' (Jude 7). The 'hideous cavity' in the sahib's back made by 'the gun that fitted the brown cartridges' and Jukes's haste to sink his yellow-brown mummified body in the quicksand are other contributory details (*WWW*, p. 195).[33]

The scene when the pony is killed and eaten is a rewording of elements of Judges 19, a chapter resembling Genesis 19. A Levite offered his concubine to satisfy the lusts of 'sons of Belial' in Gibeah, rather than suffer sodomistic rape upon his own person. They 'abused her all night'. In the morning the Levite found her corpse, placed it upon his ass and rode home, then 'divided her together with her bones into twelve pieces, and sent her into all the coasts of Israel'. In the morning Jukes finds 'poor old Pornic' lying dead. 'How they had killed him I cannot guess.' Pornic's body 'was divided, in some unclean way or other' and eaten. It is on this occasion that Dass observes, 'We are now Republic, Mister

Jukes.' Judges 19 begins its story with the words, 'And it came to pass in those days when there was no King in Israel . . .', and thus provided Kipling with a link between anarchy and sexual perversion. Although the pony is male (for a reason which I shall put forward later), his curious name has been suggested by the fact that the concubine in Judges had previously 'played the whore' against the Levite. 'Pornic' is a nonce adjective derived from the Greek *porne*, and thus means 'to do with prostitution'. The horse Pornic has been partly responsible for Jukes's landing in the deep pit, and thus may be said to have played his master false and led him astray.[34]

Once one realises that 'The Strange Ride' is a fable about the fear of sexual degradation, the threat of the 'higher centres' of the little world of man succumbing to the 'lower' visceral centres, for which domination by 'racial inferiors' is a metaphor, Jukes's own shame about seeming unmanly (*WWW*, p. 187) begins to make more sense, and one can start to interpret the dog-shooting episode which is apparently the cause of his falling in the pit.

During his fever, he is seized by an extreme loathing for the wild dogs that 'sing their hymns of thanksgiving' to the moon. The moon is the symbol of the Eternal Feminine. The votary dogs (who appear to be male) stand for deluded lovesick fools, whose appetites have been elevated into worship of the One. Like Palamon and Arcite in Chaucer's *Knight's Tale*, who simultaneously adore the divine maiden Emelye and loathe the 'foul prison' of degrading passions into which their unattainable desire has thrown them, these hounds strive for the bone. They are miserable for they can be neither pure brute nor angel. The object of their worship is both 'Sainted Diana' and 'Old Hecate'. (The phrases are taken from Kipling's poem 'The Moon of Other Days', written during this period.[35]) Jukes shoots one dog and then rides out 'to slaughter one huge black and white beast who had been foremost in song' (p. 170). Black and white figure prominently as the livery colours of the deserted mistress whose ghost drives Jack Pansay to insanity in the later 'The Phantom 'Rickshaw'.[36] The dogs trouble Jukes because they symbolise passions contending within himself; his reaction is to make war on the female principle. In his rage he faintly recollects 'standing upright in my stirrups and . . . brandishing my hog-spear at the great white moon that looked down so calmly on my mad gallop' (the symbolism is obvious here). Pornic is racing like 'a thing possessed' (*WWW*, pp. 170–1);

the violent or treacherous horse, as in 'Pig', is an emblem of unruly sexual passion, but is here used in a more complex way.

The horse and rider are in this story associated with masculine sporting-activities based on comradeship – polo, hog-sticking. Normally this comradeship offers relief from the pains of romantic entanglements and is thoroughly 'healthy' and 'clean'. However, in this case, the horse, spurred on by Jukes's vehement moon-hatred, is rendered mad too, and dashes him into the pit. Jukes has insulted the White Goddess, a rash act in itself. Inasmuch as the Moon is a goddess of fertility and childbirth, he has been violent against Nature. As a punishment, he shall be made to act in a way contrary to Nature, and the very same masculine stronghold from which he has ventured to attack her shall be converted into the agency of his downfall, for it is also the *entrée* to the homosexual underworld. Jukes is an Engineer and 'tis the sport to have the engineer hoist with his own petard – a tag which could have served as an alternative epigraph to the tale.[37]

This moon behaves oddly. The strange ride takes place on the night of 'the 23rd December 1884', when it is at the *full*. Jukes spends a day in the pit. That night, he watches the river Sutlej flowing past under the light of a *young* moon; this moon has compressed two quarters of her progress into the space of a day, which is Kipling's marker that Jukes is a liar or has hallucinated, despite the editor's disclaimer.[38]

The moon continues to menace Jukes. When he is nearly sucked under in his attempt to cross the quicksand, 'in the moonlight, the whole surface of the sand seemed to be shaken with devilish delight at my disappointment' (p. 188). On the night that Jukes and Dass plan their escape, it is after the rising of the moon that Dass hits Jukes on the head, steals the route map and disappears. From Jukes's point of view Dass is a traitor, but Dass is being loyal to the power who commands him. Long before, when Dass was a telegraph officer, Jukes, in an 'accident' about which he is oddly reticent, had given him a 'crescent-shaped scar on his left cheek' (p. 175), and has thus inadvertently branded him with the insignium of the horned moon. When the moon is in the ascendant, then, he does her bidding. Jukes recovers consciousness only when the moon is going down.

That the moon is somehow involved with the sahib's fate is hinted at by one of the items in the inventory made by Jukes, a letter addressed 'Miss Mon—'. Kipling tantalises us with this miscellany. Every item is useless, fake or fragmentary – a pipe that cannot be smoked, a knife that cannot cut, an empty envelope, a penknife that might be made of precious or base metal. A riddle with no answer? Yet Jukes hopes that someone may be able to use them to identify the man. The list suggests meaning even as it withholds it. There are keys, though broken. Two of the items are strings or threads – clues that might lead part of the way. The list is as follows.

1. Bowl of a briarwood pipe, serrated at the edge; much worn and blackened; bound with string at the screw.

2. Two patent-lever keys; wards of both broken.

3. Tortoise-shell-handled penknife, silver or nickel . . . monogram 'B.K.'

4. Envelope, postmark undecipherable, bearing a Victorian stamp, addressed to 'Miss Mon' – (rest illegible) – 'ham' – 'nt'.

5. Imitation crocodile-skin notebook . . . private memoranda relating chiefly to three persons – a Mrs L. Singleton, abbreviated several times to 'Lot Single', 'Mrs. S. May', and 'Garmison', referred to in places as 'Jerry' or 'Jack'.

6. Handle of small-sized hunting-knife. Blade snapped short. Buck's horn, diamond-cut, with swivel and ring on the butt; fragment of cotton cord attached.

Some of this defeats my guesswork and perhaps is intended to; Kipling could have introduced some distractors which make no narrative sense. Nevertheless, if we assume that the items stand for jumbled chapters in the sahib's life, that some of them are literary souvenirs, fragments shored against ruin, the following sequence can be extracted: the broken keys – the Queen of my heart – the unfaithful wife – the Destroyer and the Hell-hound – financial ruin – down to Gehenna.

'Miss Mon—' may refer to an English fiancée, a 'Moon of Other Days' – perhaps living in Kent, an idealised 'sainted Diana' figure. That he has an envelope addressed to her may mean that his letters were returned. The 'Victorian stamp' means that at some time he was in the Australian colony of Victoria, and the phrase itself suggests 'servitude to a queen'. The indecipherable postmark would be a circular one, and thus is a full-moon stamp to be set alongside the crescent-moon stamp with which Dass is marked.

The hunting-knife with the broken blade is an image of a dashing young man marred by marriage, a domestic tame-puss; it is a visual pun: 'A man may do no synne with his wyf, / Ne hurte hymselven with his owene knyf' (*Merchant's Tale*, l. 1840). But Chaucer's Januarie, who quotes this proverb to his May, *is* hurt by his unfaithful wife. The buck's-horn handle suggests both the cuckold's horns and another Chaucerian line: 'Absolon may blowe the buckes horn' (*Miller's Tale*, l. 3387) – that is, he has been rejected, like that unlucky character, in favour of a 'better man'.

The crocodile, or Mugger, is for Kipling an embodiment of a destructive force inherent in a feminine Nature; in 'The Bridge Builders' (*DW*) the crocodile is Mother Gunga, the Ganges, who exacts a toll of drowned bodies yearly.[39] Thus, a book bound in 'imitation crocodile skin' would be a suitable place to record liaisons with female types of the crocodile, predatory married women like Mrs Reiver of Simla, or the Mrs Vansuythen of 'Duncan Parrenness' (*LH*), and a consequent loss of all faith in woman. 'Garmison' is 'son of Garm', the Norse Cerberus, and links up with the other dogs in the story; in 'Garm, a Hostage' (*AR*), the dog is a faithful 'second self' who preserves the sanity of his master; but 'Jack' suggests the wild jackal or devil's dog.[40] Whether the dog is dead or a Hell-hound of the mind, the sahib, unlike the narrator of 'Bubbling Well Road' (*LH*) or Stanley in 'Garm', had no canine friend to ward off despair in the pit.

The penknife suggests both penury and suicidal impulses, by way of a reminiscence of the memorable scene in *Little Dorrit* where Mr Merdle chooses a penknife with which to kill himself upon the collapse of his speculative enterprises. Rejecting a *mother of pearl* one, he requests one with 'a darker handle . . . I think I should prefer tortoise-shell' and his body is found with a 'tortoise-shell handled penknife' beside it. He also leaves a letter with insufficient clues.[41]

The useless pipe represents the failure of even tobacco to soothe; the pipe itself is a miniature mental landscape; that it is of 'briarwood' suggests a wandering round and round in a thorny wilderness surrounding a pit, like the 'Wood of the Suicides' in the second compartment of the seventh circle.

The answer facing Jukes, then, to the question of the sahib's identity, is staring him in the face. It is 'Thou art the man' or, rather, 'Thou couldst have been the man', for the story is one which, in Kipling's fictional world, could happen to any young 'Griffin' sent out to India. 'B.K.' is one of the 'private marks' on the bales and stands for 'Brunetto Kipling', the author's possible older self, *nel mezzo del cammin di nostra vita,* rather as 'R.K.' in 'Fairy-Kist' stands for the alternative self who could be a murderer.[42] (In Chapter 7 I shall give reasons for supposing that the sahib stands for a *poet* of an older generation whose career Kipling fears to repeat.) Uncertainty hangs over the question of whether the directions found in the back of the notebook are false or not. One of Kipling's correspondents, E. L. White, drew a chart following them which he submitted to Kipling, who agreed that the path did not lead anywhere, but that it was too blamed late to change anything.[43] An ambiguous reply, allowing one to suppose either that Kipling had intended, but failed, to make the route a genuine one which Dass had stolen, or that he had deliberately made the route a false one, but, retrospectively, would have liked to have made it a true one. I suspect that 'The Strange Ride' is partly a working-out of Kipling's anxiety as to whether he should choose to be a writer about the Eastern underworld from the inside, with all the problems of establishing authenticity that this would entail. Uncertainty about the map dramatises his own inability to see into the future at the time, to decide whether it was worth risking 'having his hand on the pulse of native life' and becoming an outcast, on the chance that he would become a great artist. It was either when he had just finished or was just about to finish 'The Strange Ride' that the idea of his never-finished novel, *Mother Maturin,* took shape. In 'To Be Filed for Reference' Kipling supplied a fictitious account of the book's genesis, and half-promised that it would be forthcoming. The respectable narrator claims to be editing it from the 'treasure' of a drunken self-styled ex-Oxford man, McIntosh Jellaludin, who has paid for writing it with seven years' damnation. Describing himself as 'a Virgil in the Shades', Jellaludin has bequeathed the narrator 'the materials of a new Inferno' (*PT,* p. 330). *Mother Maturin* would have had an underworld setting. Parts of it were used for *Kim,* but that solution to Kipling's problem lay fifteen years in the future when 'The Strange Ride' was written.[44]

Since Jukes is living out a myth, though he does not realise it, his rescue is appropriately sudden, an act of grace, an overwhelming of an old goddess by a new young god. Deliverance comes on the morning of Christ's nativity, when pagan deities are routed. His good Samaritan is his *dog-boy,* whose face is 'ashy-grey in the moon-light' (*WWW,* p. 199).

In 1884 Kipling published a slim volume of imitations called

Echoes. One of them, 'The City of the Heart', after Longfellow, has a rider passing through an Indian town, bayed at by a 'yelping, yellow crew' of wild dogs:

> But I smote with the dog-whip of Work and Fact
> These evil beasts on the head,
> Till I made of my heart a wholesome tract,
> Empty and garnished.
>
> (*EV*, p. 225)

'The Strange Ride' also opposes Work and Fact to the wild beasts of the haunted heart. It is one of Kipling's earliest treatments of what was to become a ruling idea. Dunnoo is able to rescue his master because, instead of killing mutinous pariahs, he cares for a breed of dog outstanding for its affectionate nature, usefulness and intelligence. He uses a pony to pull his master out of the pit, whereas Pornic threw him in. Dunnoo is thus an intermediary between cerebral man, the 'reasoning engine', and his 'animal' instincts. He is there to demonstrate that these are not evil; they are to be controlled, not thwarted; they work, they play, they love. The energies which destroy can also save. If there was not a good sense in which man could be 'beastly', he would not be man.

None of this, of course, can Jukes bring to his consciousness, because he is not an intellectual and not trained to look closely into things. He does not even see fit to remark that he has been rescued on Christmas Day. For him the entire experience is about the discomfiture of a white man at the mercy of his racial inferiors.[45] The mode in which the story is cast, then, invites us to question whether Jukes has really understood the experience except superficially, for it is a 'seeming', and he is not the man to strip the veil from it.

Are the Hindus really Hindus? We are told by Jukes that they are, but he also notices a trait which, he says, makes them totally unlike a normal Indian crowd. 'They sat together in knots and talked – God only knows what they found to discuss – in low, equable tones, curiously in contrast to the strident babble with which natives are accustomed to make day hideous' (*WWW*, p. 185). His first description of them is of a crowd 'scantily clothed in that salmon-coloured cloth which one associated with Hindu mendicants, and at first sight, gave me the impression of a band of loathsome *fakirs*' (p. 174). In other words, these are really white

Yahoos, whose *pink* flesh-garment is the flimsiest of disguises for their naked Yahooishness. The pagan beggar and the 'white man' are brothers under the skin, and all inhabit coffins of clay. That is a knowledge which Jukes cannot face, and which Kipling, the demon-boy writing ostensibly to entertain the white masters, tells only to those who have ears to hear. All have enlisted in the legion of the damned, all men are pigs, all partake of the dunghill. The white man who thinks himself so fine is only the mushroom on it, one of Penfentenyou's 'swellings' who 'goes down' to the pit.[46] It is a judgement passed when a young man has lost his trust in man and his faith in woman and 'all the boy in him is burnt and seared away so that he passes at one step to the more sorrowful state of manhood' (*LH*, p. 406).

How old is Jukes anyway? Literally he is in his mid-thirties, that Dantean age, for he says 'Sixteen years ago, when I first landed in Bombay', a 'wandering Armenian' told his disbelieving younger self in 'Watson's Hotel with its swinging punkahs, white-robed servants' of the existence of the village (*WWW*, pp. 178–9). But he is also a palimpsest written upon a sixteen-year-old; underlying his words is a grotesque of the stranger soul entering his father's house ('What son's hotel'), a better place, surrounded by angelic ministering figures. And then comes Death, marking him early, writing his script. Kipling himself 'first landed in Bombay' in 1865, and was christened in Bombay Cathedral.

Peter Ackroyd, defending Kipling, wrote that the charge of racism is absurd, because

> in his imagination he *became* those various races and breeds . . . he sensed the Hindu within himself, just as he sensed the Cockney soldier . . . the helpless and the oppressed were always part of his own self. He may have hated the fact, and he may have tried to exorcize those interior ghosts in his more authoritarian pronouncements; but he knew of what he spoke.[47]

There is a lot of truth in that, and a sort of egalitarianism. Even in 'The Vortex', where Kipling's terror of the Empire being taken over by an Indian voice hides behind an elaborate smokescreen of farce, there is a sense in which Mr Lingnam is not just Black India but Man as he essentially is; Mr Lingnam is part of himself, the part that wants to rage, curse women, break the wheel of things. But the accusation of racism cannot be waved away. That 'he may have hated the fact' skates over the inherent racism of the idea that the loathsome self that is revealed when the 'white man' is stripped away turns out so often to be a brown man or a black devil.[48]

Kipling is locked into a conceptual framework which makes analogies between the individual human body and human society. He still thinks in terms of microcosm and macrocosm like a Renaissance man, a habit reinforced by his fondness for *The Tempest*, the poetry of Donne, and Fletcher's *The Purple Island*.[49] In this framework, the white man corresponds to the 'higher', cerebral, centres, and the brown or black man to the 'lower', which must be subdued, mastered, made to work and turned into a good servant. He is also, of course, locked into the Western symbolic language which associates blackness with evil, brownness with corruption and whiteness with good.

But, like Shakespeare and Conrad, we find him inverting the moral equations of the code; he adopts strategies of escape from the privileging of mind over matter, thinking over doing, the spiritual over the physical, angel over devil, man over beast, pure over hybrid. In similar essays in reversal, the black bitch becomes the deliverer (as in 'The Woman in his Life' (*LR*)), the brown man the knightly protector of women ('The Record of Badelia Herodsfoot' (*MI*)); dirt is 'the good brown earth', the Bona Dea, ground of delights of the senses and imagination (*SS*, I, 313); the black soil is the hiding-place not of shameful secrets but of a rare gourmet pleasure, the truffle ('Teem, a Treasure Hunter' (*TSD*)). The corrupt amphibian (toad), is metamorphosed into the hero, Mowgli (frog), or even an avatar of the great god Pan ('In the Rukh'). This is what Ruskin called in *The Queen of the Air* 'The curious reversal or recoil of the meaning which attaches itself to every great myth' (*Works*, XIX, 317).

There is a Boer War tale in *Traffics and Discoveries* – 'not one of Kipling's best stories', as Bodelsen says, called 'The Comprehension of Private Copper'. Private Copper is made prisoner by an Uitlander of English stock – 'a dark-skinned, dark-eyed stranger' who has defected to the Boers because his father has been let down by the English. To Private Copper's ear the Uitlander talks like a 'pukka Bazar Eurasian', yet has the same offensive, snobbish accent of 'the young squire of Wilmington' back home. Copper succeeds in freeing himself and capturing the Uitlander. Why Kipling takes pains to make Private Copper think the Uitlander a Eurasian only

Upon which you are to note, first, that the grave announcement, "This is the labyrinth which the Cretan Dedalus built," may possibly be made interesting even

to some of your children, if reduced from mediæval sublimity, into your more popular legend—"This is the

1a. 'The Labyrinth' (*Fors Clavigera*), read by Kipling at school; an early encounter with the enigmatic.

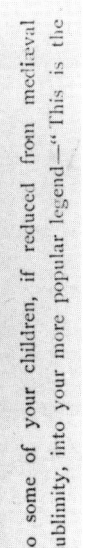

1b. *Phyllis and Demophoön*, E. Burne-Jones.

2a. 'I do 'ope you 'aven't changed your mind' (*The Windsor Magazine*, Sept. 1904, 383). Mrs Bathurst at the bar.

2b. 'The false-toother was tattooed on the arms and chest' (*The Windsor Magazine*, Sept. 1904, 386). Hooper discovers the corpses.

3a. Doré, Pl. 38, *The Inferno of Dante Alighieri*. The third compartment of the seventh circle.

3b. Brigadier-General Sir H. A. Macdonald, in L. S. Amery, *The Times History of the War in South Africa*, vol. III (1905), owned by Kipling.

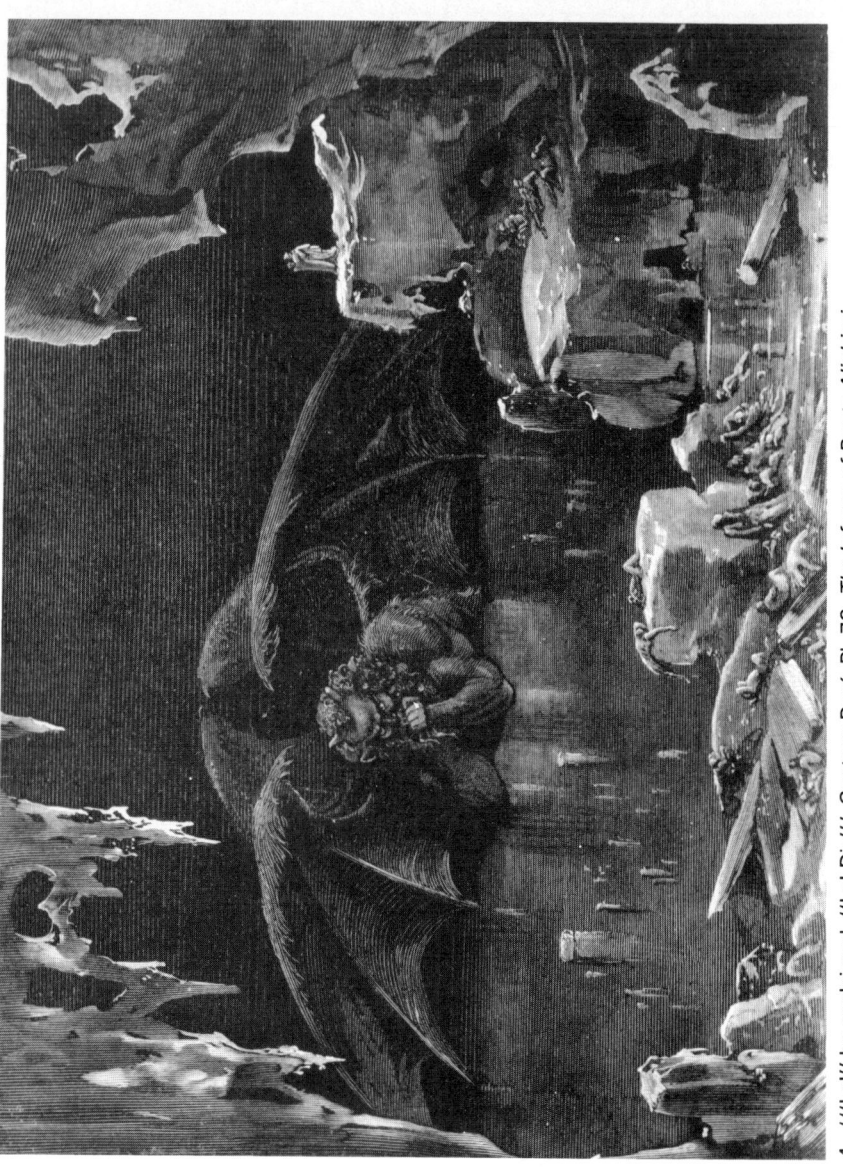

4. "'Lo!' he exclaimed, 'Lo! Dis'", Gustave Doré, Pl. 73, *The Inferno of Dante Alighieri*.

5. Old Man Kangaroo, Yellow Dog Dingo and the Great God Nqa (*Just So Stories*, p. 93). Kipling has used Doré's plate 73 for the composition, inverting Satan's arms and turning the frozen lake into a warm bath.

6a. 'Bard! Willingly would I address those two together coming.' Gustave Doré, Pl. 15, *The Inferno of Dante Alighieri*. Paolo and Francesca. A possible source for the figures of the Dingo and the Kangaroo.

6b. 'Wait till our Flying Corps gets to work!' ('Mary Postgate') The 'dire Erynnes' Pl. 27, ibid.

7. 'Behemoth and Leviathan' from Blake's *The Book of Job*, reproduced in Gilchrist's *Life of Blake*, I, p. 336. In *The Elements of Drawing* (owned by Kipling) Ruskin advised novices to study this plate.

8. Painted Jaguar, the Tortoise, the Hedgehog and the Armadillo (*Just So Stories*, p. 117).
A possible result of studying 'Behemoth and Leviathan'. Kipling's illustration for 'The
Beginning of the Armadillos'.

for the speculation to be dismissed has puzzled readers since Bodelsen directed attention to the oddity. Bodelsen suggested that the anomalies were intended to convey the idea that, by becoming helots of the Boers, Uitlanders were being *racially* degraded. Hermione Lee speaks for many when she says that what is most likely to strike the reader is the unpleasantness with which Kipling equates treachery to the English with degeneracy and the 'dubious relish with which [he] projects the racial impurity of the renegade, who, unlike the solid, loyal Tommy, goes all to pieces when captured ("'E screams like a woman")'.[50] And that does seem to be Kipling's position.

But, when Copper was the renegade's prisoner, the renegade contemptuously called him a 'po-ah Tommee', the same phrase used by a Eurasian girl who had refused to dance with Copper two years before. When the roles are reversed, he makes the prisoner repeat the words '"pore Tommy"' 'alf-a-dozen times' in order to satisfy himself that the Uitlander *does* sound like a half-caste (*TD*, p. 168). Private Copper is reaching back into his memory to match one voice with another, and we reach back into our memories too, to another personage who repeats similar words – Edgar in *King Lear*, disguised as Tom o'Bedlam, who says the words 'poor Tom' eight times in all – the Uitlander says them seven. And then, of course, we see that prisoner and captor are two sides of the same brown penny; both men are 'poor Tommies'; the Uitlander is a type of the outlaw and dispossessed, once a proud landowner with 'horse to ride and weapons to wear'. And then we *don't* see ourselves as invited to gloat over him screaming 'like a woman'. Rather, we give full weight to the words pronounced by Private Copper: 'Pore beggar – oh, pore, *pore* beggar!' The 'dark stranger' is the wild gypsy self, the 'pagan philosopher', the wronged child who screams for natural justice, the wanderer in the wilderness. And so is the man of whom the Uitlander reminds Private Copper, the 'saddle-coloured son' of the Umballa hotel-keeper whose fowls have been stolen and who complains in 'passionate, queerly-strung words' (*TD*, p. 166). The voice of Shakespeare which Kipling borrows allows a space for what conditions of war and 'the white man's burden' do not permit: fraternisation with the enemy and self-identification with the ruled; to relate them to 'poor Tom' gives them tragic dignity. And it is also true that it is *as* degenerates that they engage Kipling's empathy; the 'young squire of Wilmington' is a degenerate too, dwarfed by his archetype, a giant fertility god cut out in the white chalk, the Long Man of Wilmington.

The foregoing illustrates something of the difficulty of saying anything simple about Kipling's attitude to race, a subject which lies outside the scope of this book; at this point it must suffice to observe that anyone trying to define Kipling's ideological position on almost any matter finds him sooner or later a slippery customer.

6

Kipling and Chaucer: Mary Postgate

Lacquer and mother o' pearl – a natural combination . . . .
(Something of Myself)

Kipling's art has from time to time been described as Chaucerian, though that usually implies no more than that he is a teller of tales who delights in detail and a diversity of creatures.[1]

There are not many obvious references to Chaucer in Kipling. He wrote some parodies;[2] there is a mention in *Something of Myself*, of which more later. He owned a complete Chaucer (Routledge, 1843) and Pollard's two-volume *Canterbury Tales* (1894), but that was no more than any well-read person's library might be supposed to contain.[3] However, the existence alone of 'Dayspring Mishandled' (*LR*), which turns on the faking of a Chaucer manuscript and which has all the signs of a deep emotional commitment to the idea of what a true love of Chaucer ought to be, should be enough to alert us to the likelihood that his reading of Chaucer went deeper than the above scanty record suggests. (As 'Dayspring Mishandled' is, in my opinion, the one that really deserves to be called 'the hardest of the stories', I shall say no more about it here.) In 1912 he quotes the last verse of Chaucer's 'Trouthe' to the boys of Wellington College. By his choice of text he foregrounds the Dante-influenced, stoic poet, to whom the world is a wilderness, and man a beast unless he is also a pilgrim. Not overconcerned with strict accuracy – he misquotes, and thinks that 'buxomness' means 'gratitude' rather than 'submission' – Kipling seizes on Chaucer as a master-spirit who may teach one how to live. The poem covers, he says, 'the few facts in life that really matter' ('The Uses of Reading', *BW*, p. 81). You could say that he reads it as Chaucer's 'If'.

Some confirmation of one's impression that Kipling had a special feeling for Chaucer comes from Beresford, who in the first number of the *Kipling Journal* reported that at the age of twelve Chaucer was Kipling's *favourite* poet.[4] This was undoubtedly encouraged by the high regard in which Chaucer was held by the William Morris circle. Morris's famous *Kelmscott Chaucer*, with illustrations by Burne-Jones, was not completed until 1896, but it had been a cherished project for many years previously.

What would 'Chaucer' have meant to the mature Kipling? Undoubtedly, Kipling associated him with the genius of the language and the continuity of the national character. Dryden's 'Man of a most wonderful comprehensive nature', who had produced a compendium of national humours and portrayed 'our forefathers and great-grand-dames all before us . . . their general characters still remaining in mankind . . . for mankind is ever the same, and nothing lost out of Nature, though everything is altered',[5] would have been his. We may safely conjecture that Kipling would not have dissented from the nineteenth-century consensus: 'The most practical of all the great poets. . . . His poetry reads like history. Everything has a downright reality'. 'His humour is . . . entertaining, profound and good-natured'; 'His large, free, simple clear yet kindly view of human life'; 'Tender to tearfulness – childlike, and manly, and motherly; / Here beats true English blood richest joyance on sweet English ground.'[6]

Yet there were some voices which did not so much contradict the mainstream view as fail to reiterate it, emphasising marginalised qualities: Chaucer's vision rather than his realism; his hidden meanings rather than his simplicity; grotesquerie rather than humour or 'genial' satire. Where Leigh Hunt saw nothing in the Cook's 'mormal' but a masterly touch of naturalism – just the sort of thing that a Cook would get from continually tasting sauces and syrups – these others steered readers towards seeing it as also an outward and visible sign of the Cook's moral corruption. One of these was Ruskin; the other was William Blake. Both, as it happens, were voices which were particularly available to Kipling. (See Appendix II for a discussion of Kipling's reading of Blake.) I find his 'Chaucer' closer to theirs than to Arnold's, though my argument does not hinge on proof that he read their Chaucer criticism. But, since what Kipling made of Chaucer may seem to some readers at odds with what one might have expected of a late Victorian, these minority voices are worth hearing.

Ruskin saw Chaucer as representative of 'a strange, but quite essential' characteristic of the English – 'a delight in the forms of burlesque which are connected in some degree with the foulness of evil'. Though one of the wisest and most moral of writers, Chaucer would 'stoop to play with evil'. Yet the English genius is enfeebled when this trait is absent. In other words, Chaucer was never being more English than when he delighted in dirt. Ruskin uses words like 'foul' and 'evil' rather than 'ribald', 'broad', 'earthy' or 'coarse', the terms more usually employed when Victorian critics attempted to account for *The Miller's Tale*.[7]

Blake's Chaucer criticism is contained in his *Descriptive Catalogue of Pictures*, where he explains the aims and meaning of his fresco *Sir Jeffery Chaucer and the Nine and Twenty Pilgrims on their Journey to Canterbury*.[8] He seems to be straightforwardly following Dryden in claiming that Chaucer's supreme gift was for depicting with accurate minuteness the manners and even dress of our forebears while at the same time hitting off the universal: 'Chaucer's characters . . . are the physiognomies or lineaments of universal human life. Names alter, things never alter.' (Compare Kipling's 'Men and Things come round, eternal as the seasons'.) But what Blake emphasises is the allegorical nature of the journey: 'Every age is a Canterbury Pilgrimage; we all pass on, each sustaining one or other of these characters.' By 'characters' Blake means not 'personalities' but delineations of 'visions' of the 'eternal principles'. Where society separates them from humanity and erects these into gods, as did the Greeks, they become 'destroyers' and Blake sees it as his task to restore to them their humanity without sacrificing their eternity. So the Shipman is a reappearance of Ulysses. The Pardoner is the Age's Knave, 'sent in every age for a rod and a scourge . . . suffered by Providence for wise ends', and the Summoner 'a Devil of the first magnitude'. For Blake these 'eternal attributes' have been split into dualities: the Ploughman is 'Hercules in his supreme eternal state', while the Miller is his 'spectrous shadow', mere 'brutal strength and courage'.

Allowing Ruskin and Blake, then, to colour our concept of what Kipling made of the Chaucerian, we find, on returning to Kipling's work, that the two writers have narrative devices in common – the *faux-naïf* narrator, the collection of tales which 'interlace' with one another, the alternation of prose and verse as in the *Boece*, 'abridgement formulas' (Kipling's 'But that is another story' matching Chaucer's 'Of al this make I now no mencion'[9] and the like). There are many others from whom Kipling could have picked up the same strategies, but, since he did read Chaucer with attention, Chaucer may be credited with a portion of influence.

In addition to these general resemblances, we also find semi-quotations from Chaucer dotted around Kipling's work. One such is his use of 'solace' in 'My Son's Wife' (*D of C*, p. 353), where, besides being the bogus sympathy provided by loves of the 'Souls', it is also sexual pleasure, the 'solas' of *The Miller's Tale*. Another is 'old cold Saturn' in 'A Doctor of Medicine' (*RF*, p. 264), which derives from 'Pale Saturnus the colde' who 'Foond in his olde experience an art' (*Knight's Tale*, ll. 2443–5). But more important are the reappearances in his work of Chaucerian plots and characters. One of them has long been recognised as a distinct possibility. There has been some dispute as to whether *The Pardoner's Tale* was a source for 'The King's Ankus' (*JB2*), since there is a closer analogue in the *Jatakas*. Given Beresford's testimony, however, the question-mark is an unnecessary one. It is obvious that Kipling knew both, and that the plurality of sources served to confirm for him the universality of the tale. In a sense he was returning Chaucer to his origins. Folklorists had established that European folk and fairy tales had come from India – the point at issue was what fraction, with some holding out for 100 per cent. It was a commonplace in Kipling's youth that Buddhist popular literature, by making Gautama the gathering-point for a collection of tales, had brought together the most diverse material, including the beast fable and comic droll, all leading characters being able to be regarded in some sense as reincarnations. In so doing, the followers of Buddha had 'invented the Frame as a method of literary art'. Later collections – *The Arabian Nights*, Boccaccio's *Decamerone*, Chaucer's *Canterbury Tales* – were said to be 'directly traceable' to this method.[10]

The Pardoner's Tale operates on the same kind of level of natural supernaturalism, which I have called a defining feature of Kipling's storytelling. The three literal-minded rioters who take an oath to find and kill Death are first warned by a boy that his 'dame' has told him always to be careful as Death is to be met with at any time. The taverner confirms this: 'By Seinte Marie! . . . The child seith sooth', adding that a mile away is a 'great village' where Death may be found. Halfway to their destination, the rioters arrive at a stile over which they are about to climb when an old man appears, telling them that, since they are 'so leef to finde Deeth' they may go 'up this croked way' where he will wait for them. There are many features here which one finds in Kipling's mature art. There is an off-stage Madonna – the 'dame' and the

'Seinte Marie' whose wise commands are perverted to the ruin of
the blasphemers. There is the wise child who at the same time is
the rioter's boy – part angel, part limb of Satan. There is Death's
'village', archetype of sinister villages in Kipling – 'The Village that
Voted the Earth was Flat', 'The Village of the Dead'. There is the
stile – the dividing-line between the natural and the supernatural,
which has its counterpart in Kipling's bridges and golf-courses –
the 'links'. And there is entrapment by the idle word – the young
men 'seek death' in a sense other than they intended.[11]

The Pardoner himself is a literary ancestor of Kipling's sexually
ambivalent deceivers,[12] but he is only one example of the metagrobolised Pilgrim. The Shipman, for instance, is the archetype of the
unscrupulous old McRimmon, the 'Blind Deevil o' the Black Bird
Line' ('"Bread Upon the Waters"', *DW*). He enriches himself by
salvaging a boat which 'towed like a barge' and which is nicknamed
'The Hoor o' Babylon' because her fresh paint conceals a 'red
weeping crack you could put a penknife to'. Chaucer's crafty
Shipman similarly bothered little about 'nyce conscience'. He owns
a barge named after a public sinner – 'the Maudelayne', who in her
character as saint was also a weeper.

Another commentary upon a Chaucer text is Kipling's grimmest
Indian love story – 'Beyond the Pale' (*PT*), *The Miller's Tale* being
the base. The story of Alison, the wanton carpenter's wife, is
usually read as an 'earthy' comedy. Absolon, the genteel parish
clerk, desires her, but she has chosen Nicholas, the student lodger.
She insults Absolon by giving him her buttocks to kiss; he, shocked
out of his romantic notions and believing that his soul now
belongs to the Devil, returns with a red-hot ploughshare intended
for her. He brands Nicholas instead when the latter farts
at him.

An orthodox drawing out of the 'moral' goes something like this:
the story revels in chaos in order (finally) to celebrate common
sense. The men deserve to be punished for pretentiousness, vanity,
squeamishness, immaturity and jealousy. A more up-to-date reading extracts a proto-feminist message from the story: Alison's merry
giggle of 'Tehee!' at her trick and her freedom from authorial
censure evidence Chaucer's (perhaps momentary) recognition of
women's right to humiliate men in a light-hearted and girlish
fashion.[13]

These cheerful readings tune down the darker, Swiftian side of
the tale. The Miller tells the company that 'An housbonde shal nat

been inquisitif / Of Goddes privetee, nor of his wyf. / So he may finde Goddes foison there, / Of the remenant nedeth nat enquere' (ll. 3163–6). The blasphemous pun on 'privetee', which draws a parallel between a woman's genitals and the secrets of God, runs throughout the story. All disasters in the tale occur because of inquiring too closely into a 'privetee' of one sort or another. The carpenter's servant peeps through the cat-hole in Nicholas's door, thus initiating a chain of events which leads eventually to his master's cuckolding. If the carpenter had stuck to his own principles and refused to look into 'Goddes privetee', all might have been well. But, when Nicholas claims to have a privileged view of the Almighty's intentions, the carpenter cannot resist wanting to know them, the result of which is that he finds himself one night sitting in a tub suspended from the ceiling awaiting a second Noah's flood, while his wife and Nicholas are besporting themselves with 'mirth and solas'. Finally, Absolon looks literally into a woman's 'privetee' and discovers Hell-mouth; he weeps 'as a child that is ybete', which isn't funny at all.

If woman has a secret that should not be inquired into, at the risk of damaging man's happiness, then so has God. The forbidden question is, 'Since you so arranged things that we are born *inter faeces et urinas*, and thus caused us to associate birth with excrement and pleasure with shame, is it possible that you hate your creation?'[14] The Miller has a simple man's answer to the question: be grateful that sex is a pleasure and don't inquire further. The narrator warns his audience not to take game for earnest, which may be taken as a directive that the story is no joke, though for some people it is best to take it as such. It is also a variation on the theme of the dual diabolic–angelic character of women, of which Alison's black and white clothes are the emblem. That she goes unpunished evidences both the narrator's suspension of judgement upon her in particular and male vacillation between two totally contradictory views of woman in general: '*hominis confusio*' and '*mannes joye and al his blis*', as Chanticleer says in *The Nun's Priest's Tale* (ll. 3164–6).

Kipling found, I believe, an affinity between the tragic aspects of Chaucerian humour and his own, and read *The Miller's Tale* for the tragedy, as the following examination of 'Beyond the Pale' will attempt to show.[15] What he offers is not a straight transference of the story to an Indian setting but a variation on a Chaucerian theme. Narrative events are deliberately changed. The rival men are subsumed into one protagonist who has some of the qualities of both Absolon and Nicholas.

Like Chaucer, Kipling uses an unreliable narrator. The first few sentences run, 'A man should, whatever happens, keep to his own caste, race, and breed. Let the White go to the White and the Black to Black. . . . This is the story of a man who wilfully stepped beyond the safe limits of decent everyday society, and paid for it heavily' (*PT*, p. 171). Like *The Miller's Tale*, 'Beyond the Pale' is about the dangerous mixture of black and white; the beginning, so often taken as evidence of straight racism, is of course two-edged, and the reader's sympathies are immediately enlisted against the safe, decent and everyday. Trejago, the reckless hero, 'knew too much in the first instance; and he saw too much in the second' (ibid.).

Like Absolon, he uses a go-between and stands under a window singing to an idealised beloved, in his case, Bisesa, a beautiful Indian child widow. However, he also doubles Nicholas's part, for his serenade, unlike Absolon's, is successful (*song* plays an important part in both narratives) and he becomes Bisesa's secret lover. He is dressed in a *boorka* – a garment which 'cloaks a man as well as a woman' (*PT* p. 174). (Absolon dresses in somewhat effeminate clothes.) To get to her house Trejago goes down a 'narrow, dark Gully' lined by high walls 'where the buffaloes wallowed in the blue slime', and stumbles over a big heap of cattle-food. The cattle-food is there, of course, to hint to the reader that Trejago has been ensnared by the biblical 'strange woman' and is going as an ox to the slaughter. Then he sees 'that the Gully ended in a trap, and heard a little laugh from behind the grated window'.[16] (Alison chuckles 'Tehee!' as she claps shut the window.) Chaucer's Alison sings like a swallow and is 'ful brighter' in 'the shining of hir hewe / Than in the Tour the noble yforged newe', the Tower of London being then the site of the chief London mint (*Miller's Tale*, ll. 3255–6, 3258). Bisesa also sings and is 'as ignorant as a bird' (*PT*, p. 175). When she sobs, believing herself deserted, that she is 'only a black girl', the narrator adds parenthetically, 'She was fairer than bar-gold in the Mint.' She puts an end to their relationship, but Trejago returns, to find Bisesa at the window, holding out the stumps of her wrists towards the young moon, her hands having been cut off when the illicit romance was discovered:

some one in the room grunted like a wild beast, and something
sharp – knife, sword, or spear, – thrust at Trejago in his *boorka*.
The stroke missed his body, but cut into one of the muscles of
the groin, and he limped slightly from the wound for the rest of
his days. . . . Something horrible had happened, and the thought
of what it must have been comes upon Trejago in the night now
and again, and keeps him company till the morning.   (p. 178)

The wounding of Trejago in the groin, which several commentators
have seen as a euphemism for actual castration and which he calls
a 'riding strain', corresponds to Absolon's onslaught on Nicholas:
'And he was redy with his iren hoot / And Nicholas amydde the
ers he smoot' (*Miller's Tale*, ll. 3809–10) But Trejago also has
experienced something analogous to Absolon's horrified reaction
to feeling 'a thing al rough and long yherd' upon kissing Alison's
supposed lips. Kipling, however, by changing the Chaucer original
and making the woman suffer because of the man, has altered the
meaning. It is Trejago's discovery of the 'brutishness' of sexual
appetite which emasculates him, his mistake being to have deluded
himself into thinking that passion enables one to transcend Darwin-
ian evolution, live outside time and 'ride, ride forever ride' in the
instant made eternity. Bisesa is an *'endless* delight' to him, but 'after
a month of this folly' he has to pay attention to the ordinary
world – which neatly encapsulates the confusion. 'This folly' ends
in mutilation of both man and woman. As he is about to bring
such awareness into his consciousness he is smitten down, in the
Carlylean manner, for 'What hand will not smite the foul plunderer
that grubs [the flowers] up by the roots, and, with grinning,
grunting satisfaction shows us the dung they flourish in!'
   The Miller's Tale is a palimpsest over which 'Beyond the Pale'
has been written in darker and more violent colours in order to
make us question whether it is really about exotic Indian behaviour.
(In a reversal of the process, in 'On Greenhow Hill' [*LH*] the
English landscape is overlaid on the Indian one, in such a way as
to emphasise their resemblances and virtual identity.) Bisesa asks
'exactly as an Englishwoman would do' if Trejago loves her (*PT*,
p. 176). You can take that to be ironic, and that Trejago is a fool to
think that Indian women are like Englishwomen. But the deeper
irony lies in the fact that his notion really is true. Indian behaviour
is human behaviour, with the lid off.
   At this point, the reader may be wondering whether there is

any external evidence that Kipling concealed Chaucerian types in his work, and, as it happens, there is. In *Something of Myself* he confesses to having been spotted doing it by a *Manchester Guardian* reviewer (H. B. Charlton, the Shakespearean scholar).

> I wrote a tale ('The Wish House') about a woman of what was called 'temperament' who loved a man and who also suffered from a cancer on her leg – the exact situation carefully specified. The review came to me with a gibe on the margin from a faithful friend: 'You threw up a catch *that* time!' The review said that I had revived Chaucer's Wife of Bath even to the 'mormal on her shinne.' And it looked just like that too! There was no possible answer, so, breaking my rule not to have commerce with any paper, I wrote to *The Manchester Guardian* and gave myself 'out – caught to leg.' The reply came from an evident human being (I had thought red-hot linotypes composed their staff) who was pleased with this tribute to his knowledge of Chaucer. (*SM*, p. 212)

This passage is worth studying in detail. What is clear is that Kipling acknowledges that he has created a modern Wife of Bath in 'The Wish House' (*DC*); what is doubtful is whether he thinks the process was conscious or unconscious. 'Carefully specified' suggests the former. Evidently the 'faithful friend' (it would be interesting to know who this was – I suspect his sister) thinks so too; this friend knows that he has an interest in the Wife of Bath and that he engages in games of wits against his readers. But, even if Kipling did not discover that he had revived the Wife until Charlton's review, this would still be a testimony to the power that the Chaucerian figure and framework exerted over his creative processes.

It has often been observed it was *not* the Wife of Bath who had the mormal but Hogge the London Cook. Yet Kipling knew this perfectly well – or at least he did when he wrote *Kim*, where the ulcer-on-the-leg motif first appeared, this time inflicted on a male *scullion*. As the scullion evidently has a wife who 'pesters' Kim, we may take the unsavoury pair to be derived from the Cook and his tale, which breaks off at the point where a wife who 'swived for her sustenance' is introduced.[17] What Charlton had apparently arrived at by widdershins thinking was that Kipling's Grace Ashcroft (the heroine of 'The Wish House') is a hybrid creation –

Chaucer's Wife with some qualities of the Cook thrown in plus a *tertium quid* owed to Kipling's own inventiveness. He has given her the 'temperament' – that is, sexual appetite – of Chaucer's Wife, but he makes her also a retired London cook, so that she has Hogge's 'mormal' too. The anecdote is, in fact, a *verb. sap.* concerning his methods.

The word 'shin' would seem to be the slightest of verbal clues, and yet, as we have seen, Kipling with mock ruefulness acknowledged it to be a blatant giveaway. Once readers have noticed it, it is easy to see other signs of Grace's origin in Chaucer. The Wife has five husbands whereas Grace has had only one, but both have been promiscuous in their youth, and there are parallels between Grace's husband and lover and the Wife's fourth and fifth husbands. 'My fourthe housbonde was a revelour / That is to seyn, he hadde a paramour', says the Wife (*Wife of Bath's Tale*, (ll. 453–4); she pretends to weep at his funeral 'As wives mooten, for it is usage' (l. 589); her fifth husband, the clerke Jankin, is the one whom she is least able to manage, but she confesses, 'I trowe I loved him best, for that he / Was of his love daungerous' (i.e. imperious; ll. 513–14). Grace's husband was a 'rover' (p. 119); she lays flowers on his grave 'for the look of the thing'; of her lover, Harry Mockler, who causes her much suffering, she says, 'I'd found me master, which I 'adn't ever before. I'd allus owned 'em, like' (p. 122). And the Wife's famous lines, in which she asserts that in old age it still 'dooth myn herte boote' to think that 'I have had my worlde as in my tyme', are matched by Mrs Ashcroft's 'I've me 'eart left me still' and her friend's reply, 'That's somethin' to look back on at the day's end.'

With the Chaucerian original in mind, it becomes difficult to regard 'The Wish House' as simply an exposition of woman's capacity for self-sacrifice, despite his giving his heroine the name of Grace, and despite her taking her lover's cancer upon herself. It is a rather tougher story about the obsessiveness of woman's sexual desire and her exerting what Chaucer called the 'maistrie' – the power – through self-inflicted wounds. (The Wife eventually triumphs over her fifth husband because, having provoked his physical violence, she makes him feel guilty, thinking that he has killed her; when he asks her forgiveness she gives him a return blow.) The preface poem, 'Late Came the God', in which Woman is said to be 'Resolute, selfless, divine', is a counter-truth. It is always prudent to appease the Furies by naming them Eumemides

(Kindly Ones), or to say with the sly Nun's Priest, 'I kan noon harme of no woman dyvyne.'[18]

Grace Ashcroft is only one of Kipling's 'metagrobolisations' of the Wife; the character haunted him. He even owned a piece of her. When the young Rupert Croft-Cooke visited him in 1922, Kipling read him 'a purple patch from Chaucer' which Croft-Cooke was never subsequently able to identify. He was also allowed to handle a 'page of Chaucer's own manuscript . . . a little of the Wife of Bath's Tale framed between two pieces of glass'. This had been brought either by or for Kipling in 1919 from Maggs the antiquarian booksellers.[19]

It is again Blake who can best help us approach Kipling's Wife of Bath. Turning to the female pilgrims in his *Descriptive Catalogue* he writes,

> The characters of Women Chaucer has divided into two classes, the Lady Prioress and the Wife of Bath. Are not these leaders of the ages of men? The lady prioress, in some ages, predominates; and in some the wife of Bath, in whose character Chaucer has been equally minute and exact, because she is also [i.e. as well as the Pardoner] a scourge and a blight. I shall say no more of her, nor expose what Chaucer has left hidden; let the young reader study what he has said of her: it is useful as a scarecrow. There are of such characters born too many for the peace of the world.[20]

Elsewhere he speaks with contempt for those who 'think that the Wife of Bath is a young, beautiful blooming damsel. . . . the Fair Wife of Bath and that spring appears in her cheeks', and refers doubters to the self-description of the Wife, who is 'no modest one'. It is clear that he considers that Chaucer intended her to be a reincarnation of Rahab, the eternal harlot, not merely a shrew, and it is this 'veiled meaning' to which he refers the adolescent reader.

That Chaucer's Wife is a biblical type is an idea which study of medieval pulpit sermons and iconography has made familiar to twentieth-century academia. Perhaps Victorian readers were aware of it in a vague way, but no nineteenth-century commentator on Chaucer spells it out quite so clearly as Blake, for all his claim to be respecting Chaucer's secrecy. The Wife has stockings 'of fyn scarlet reed' and 'shoes ful moyste and newe. / Boold was hir face, and fair, and reed of hewe.' All the pilgrims have horses, but she is singled out as having 'a paire of spores sharpe' on her feet, and these suggest her indomitable sexual appetite and her function as scourge (*General Prologue*, ll. 445–76). Her trade is weaving, which can imply either virtuous thrift or the ensnarer's craft. She thus has some of the qualities of the 'strange woman' and some of the Scarlet Woman of Revelation 17, Babylon, the Mother of Harlots, who appears drunken with the blood of the saints and mounted on the ten-horned beast.

In reconstructing the Wife, the most noticeable feature that Kipling takes from Chaucer is her shoes, though, as in the case of 'The Wish House', this is not always present. He compounds the scarlet colour of her stockings with the idea of the 'moyste' (i.e. supple) leather shoes to produce an emblem expressive of whoredom, bloodlust and female dominance, either singly or in combination. This is the woman with red feet, red shoes or shoes that are wet with blood – Kipling develops the idea suggested by the Chaucerian 'moyste'. Sometimes she dances like a fairy, which evokes the dancing fairies of the Wife's tale, servitors of the Loathly Lady of the Well at the World's End, and (when this figure appears in an Eastern setting) the seductive and red-lac-footed peri who partakes not a little of the bloodthirstiness of the goddess Kali.

The first occasion on which I detect Kipling's definitely having the Wife in mind is in his description of Amber, once the 'Queen of the Pass', the ruined city which Kipling visited during the late-1887 tour that also took him to Chitor. Looking down from the top of the palace, he sees the city lying like the body of an old courtesan, that favourite comparison of those affecting the Zola-esque: 'The drip-stones of the eaves were gap-toothed, and the tracery of the screens had fallen out so that zenana-rooms lay shamelessly open to the day' (*SS*, I, 22).[21] The old seductress, rejuvenated, appears half a year later as 'the Patient East' in a sketch called 'The Burden of Nineveh'. She is, of course, all that is *not* Patient Griselda, with whom Chaucer's Clerk contrasts the Wife. Here the red feet appear for the first time:

'What is the matter with my feet?' said the Patient East putting out a gold-ankletted foot that had been set on the neck of some few not altogether undistinguished persons. 'Well', said the

M.P. 'I observe that you adhere to that poetical, but still barbarous, custom of dyeing the soles. Lac dye, is it not?' The Patient East smiled inscrutably.[22]

In his 1889 *From Sea to Sea* travel sketches he describes the slaughter-houses of Chicago; this illustrates very well his early, overemphatic use of emblem:

> Women come sometimes to see the slaughter, as they would come to see the slaughter of men. And there entered that vermilion hall a young woman of large mould, with brilliantly scarlet lips, and heavy eyebrows, and dark hair that came in a 'widow's peak' on the forehead. She was well and healthy and alive, and she was dressed in flaming red and black, and her feet (know you that the feet of American women are like unto the feet of fairies?) her feet, I say, were cased in red leather shoes. She stood in a patch of sunlight, the red blood under her shoes, the vivid carcasses stacked round her, a bullock bleeding its life away not six feet away from her, and the death-factory roaring all round her. She looked curiously, with hard, bold eyes, and was not ashamed. Then said I: 'This is a special Sending. I have seen the City of Chicago.'   (II, 166–7)

'Sending' requires some comment. During Kipling's lifetime it had the specialised meaning of a telegraph or wireless transmission. In 'The Sending of Dana Da' (*SI*, p. 310), the narrator explains that it is a term drawn from Icelandic wizardry, a revenge-wish which wanders about as a 'little purple cloud' until it finds the 'Sendee' and kills him. In 'The Last Rhyme of True Thomas' (*DV*, p. 378), 'Sendings' are interchanges between the poet's mind and the natural and supernatural worlds, which materialise as images in writing. A Sending, then, may be good, bad or neutral, and may be literal or metaphorical. The sahib in 'Morrowbie Jukes' is a Sending, and appears because of the presence of the former telegraph operator, Dass. Boy Niven in 'Mrs Bathurst' is both transmitter and Sending.

The apparitions in *Puck of Pook's Hill* and *Rewards and Fairies* are Sendings, mostly benign, but one of them, Queen Elizabeth in 'Gloriana' (*RF*), is the red-shoed lady again. Dan and Una have seen Queen Bess's 'little green shoes' in a glass case at Brickwall House (p. 35). This is another of Kipling's realistic–symbolic names;

'Brickwall' – an actual mansion – is the dead-end, the trap. Queen Bess appears, and recounts the story behind them. The shoes prove to be the ones in which she has danced while trying to decide whether to accept the self-sacrifice of two chivalrous young noblemen, whom she knows to be ready to die for Queen and country. The shoes burst at the moment when she hardens her heart and sends them to their doom. 'Green shoes', then, represent the tender and nurturing appearance of the Queen. She seals their fate with a kiss, warning them two-facedly that 'Sweetheart, a Queen has no heart' (p. 48). When she appears as a ghost to Dan and Una her shoes are 'red-heeled', which, in the course of her re-enactment of the story, are called simply 'red'. Finally, as her ruthlessness and guilt become manifest, she 'stamped her red foot' (pp. 32, 43, 47). Gloriana has 'blood on her shoes', as Nature is red in tooth and claw. She is Belphoebe, the Moon, the Virgin Queen for whom men give their lives, and who has the alternative character of Hecate, dark witch of the Underworld. But, unlike the bold, bloodthirsty Chicago harlot type, she exercises power with some responsibility. Dan's judgement on her is 'I don't see what else she could have done' – that is, in the interests of fulfilling England's destiny. (This is a good example of Kipling's writing for adults on one level and for children on another, as well as of the darkening vision of *Rewards and Fairies* when compared to *Puck of Pook's Hill*.)

Blake anachronistically dressed his Wife in Elizabethan costume, for she represented to him the 'voluptuousness and folly' that 'began to be accounted beautiful' after Elizabeth's time, as opposed to the elegance of medieval beauty. For neither Blake nor Kipling is Queen Elizabeth the 'Good Queen Bess' of the history books. Both the Chicago Sending and Gloriana have fairy-like dancing feet, and are Fatal Women, Fatae Morganae, Faerie Queenes. Kipling has not idiosyncratically invented these connections. They were commonplaces among nineteenth-century folklorists, and are to be found, for instance, in the editor's notes to Charles Nodier's *La Fée aux miettes*, the story which supplied the epigraph to 'Dayspring Mishandled'. Spenser's Gloriana and Morgan-le-Fay are there explicitly equated as variants of pagan Nature-goddesses.[23]

But the most complex example of the bloody-shoed woman, and the one in which her origins in Chaucer's Wife are of the greatest interest, is found in the notorious 'Mary Postgate' (*D of C*, 1915), called by Oliver Baldwin 'the wickedest story ever written'. Because it also displays Kipling's technique at its most trenchantly brilliant, it is a 'case'. The documentation of Chaucerian influence up to this point has been the prologue to a reading of this tale, to which the Chaucerian allusions offer a way of approach.

The tale was written after the first German bombings of British civilians, and Kipling was probably still working on it when the Germans first used poison gas on the Western Front and the *Lusitania* was sunk.[24] Mary Postgate, the crippled Miss Fowler's lady companion, is a middle-aged, camel-like spinster, a 'public aunt' to the village and the 'butt and slave' of Miss Fowler's 'unlovely' orphan nephew, Wyndham (Wynn). Upon the outbreak of the war he joins the Flying Corps, but his plane crashes before he can engage in active combat. The two women take the news of his death with stiff upper lips; the war has seemingly left them unable to break down and weep in a natural way. After the funeral Miss Fowler proposes that his possessions should be burned, so that 'no one can handle them afterwards'. While going to buy paraffin for the incineration, Mary meets the village nurse; they hear what they fancy to be a gun fired behind the local pub, the Royal Oak. Rushing to investigate, Nurse Eden finds the 'ripped and shredded body' of little Edna Gerritt, the publican's daughter, lying under the tiles of a collapsed stable. Mary assumes that the child has been killed by a German bomb, though Hennis, the local doctor, tells her that the stable had collapsed owing to dry rot. Later, while burning Wynn's gear in the garden, she sees an injured German airman whose plane has apparently crashed. He begs her for help in broken English and French. Mercilessly she refuses, recognising him as Edna's killer. She threatens him with a 'huge revolver' loaded with dum-dum bullets, taking an 'increasing rapture' in watching his death-agony; after this mockery of sexual climax, she 'scandalised the whole routine by taking a luxurious hot bath before tea' and lies 'all relaxed' on the sofa looking, says Miss Fowler, 'quite handsome!'

Defenders of the story have tried to close the gap between the technical mastery and its perceived glorification of cruelty. Most start from the premise that Mary is a fictional character and that her emotions cannot be identified with those of Kipling himself. According to this reading, the story illustrates the dreadful change that has taken place in the national character as a result of 'German frightfulness'. In Bodelsen's words, 'This is what it has come to, that a kindly and respectable English spinster finds herself turned

into a torturer.' A sophistication of this is Malcolm Page's suggestion that there is doubt as to the airman's nationality; he could be
a Frenchman.[25]

Norman Page, in an article which importantly advanced
interpretation of the story, rightly objected to reading it as a simple
tale about the effect of the war on the gentle English psyche.
'"Kindly and respectable" [Bodelsen's description] hardly squares
with the characterization of the repressed and distinctly odd Miss
Postgate.'[26] He also disposed of Malcolm Page's suggestion: a real
Frenchman would not have said 'Che me rends', as the airman
does in the story, though, as we shall see later, the insight, that
there is doubt as to the airman's nationality, turns out to be true,
though not in quite the way Malcolm Page argued.

Norman Page also said that the airman is a hallucination. Others
had done so before him. Randall Jarrell assumed it, without giving
reasons. John Bayley thought it possible, but opted for irresolvable
ambiguity.[27] But Page was the first to argue closely that he is
definitely fictitious. He drew from this the conclusion that Kipling's
real theme is 'the power of the disordered imagination'; he quoted
approvingly the view that Mary is possibly 'an hysterical and
perhaps even a crazed female'.[28] This, in his view, gave Kipling a
certain moral distance from his creation. Page, in my opinion, was
right about the airman, for all the reasons that he gave, and for a
few additional ones as well, but I cannot altogether agree with his
conclusions. Mary is mad – I would say a great deal madder than
has been supposed – but Kipling partly approves of the emotional
logic and visionary insight into the moral issues involved that her
madness vouchsafes her.

It is not hard to extrapolate a defence of the story's morality
from the hallucination reading. First, it deflects the story from the
political actualities of the First World War to ontological questions.
Secondly, if there is no airman, then Mary has, from a utilitarian
point of view, done nothing immoral. It is true that she stands
condemned by that branch of ethics which makes no distinction
between action and intention, between adultery and lusting-after,
theft and covetousness. If she believes that she has let an airman
die in torture, then, by that argument, she has as good as
done so. But there have always been difficulties in pursuing the
consequences of such an ethic. *Measure for Measure* (a play often in
Kipling's mind) entirely hinges on these difficulties. Should Angelo
be put to death when he has not actually deflowered Isabella or

had her brother executed but merely thinks he has? And, if there are problems with deciding how to judge Angelo, a responsible agent, how much more should we suspend judgement on a deranged Mary Postgate, for she is not answerable for her thoughts. She is 'guilty but insane'; anti-German war hysteria is thus 'placed'. Doctor Hennis, who sees Edna's death as an accident, is then the sane central consciousness.

As should by now be clear, I do not find these arguments totally satisfactory. Page in the very meticulousness of his convincing proof that the airman is an air man has thrown up a new problem: why has Kipling taken such pains to delude the reader into thinking, with Mary, that he is real? (John Bayley's answer in *The Short Story*, that the question is irrelevant, strikes me as a last resort.) Nor do the above defences satisfactorily meet the case made against the story nearly fifty years ago by Boris Ford, for whom 'Mary Postgate' was not merely brutal but emotionally dishonest as well:

> On the whole, Kipling despised women; but in one or two of his tales he is glad to use them to vent feelings that he would be ashamed to attribute to a man, and above all to describe as being possible to himself. And one feels, in this story, that he is quite conscious of vicarious enjoyment in dealing with a woman whom he can safely allow to be contradictory and irrational.[29]

For Ford, Kipling, 'like Mary Postgate "ceased to think and gave himself up to feel" when he undertook this story'. It is not a sufficient answer to document its conscious and careful crafting, for, unfortunately, craftsmanship is not inseparable from coarseness of feeling. Nor do I think that Ford's essential point can be refuted – that in inventing Mary Postgate Kipling was using a woman as the instrument of his hatred of Germans. One can quarrel with some of his formulations – that loose 'on the whole' won't do; for Kipling, to whom any strong emotion lay a hair's-breadth away from its opposite, despisal, admiration and fear can coexist. Nor did Kipling habitually shunt retributive feelings onto women, as 'Sea Constables', another story in *A Diversity of Creatures*, shows; and in any case he did not do so in the simple way outlined above. Remembering encounters with the soldiery of Fort Lahore in the 1880s, Kipling spoke of his anger at the 'unnecessary torments' endured by the private soldier because of 'the Christian doctrine which lays down that "the wages of sin is death"' and which obstructed the inspection of bazaar prostitutes or the instruction of the men in taking precautions against venereal disease: 'Visits to Lock Hospitals made me desire, *as earnestly as I do to-day* [my italics], that I might have six hundred priests – Bishops of the Establishment for choice – to handle for six months precisely as the soldiers of my youth were handled' (*SM*, p. 56). This grotesque fancy, unashamedly cherished for over fifty years – a lost legion of poxed priests, an ignoble 600 left to the tender mercies of Kipling in their Valley of Death – reads like the germ of a Kipling revenge story which, we may be grateful, he never wrote. The main difference, it seems to me, between that and the feelings which he attributes to his Mary Postgate is that, whereas she is implacable, Kipling would presumably let his priests off after their *saison en enfer*. (The mythic 'six months' appears again.) Kipling revolts against using women (the prostitutes) as instruments of retribution, while at the same time *he* would use them to punish the uncharitable who would make of them such instruments.

But Ford's central point, that there is some kind of self-identification of the author with his creation, seems to me to be a crucial insight about the story, which poses the same sort of problem as Browning's tendency to choose as personae in his dramatic monologues failed questers, charlatans, casuists, cheats and madmen. Kipling salutes her with fear and some admiration as a demonic handmaid of the Lord. She is akin to one of the fierce women in the Bible, Judith – or Jael, the 'office name' that he gave to his 'slim smooth black treasure' of a fountain pen 'picked up', he said, in Jerusalem (*SM*, p. 230).[30]

Mary is a developed and credible personality – one of Kipling's most developed personalities. But she is also one of his greatest role-players, and she calls into question the concept of personality. As Kim asked of himself, 'What is Kim?', she could ask of herself, 'What is Mary?' – if she had a mind to. Her story is a type of apocalypse; the subject is Armageddon and three of the Four Last Things – Death, Judgement and Hell, with Heaven omitted. It is a story about transition; one age passes away and a terrifying new one, of which the harbinger is the Scarlet Woman, comes into being. Kipling registers this change in terms of the alteration in the predominance of one kind of woman over another. Blake had written that Chaucer had divided the characters of women into two classes: 'The lady prioress, in some ages, predominates; and in some the Wife of Bath.' Mary Postgate begins as an avatar of the Prioress; she ends as one of the Wife. She also passes through states of playing the Sybil of Christian eschatology, a Moira or Fate, and one of the persons of Ruskin's triple Fors Clavigera, Fortune bearing a nail, the Jael-figure administering the law of Lycurgus. She also plays Kali. The original title of the story was 'The Destructor'.

The starting-point for the journey towards this conclusion is the ambiguous title: 'Mary Postgate'. This suggests someone at once virgin and maternal, which she is; her caring for Wynn and honorary aunthood are substitutes for the actual motherhood she is denied. But 'Mary' can mean 'bitter' as well as 'lady', and, as said in Chapter 1, it is a dualistic name in Kipling. In the poem 'Mary Pity Women', the deserted Cockney mistress wishes that 'the Wrath' would strike her faithless man. In 'The Bridge Builders' the old gods claim that the woman called Mary of the 'new faith' (Christianity) is really Kali, goddess of destruction, under a false name (*DW*, p. 34). And what of 'Postgate'? The name sounds genteel, prunes-and-prismy, with overtones of 'sticking to one's post'. But in Kipling 'the Gate' can be entrance to either Heaven, Hell, Eden or Gesthemane, as in 'The Gate of a Hundred Sorrows', 'On the Gate' and 'Mrs Bathurst'. 'Mary Postgate' is the female figure who awaits man after he has passed through 'the Gate', and what sort of figure depends on which sort of gate. Is she Miss Meadows, the True Romance, or does the gate have written over it 'All hope abandon, ye who enter here'?

A literary precedent for combining the two kinds of Mary, such sweetness with such ferocity, is Chaucer's Prioress; there are parallels between Kipling's story and her tale; the disparity between the violence of the latter and the ostensible character of the teller has often been remarked upon in this century, though in Victorian times it was regarded as one of the most perfect, tender and edifying of all the Canterbury Tales. One line – 'Oh martir, sowded to virginitee' – was chosen by Matthew Arnold in 'The Study of Poetry' (1880) as one of the 'touchstones' by which he measures Chaucer's particular poetic virtue.

The Prioress's Tale is, like 'Mary Postgate', a story for Holy Innocents' Day, 28 December, and tells of a child martyr, murdered by 'cursed Jews' and thrown into a privy because of his devotion to the Virgin; the circumstances of his slaying (around Christmastide, in a street),[31] are near to those of the death of Edna Gerritt.

(Wynn's death takes place during a wet December and Edna is killed five days after his funeral in a stable attached to an inn just off a village street.) In 'Mary Postgate' the Germans, called 'bloody pagans', take the place of the Jews as child-murderers. The latter are brought to justice 'With torment and with shameful deeth' by the provost of the city, who pronounces sentence:

> 'Yvele shal have that yvele wol deserve';
> Therfore with wilde hors he dide hem drawe,
> And after that he heng hem by the lawe.
> > (*Prioress's Tale*, ll. 1822–4)

The Prioress, praised for her tender-heartedness in the ironic *General Prologue* to the *Canterbury Tales* (ll. 119–62), contemplates the savage death of the wicked Jews with pitiless satisfaction. Like Mary, she is telling a story that she believes to be true. (Mary's telling is in her head, of course, not to an audience.) Moreoever, the Prioress has several other traits which Kipling seems to have borrowed in his composition of the figure of Mary, who is recommended to Miss Fowler as thoroughly conscientious, tidy, companionable, and ladylike:

> Some of Miss Fowler's tales . . . were not always for the young. Mary was not young, and though her speech was as colourless as her eyes or her hair, she was never shocked. She listened unflinchingly to every one; said at the end, 'How interesting!' or 'How shocking!' as the case might be . . . . (*D of C*, p. 419)

The Prioress is, like Mary, thoroughly conscientious ('al was conscience'), tidy (she has cleanly table manners and her wimple is pleated 'ful semyly'). She is a companion (one of Chaucer's 'myrie compaignye)' and lady-*like* (she does not really belong to the gentry but is 'estatlich of manere'). Mary's eyes are colourless; the Prioress's are 'greye as glas'. Mary has a 'long back'; the Prioress is 'nat undergrowe'. The Prioress also listens 'unflinchingly' to tales which are 'not always for the young', since she never expostulates at the bawdy of the Miller or the Friar, and she, too, has a polite ejaculation: 'By Seinte Loy.' Mary's imperfect command of languages – she speaks to the airman in bad German – has its counterpart in the Prioress's inability to speak any French but that of 'the scole of Stratford atte Bowe'. The Prioress is sexually attractive and wears a badge saying 'Amor Vincit Omnia'. Even beauty comes to Mary in the end, and she, too, could wear that badge – with Kipling's gloss, 'So close must any life-filling passion lie to its opposite.'

Of course there are several important ways in which Mary is not like the Prioress, the most obvious being that she is not elegant. She is a *type* – that is, an imperfect copy of the original. Other literary figures have taken part in her making – Austen's Miss Bates, for instance.[32] But an examination of them lies outside the scope of this book.

Miss Fowler, too, is a figurative character. If Mary is her companion, then she is in some sense a Chaucerian author-type and the unseemly stories she tells other Canterbury Tales. She has a catch-phrase – 'That disposes of *that*' – akin to Chaucerian formulaic abridgements such as 'but shortly to the point' or 'ther is namoore to telle'. She is the daughter of a 'minor Court official'; Chaucer was a minor Court official too: Miss Fowler could then be regarded as 'Chaucer's daughter' in the same metaphorical sense as Kipling has one of his characters describe Jane Austen as 'fruitful in the 'ighest sense of the word. . . . She *did* leave lawful issue in the shape o' one son; an' 'is name was 'Enery James' ('The Janeites', *DC*, p. 154). She is born in the 1840s, five centuries to the decade after Chaucer, whose birth-date has been ascribed to various years in the 1340s. But her father has served at Court 'in the days when the Great Exhibition had just set its seal on Civilisation made perfect' (*D of C*, p. 419). The word 'perfect' should warn us. The Great Exhibition marked for Ruskin the nadir of art and a surrender to the spirit of rampant commercialism. The moving spirit behind it had been Prince Albert, Victoria's German consort. The Great Exhibition is Kipling's shorthand for a period of complacency, when Britain had been lulled into believing that Babe and Cockatrice might live together. Miss Fowler's crippling symbolises the impotence of the genuine Chaucerian spirit and its degeneration into the malignant laughter that issues from bitter springs. The fowler sets the snare; there are indications that she is a puppet-mistress who gradually relinquishes control over her 'companion'. She wears a ring on the third finger of one hand but is not married. Did her fiancé die? Is Wynn really her unloved illegitimate child, conceived when she was at the (to Kipling) dangerous age of 'nearer fifty than forty', just before the menopause, and, like Helen Turrell's son in 'The Gardener', passed off as a nephew?[33] The important thing is that the reader should live in uncertainties. It is enough to think that Miss Fowler might be covering up a guilty family secret.

Chaucer was also the author of *The Parlement of Foules*, and the name 'Fowler' has an echo in the curious name of the doctor – Hennis. The doctor is strangely protective of Miss Fowler, and is in a sense her man. 'Hens' are 'Hennes' in the spelling of Chaucer, whose *Nun's Priest's Tale* is a fable of human nature entirely rendered in terms of the poultry-yard.

Chanticleer in that story has several traits in common with Wynn Fowler. The former lords it over his hens; he is conceited about his natural technical expertise: 'By nature he knew each ascencioun / Of the equynoxial in thilke toun; / For when degrees fiftene weren ascended, / Thanne crew he' (ll. 2855–8) he 'deigned nat to set his foot to grounde' and his inordinate pride is nearly his downfall. Wynn, like Chanticleer, is a cock-of-the-walk who loves to 'swell and exalt' himself before his womenfolk, whom he despises, though unlike Chanticleer he does so nakedly, without the cover of gallantry. He parades his knowledge of charts, 'dials and the sockets for bomb-dropping till it was time to mount and ride the wet clouds once more'. Chanticleer's legs and toes were 'like asur'; Wynn lands one morning from the sky 'blue with cold'. Chanticleer recounts a premonitory dream of a man whose dead body is found in a dung-cart; Wynn accomplishes his literal downfall in a 'flying chariot' which is called a 'stinking thing'. (In 'Teem' motor cars are called 'stink-carts'.)

I shall leave for a moment the Chaucerian parallels and return to Norman Page's argument. He pointed out that no arrangements are made for the burial of the airman's body, a strange omission on Mary's part. He showed that Kipling's use of interior monologue means that there is no evidence for the existence of the airman outside her imagination. The following passage (not used by Page), containing the airman's first words to Mary, illustrates his point very well:

'Laty! Laty! Laty!' he muttered, while his hands picked at the dead wet leaves. There was no doubt as to his nationality. It made her so angry that she strode back to the destructor, though it was still too hot to use the poker there. Wynn's books seemed to be catching well. She looked up at the oak behind the man; several of the light upper and two or three rotten lower branches

had broken and scattered their rubbish on the shrubbery path.
On the lowest fork a helmet with dependent strings, showed
like a bird's-nest in the light of a long-tongued flame. Evidently
this person had fallen through the tree.   (*D of C*, p. 437)

Kipling gives the reader some hefty nudges ('no doubt', 'evidently')
that the narrative consciousness is unreliable, and supplies an
alternative explanation of what is occurring . The 'helmet' which
is showing '*like* a bird's-nest' *is* a bird's nest, and the branches
have broken because they are rotten. (The significance of their
being rotten *oak* will be enlarged upon later.) But the description
of the burning of Wynn's books contains within itself another
explanation as to why Mary's airman would be imaginary.

It is emphasised several times that she has a 'large nose' and an
acute sense of smell. 'Postey, I believe you think with your nose',
says Wynn when Mary complains that his biplane 'smelt very
badly'. As she returns with the paraffin, thinking of Edna's death,
'her large nostrils expanded uglily'. She waits for the airman to
die 'brows knit and nostrils wide'. An acute sense of smell is, for
Kipling, one mark of the instinctual artist; the eponymous dog-
hero of 'Teem', the last story to be published in Kipling's lifetime,
is able to exercise his art of truffle-hunting by virtue of his champion
nose. 'Teem' is an allegory of his artistic career; Teem is himself
having fears that he may cease to be before his pen has gleaned
his teeming brain.[34] Mary's acute nose is a sign of her ability to
smell out evil; her nostrils flare at crucial points where she is acting
as detective. But the nose has a more functional quality. The
incinerator in which she burns Wynn's possessions lies in a 'dank
little laurel shrubbery' 'under the drip of three oaks'. 'As she lit
the match that would burn her heart to ashes, she heard a groan
or a grunt behind the dense Portugal laurels' (pp. 435–6). The
detail of the 'Portugal laurels' was praised by Edmund Wilson for
its juxtaposition of the mundane and specific with ' "The match
that would burn her heart to ashes" . . . a phrase on another
plane'[35] and it is often singled out for admiration when Kipling's
art is assessed. Well-deserved admiration too – and it is also a case
of Kipling's byzantine ingenuity condensing into its opposite:
simplicity.

The Pythian Sibyl was said to breathe in fumes of burning laurel
leaves before prophesying; Kipling would have been familiar with
this from his knowledge of classical myth. But the bay laurel,

Laurus nobilis, in fact has no hallucinogenic properties, and from as far back as the late eighteenth century it was proposed that the vision-inducing leaves, if there was a factual basis to the myth, came from some other laurel-like plant, such as the *Prunus laurocerasus*, the 'common laurel'. The leaves contain Prussic acid, as do those of other *Prunus* 'laurels', such as the Portugal laurel (*Prunus lusitanica*).[36] Miss Fowler's laurel bushes are 'not five paces from the flames', and therefore singed and giving off fumes which Mary's flaring nostrils inhale. The Prussic acid which they exhale stands for a homoeopathic hatred; a natural poison to counteract the evil of Prussian poison gas. She does not see the airman, who is half-hidden behind a laurel, until the fire begins to burn. Elsewhere in Kipling, as a preliminary to seeing visions or receiving 'Sendings', there is often some drug – alcohol, ether, benzoin pastilles or opium – which promotes them by interaction with fever or stress. Mary, her imagination heightened by the recent sight of the dead child and intoxicating fumes, becomes a quasi-Sibylline prophetess; she presides over a pyre lit with 'sacrificial oil' in a 'sanctuary' of laurel and oaks, the tree of the Dodonian oracle. This is why she talks in tongues not her own. The airman 'speaks' through her. But she is also the Roman Sibyl who burned the books of the laws and the Sibyl of the *Dies Irae*.

Kipling, with slight metrical variation, used the tercets of the famous Latin Sequence (an obligatory part of the Catholic Mass for the Day of the Dead until 1969) as a model for his 'Harp Song of the Dane Women'. He quoted the opening lines at the climax of 'The Conversion of St Wilfrid' (*RF*, pp. 241–2) –

> Dies Irae, dies illa
> Solvet saeclum in favilla
> Teste David cum Sibylla

– where the Sequence is played on the organ by a mysterious lady in black, to the awe and delight of Dan and Una, to whom foreknowledge of death has been introduced so gently that they do not yet realise it.

The Roman Sibyl burned books, as Mary is doing; her world, like that of the Sibyl of the *Dies Irae*, is turning to ashes: 'Now Wynn was dead and everything connected with him was lumping and rustling and tinkling under her busy poker into red black dust and grey leaves of ash' (*D of C*, p. 439). The incinerator ('destructor') is described as if it were a miniature Childe Roland's Dark Tower and Gehenna combined; it has a grated trap, like the window in 'Beyond the Pale': 'an open-air furnace for the consumption of refuse; a little circular four-foot tower of pierced brick over an iron grating'. She has bought paraffin from a Mr Kidd and thinks first that the grunts behind the laurels are sheep. She is celebrating the day that separates the *oves* from the *haedi*, the sheep from the goats.[37]

But the Sibyl is not the only famous female book-burner. The Wife of Bath, exasperated by her fifth husband's tales of wicked women, tears three leaves out of his book and hits him so hard that he falls in the fire. Later she makes him burn the offending volume. In 'Mary Postgate' numerous books belonging to Wynn are burned, and the authors are named: 'Hentys, Marryats, Levers, Stevensons, Baroness Orczys, Garvices, schoolbooks, and atlases, unrelated piles of the *Motor Cyclist*, the *Light Car* and catalogues of Olympia Exhibitions' (p. 433). Many of these are masculine books which exclude women from the world of action or which imply that woman is man's ruin. The titles of Garvice's novels include *Eve, Just a Girl, Linked by Fate* and *Love the Tyrant*; Mary would see only the titles. There is one odd female – the writer Baroness Orczy. Why *she* should be thrown in with the men will be suggested later. And what do the *Light Car* and 'catalogues of Olympia Exhibitions' suggest? The words convey an interest both in mastering things mechanical and in pornography; the *Light Car* suggests the light woman when juxtaposed with 'Olympia Exhibitions' – motoring-shows or Manet's famous *grande horizontale*? (In Kipling cars are almost invariably females.) The possible pun conveys the following idea to Mary: that Wynn *exploits* women.[38]

Miss Fowler orders Mary to burn the 'things' so that they are not handled by strangers, but we never hear her reasons for agreeing to this. Norman Page pointed out that, in burning all that remains of Wynn, Mary is avenging herself on him, 'in unconscious retribution for the petty cruelties directed at her over many years, the memories of which have been revived by all the bric-à-brac of his childhood and adolescence'.[39] Page also drew attention to the fact that Mary's image of the German airman is constructed out of Wynn, with a few stereotypical 'Hun' features added, and that he appears only when she is thinking of him.

But why *unconscious*? Is it not possible that Mary is very aware of her hatred, but is trying not to think of it? We are told again and again that she has a 'trained mind' which does not 'dwell on these things'. (John Bayley has drawn attention to the importance of the word 'mind' in the story.[40] And throughout we are given hints that she is using her 'trained mind' to conceal her thoughts from other people and to banish them from her consciousness, which is not the same as having unconscious feelings. Indeed, to put the matter in this way forces one to notice the following peculiarity: after Wynne grows up, nothing that we are told about Mary's feelings for him, which we assume to be those of love, could not be equally well construed as feelings of hate.

Whenever asked what she is thinking she evades a straight answer, claiming that she is stupid or literal-minded. 'What do you ever think of, Mary?' asks Miss Fowler suddenly. 'Oh, Wynn says he wants another three pairs of stockings – as thick as we can make them.' Reflecting on 'woman's work' as she rakes the fire, her internal monologue goes: 'A woman's business was to make a happy home for – for a husband and children. Failing these – it was not a thing one should allow one's mind to dwell upon – but – but – '.

There are many things that Mary is trying not to think of. One of them, I suggest, is that she has wished for Wynn's death, which has followed immediately upon it. A supernatural reading would say that she has inflicted a Sending upon him. But Kipling is no more committed to a belief in telekinesis than to a belief in sea-serpents or sea-gypsies. He is dealing with that strange state of mind in which one rejects with one's reason the idea that one possesses supernatural powers without being able to shake off the hold such a thought has on the imagination when a wish has been 'uncannily' fulfilled. The theme of 'Mary Postgate', like 'Friendly Brook', is 'Run silent, run deep.' Mary thus subjects to criticism the virtues of silence and consuming one's own smoke. Readers who fall into Kipling's trap and intepret Mary's behaviour as her steely self-command over her deep grief are both confirming Kipling's point about the virtual interchangeability of the passions of love and hate and illustrating the hold over the communal imagination of the myth of woman as Patient Griselda – infinitely capable of taking without complaint all the abuse that man heaps on her. But 'Grisilde is deed and eek her pacience.' There comes a point when woman has had enough.

There are good reasons for Mary to hate Wynn. He has never said an affectionate or grateful word, for all her slaving for him, but on the contrary has thumped her and torn strips off her, especially after becoming an airman: 'You're lamentable', he says when she fails to master his chart; 'You are less use than an empty tin can, you dowey old cassowary.' When Miss Fowler remonstrates he retorts, 'But Postey doesn't mind. . . . Do you, Packthread?' Ominously Mary does not agree, but answers, 'Why? Was Wynn saying anything?' Wynn's last recorded words to her, just before he flies off, are that she has less brain than a white mouse. '"Ah!" said Mary as the stinking thing flared upward. "Wait till our Flying Corps gets to work!"' The 'stinking thing' is both Wynn's plane and Wynn himself, who besides being rotten before he is dead has sealed his fate by his idle words. 'The white mouse eye can sparkle as well as the eagle's with rage.'[41] Whose Flying Corps is going to work? England's embryo RAF or the white mouse's avengers, black flittermice from the Pit, Alecto, Tisiphone and Megara? (Doré's Dante gave the Furies leathery bat-wings.) Mary then pushes Miss Fowler home, refusing male assistance: 'It's all downhill.' *Facilis descensus Averni.*

After this effort we are told, 'The exertion had given her colour and the wind had loosened a wisp of hair across her forehead.' These are easily misinterpreted signals of a deeper disturbance; Mary's *complexion* is changing both in the modern and in the medieval sense; she is acquiring the ruddy face of the Wife and Maenadic wild hair like Maisie in *The Light that Failed* and Miss Copleigh in 'False Dawn'.[42] On the morning that Wynn passes overhead in his flying-machine for the last time, 'A little blur passed overhead. She lifted her lean arms towards it.' The reader is led to think that Mary is stretching out her arms lovingly, but when a woman in Kipling holds out her arms (Bisesa; Diamonds and Pearls in 'Love o' Women') she usually brings death. The blur is both the plane and Mary's Sending as she 'wipes it out'.[43] When Mary hears about Wynn's death, the room whirls. She is discovering her witch-like powers. The sensation is something like Macbeth's shock on hearing that he has become Thane of Cawdor.

Mary's laconic response to Wynn's death, 'It's a great pity he didn't die in action after he had killed somebody', is generally held to indicate her inability to express her deep grief in appropriate language. But, if she hated him, the words open up dark possibilities: 'If I had known that my wish would be granted before he had killed a German I would have been more patient.' Or, if the 'somebody' is herself: 'Now that he is dead I realise that I did not

want to be his murderer. It would have been better if he had
finished the job of killing me, having broken my heart. Then he
would *really* have deserved to die.'

At this point Mary simply desires his annihilation and does not
intend to inflict punishment beyond the grave. The distribution of
his 'Service things' – which are not burned – and his civilian clothes
is a chillingly symbolic act of ritual dismemberment, perpetuating
and distributing the useful side of Wynn: the part connected to
his work. After she sees Edna Gerritt's body her consciousness is
altered and she assumes a new role, which consideration of her as
a type of the Wife of Bath will help us to analyse.

One of the two possessions of Wynn's that she retains points
forward to this new role. This is his belt, defining her role as
Scourge and that she now has the 'maistrie' (wearing the trousers).
The Wife claims that she has been the 'whippe' to her husbands
and the 'purgatorie' of her fourth (*Wife of Bath's Tale*, ll. 175, 489).
Mary is linked to imagery suggesting 'Bath' on three occasions.
She pushes Miss Fowler around in a bath-chair; she gives her an
'eleven o'clock glass of Contrexeville' (a spa water; the time – the
eleventh hour – is ominous too), and, finally, takes a hot bath.
Then, to return to the starting-point, she is associated with red
footwear. Edna's death is bloody in the extreme; Nurse Eden's
uniform is soaked, and Mary stands near her 'dripping hands'.
Upon Mary's return Miss Fowler exclaims, 'What *have* you got on
your boots? They're soaking wet. Change them at once.'

Mary not only obeys but wraps the boots in a newspaper and
puts them in the string bag with the bottle of paraffin. She has
been walking in the rain, but Miss Fowler's question and Mary's
behaviour make sense only if the reader understands that Mary's
boots are wet not with water but with blood. We never read of her
burning them; they remain in the bag, like the relics of a martyr,
and their shrouded presence colours the imagery of her thoughts;
she, as it were, hears 'the voice of the child's blood crying yet'.[44]
'Wynn was a gentleman who for no consideration on earth
would have torn little Edna into those vividly coloured strips
and strings. . . . It was no question of reading horrors out of
newspapers' (*D of C*, p. 438). The horror is inside the newspaper
in the string bag.

The imagery of 'strips and strings' is one aspect of the extent to
which thread, cloth, clothes, knitting and woven materials are
mentioned in the story. (Mary is nicknamed 'Packthread' by Wynn

and becomes 'his sewing woman'.) The equating of little Edna to 'strings' is another application of Carlyle's clothing-metaphor in *Sartor Resartus* – human tissue is just woven world-stuff – but there is also in the cloth-imagery a specially pointed reference to the Wife's trade. The Wife cites the old adage that spinning, deceit and weeping are God's gifts to women; as said before, 'spinning' has an emblematic function, and to the connotations of industry and harlotry must be added that of the Fate that weaves man's destiny.

Mary is compared to a camel. With his story of Patient Griselda, the Clerk of Oxford attempts to refute the Wife; in his *envoi* he sarcastically addresses all women whom he fears might try to imitate her: 'Ye archwyves, stondeth at defense, / Syn ye be strong as is a great camaille' (*Clerk's Tale*, ll. 1195–6). Mary, like the Clerk's 'great camaille', is treating him as the Wife treated her three old husbands – that is, making him *discharge a debt*.[45] The commercial metaphor, parodying St Paul's admonition that husbands and wives should not 'defraud' one another, runs all through the Wife's prologue. Each old husband disgusted her physically ('In bacon hadde I nevere delit'), but she exults at the thought of how she acted as the tribulation upon his flesh and made him 'paye his dette' at night in sexual servitude. Mary contemplates with loathing the rolling head of the airman, 'pale as a baby's, and so closely cropped that she could see the disgusting pinky skin beneath' (*D of C*, p. 436), and her murmured 'Go on. That isn't the end' (p. 441) just before the airman's death-rattle is her counterpart to the Wife's making her husbands 'swinke' in bed and weep.

But Kipling has some more traps to spring. Not only has Mary hated Wynn and willed his death. In addition, as Page points out, the air man is said by Mary to look like Wynn. In her mind he is both Wynn and 'the enemy he failed to kill'.[46]

Once one sees this, much apparently irrelevant detail is explained. For instance, Miss Fowler says that Wynn was 'always utterly unreliable at funerals' – that is, he had a tendency to laugh. This could be enough to suggest to Mary that he might refuse to lie down after his own, and she often speaks of him as if he is still alive. When Mary goes to get Wynn's pistol, which formerly frightened her, she reflects, 'Wynn would be pleased to see how she was not afraid.' At first this seems to be an unambiguous sign that she is still devoted to Wynn, until one notices that, oddly, on her return to the garden, the airman *does* attempt to look pleased:

'The mouth even tried to smile.' But upon Mary's production of the pistol 'the corners went down' (pp. 437–8). Then one recollects that Wynn formerly exercised power through reducing Mary to 'helpless laughter' and sees that 'pleased' is as ambiguous as the Chaucerian 'gentil Pardoner' or 'worthy woman'. This time the laugh is on Wynn.

He is interchangeable with the airman because Mary perceives him as *Germanic* in his brutality and contempt for women. It is through his cruelties that she is able to imagine what German frightfulness would be like. Barbarity towards women is absolutely at the centre of Kipling's claim that the German nation is a lesser breed. It can be found as far back as the *Plain Tales* story 'The Bronckhorst Divorce Case', where the cruel husband is given a 'Prussian' name. (When he is 'cut to ribbons' for the hateful treatment of his wife, his broken body is described as 'it', like the airman's in 'Mary Postgate'.) If Germany won the war, Kipling warned an audience in a 1918 speech titled 'The Menace of the Modern Thing: When the Veil is Lifted', 'Women will be the mere instruments for continuing the breed: the vessel of man's lust and man's cruelty.'[47]

For Kipling, cruelty to women and child-murder are crimes different only in degree. The same person who commits the one is capable of the other. One looks again at Mary's comment on Wynn: 'Wynn was a gentleman who for no consideration on earth would have torn little Edna into those vividly coloured strips and strings. But this thing hunched under the oak-tree had done that thing.' The meaning Mary attaches to that statement may be paraphrased as follows: Wynn would never have actually torn a child to pieces. (He was never *physically* destructive – not even with his toys.) His public-school training and the code of the British barbarian ensured that there were some things that 'just aren't *done*'.[48] But underneath he had a diabolic nature – the prince of darkness is, after all, a gentleman. The only thing that separates Wynn from the airman is a veneer of civilised behaviour.

When the reader realises that the airman is a figment of Mary's imagination, what ought the reaction to be? Relief that 'it was just an accident' after all, and that German-hating can be hived off to crazy females? Not exactly. '*But* it was a fact', as Mary says to herself, that Edna's body has been horribly shredded. That, at all events, is no hallucination. If Edna has not been killed by a German, an accusing finger still ought to point at those responsible;

Doctor Hennis is sure that the stable collapsed through criminal negligence. He says, 'That accident at the "Royal Oak" was due to Gerritt's stable tumbling down. It's been dangerous for a long time. It ought to have been condemned.' The beams 'were dry-rotted through and through' and she was cut to pieces by the falling beams and tiles (*D of C*, p. 434). The person immediately responsible was Edna's father, who ought to have kept his property in repair, or, if he was a tenant, then his landlord should have done so. It is at this point that the story lurches into allegory.

Kipling's indictment in 'Mary Postgate' is essentially the same as that of his famous war epitaph:

> If any question why we died
> Tell them, because our fathers lied.

The beams of the Royal Oak stable stand, in Kipling's scale of values, for the institutions of this sceptred isle, corrupted by 'Common Form', the complacency of the aristocracy, represented by the Balfours and the dilettante upper-class lilies of the field, the 'Souls'. That it is the *stable* which collapses suggests a special area of corruption, one which extends right into the garden of the Big House; the rotten branches of the shrubbery oaks are related to the stable beams. The 'stinking thing' is a Fouler of its own nest as well as a Fowler and has harboured – maybe given birth to – this 'Thing'; if Gerritt is her tenant, *she* should have seen to the repair of the stable. (There is more to be said about the stable.)

The equation of old wood with England's 'Old Corruption' is traditional.[49] Kipling uses it, notably in 'Below the Mill Dam' (*TD*), where the pre-Domesday waterwheel stands for the creaky machinery of British political life. (In that story, written in 1902 when Kipling was more buoyant, the Mill is revivified by an electric turbine); it is, like 'The Mother Hive' (*AR*) one of Kipling's pre-war right-wing allegories whereby he tried to warn England of the menace of the enemy within – Fabian socialists, Irish Nationalists, Little Englanders, suffragettes: any group whom he saw as softening up England for the Hun. One of his abiding sources of bitterness was that he played the role of Armageddon's Cassandra.

Kipling sets the story in the heartland of the caste which he held responsible for the war. He never locates Mary's village exactly.[50] But it is identifiably in Wiltshire; 'What a blessing it didn't happen in Salisbury!' says Miss Fowler of Wynn's accident, and Salisbury is presumably the 'county town' of Dr Hennis's destination. Wynn's training-centre, which must be the recently opened Upavon Flying School on Salisbury Plain, is said to be less than thirty miles from Mary's village.

After their retirement from India in the 1890s, Kipling's parents settled near the Wiltshire village of Tisbury, and it was there that they died in the winter of 1910–11. Kipling had to supervise his mother's funeral arrangements; personal bereavement certainly would account for unhappy associations of Tisbury after 1910; in the ruthless burning of family letters that Kipling perpetrated after his father's death can be seen the origin of one strand of the fabric of 'Mary Postgate'. The roll-call of deaths that Mary cites to herself ('dead as dear papa in the late 'eighties, aunt Mary in 'eighty-nine. . .') could be matched by a list of Kipling's dead relatives and mentors.

But the salient fact about Tisbury for 'Mary Postgate' is that nearby was the Pre-Raphaelite-designed country house Clouds, where had lived a prominent Souls family, Sir Percy and Lady Wyndham, friends of Kipling's parents and of his 'Uncle Ned' Burne-Jones. It was at Clouds that Lockwood Kipling died. Of Kipling's relationship with the Wyndhams Angus Wilson comments, 'So far as I know Kipling was on good terms with them but, when his father died at "Clouds" in 1911, he speaks of them particularly as friends of his parents. As he increasingly grew impatient with the Tory old guard's Imperial policy and Balfour's cultured *fainéantisme*, so he must have tolerated the Souls less easily.'[51]

His parents' deaths seem to have released Kipling from inhibitions about attacking Soulism even if he always remained on polite terms with individuals who had been their friends. In 'My Son's Wife' (1913), also in *A Diversity of Creatures*, he satirised the sexual infidelities of the Souls; he calls their political credo and personal morality 'the disease of the century'. And in 'Mary Postgate' he gives to young Fowler the first name of Wyndham. Moreover, there is a Sir Percy hidden away in the story too – the hero of Baroness Orczy's 'Scarlet Pimpernel' fake-historical 'Wardour Street' novels, a class of fiction which Kipling despised (*LR*, p. 6).[52] The last item in the inventory of Wynn's possessions is 'jig-saw puzzles', which is Kipling's marker that the list itself is one. The verse that everyone knows about Sir Percy is the one ending

Is he in heaven? Is he in hell?
That damned elusive Pimpernel.

It is a question that Kipling poses to himself about the Sir Percy
Wyndham caste – his father's friends at Clouds, Fonthill and
Wardour Castle. The caste is a gentlemanly one which would never
dream of killing a child, but which has ignored his warnings, lived
in cloud-cuckoo-land, weakened England and paved the way for
the war. These *gentlemen* don't join the poor bloody infantry and
face the hell of the trenches. They soar above these things in the
'wet clouds' (My italics; Kipling's son had joined the Irish Guards,
not the Flying Corps); 'Wynn says it's much safer than in the
trenches', says Mary (*D of C*, p. 424). Kipling was not anti-Flying
Corps, of course, but he would not have admired anyone who
joined it for its glamour and supposed safety.

The commonsensical doctor sees a literal truth. Mary, in her
character as visionary, brings together the literal and metaphorical;
the crashing of the stable and the dropping of a bomb are not two
completely different explanations for Edna's death but *related* ones.
One is due to a sin of commission, the other to one of omission.
'There was no doubt as to his nationality' is itself a sentence open
to doubt, for he is both Wynn and airman, yet she has attained to
a truth, for 'Germans' are also 'germans', our brothers, sisters,
cousins. Even the Royal Oak, the sovereign's family tree, is deeply
implicated in the guilt of being German through blood ties. (It was
during this period that the House of Saxe-Coburg-Gotha changed
its family name to Windsor.) 'I'd have you know that these waters
of mine / Were once a branch of the river Rhine', the Thames tells
its bridges (*DV*, p. 709) in the poem Kipling wrote for a school
history of England.

The story emerges as more brilliantly crafted than before, both
in its economy of implication and in its weaving a unity out of so
many disparate elements. The chief aesthetic flaw is Kipling's use
of rotten wood as a symbol of the institutions of England.[53] Here I
think he failed to make the realistic surface of his tale mesh fully
with the allegorical dimension. A German pilot dropping a bomb
on a little child is simultaneously both a literal killer and a type of
the threat to all family life. (I am putting aside here the question
of whether Kipling was justified in believing the atrocity stories
put about at the time.) A rotten stable collapsing is a literal killer,

but cannot stand in the same way as a *typical* threat. This might have passed muster if Kipling had been writing a straightforward fable like 'Below the Mill Dam', but he is here pushing his hybrid method to its limits; his motif has to take a weight of significance under which it totters. He has tried to place the imaginary pilot and the real stable on the same axis of evil.

At the same time, the foregoing reading raises in a new form the problem of the gap between the morality and the artistry. If anything, he is revealed as even more deeply enmeshed in hatred and self-contempt than before. The theme of 'Mary Postgate' is the enemy within, the deep-struck 'rottenness in the people's loins'. The line 'When the English began to hate', in the *envoi* poem, does not refer merely to hatred of Germans, but also to hatred of germans, to civil war. The English have begun to hate their own families. At the heart of 'Mary Postgate' is familial guilt as *infandum* as the secret of the Alvings or that of the House of Atreus, and a subtle disloyalty to the Crown. I suspect that Oliver Baldwin's description of 'Mary Postgate' as the 'wickedest story' has behind it recognition of the secret references to the Clouds set and a sense of outrage at the unfairness of Kipling's implied accusation.

Mary Postgate troubles Kipling because she is a visionary artist akin to himself. She has his acute sense of smell; she has done what he has done – created and destroyed the airman by the power of her imagination, and, like him, she has the virtue of keeping silent and conserving her vitality. Poking a fire – one of her last actions in the story – is the operation to which Kipling compared the ruthless 'raking out' methods of composition by which readers might feel the force of the unsaid. Throughout Kipling there appears the figure of the artist who is a destroyer – the 'I' who discovers his brotherhood to the Agent-General, Ortheris picking off the deserter 'with the smile of the artist who looks on the completed work' (*LH*, p. 96). If the spinster is a thwarted mother, then so is the artist, who speaks of his books as though they were his children, appropriating the language of conception, gestation, labour and birth. The artist, too, in the memorable phrase applied by Howitt to Keats, finds a quasi-sexual relief in 'a vivid orgasm of the intellect . . . like madness'. And like Mary, Kipling is unable to take part in the fighting except vicariously, through his son's presence at the front and through writing. As Mary knits socks, he weaves yarns. Like her, he is imprisoned in a small rural village, frustrated in his energies, and able only to send out the conceptions of his brain.

Yet there are a crucial respects in which she is not like him. Sensitivity to nasty smells is an ambiguous quality. 'You never like anything that isn't made just for you', Dick tells Maisie when she objects that the sea is 'so smelly' (*LF*, p. 5). The same might be said of Mary's reaction to the plane. She has blood on her shoes, which, in Kipling's iconography, means that she is guilty. And that, too, is what she is trying not to think about. For, as Wynn's 'buttoned-up' colleagues say to her at the funeral, he was 'a first-class fellow – a great loss' (*D of C*, p. 427). When she sees Edna's body the awareness stirs within her that in pursuing a private revenge she has, in intention at any rate, removed from the scene someone who could have saved Edna's life. So *she* is entangled in Edna's death and has a debt to pay too. The German airman is produced by her uncomfortable conscience as repayment.

She burns all of Wynn's childish things, good and ill together. She makes no distinction between rubbish and the authentic, between Baroness Orczy and Robert Louis Stevenson, between *The Scarlet Pimpernel* and *A Child's Garden of Verses*. Has she unthinkingly burned *The Wrong Box*? She may have destroyed the record of Wynn's misogyny, but also that of his innocence and spirit of adventure. Garvice's most famous book was *In Wolf's Clothing*. Is that what Wynn has been all the time – a little lost sheep masquerading as a brute? (Even The Scarlet Pimpernel is a misjudged hero, disguising his bravery as foppery.) She notices that Wynn has kept Miss Fowler's and her own photograph 'borne off in fun and (good care she took not to ask!) had never returned; a playbox with a secret drawer . . . a packet of all the letters that Miss Fowler and she had ever written to him, kept for some absurd reason through all these years' (*D of C*, p. 431).

Why has Wynn kept the photographs and the letters? Kipling distrusted the keeping of letters, for he knew that they can be used 'to make a monkey' out of the sender if they fall into the wrong hands; he encouraged Rider Haggard on one occasion to open his heart to him, assuring him that all letters from him were burned.[54] Mary is nonplussed, and can only ascribe 'some absurd reason' to Wynn; she suspects some cruel joke. But that 'secret drawer' should make us pause. Could it be that Wynn is not as brutally 'Germanic' as he sounds; that Mary's years of love for him, the horseplay and grief and joy over his reports, have counted for something; that the unlovely Wynn – who found a mother-substitute at the age of eleven (very late, but was it *too* late?) – did have a kind of inarticulate affection for Mary, which maybe even he himself did not recognise? He has gone to the war, and will be *doing* something that, irrespective of his apparent motives and his utterances, will combat Hun cruelty to women and protect the family. Could he be a Chanticleer in reverse, telling women to their faces that they are man's confusion, but in the secret drawer of his heart saying that they are man's joy and all his bliss?

In 'The Bronckhorst Divorce-Case', the narrator tries to excuse the 'heavy-handed jest' favoured by Bronckhorst, which, he supposed, Bronckhorst 'had first slipped into . . . meaning no harm, in the honeymoon, when folk find their ordinary stock of endearments run short, and so go to the other extreme to express their feelings. A similar impulse makes a man say, "Hutt, you old beast!" when a favourite horse nuzzles his coat-front' (*PT*, p. 247). How do we know that it is not this impulse that makes Wynn say, 'Hullo, Postey, you old beast'? The tale's answer is that we don't, because only the person concerned and God, if there is a God, can possibly know.

Mary may have made a mistake in failing to recognise her champion under the disguise of the bully. What she has done is to rush to judgement. Her Sybilline prophecy is premature. She burns wheat and tares together before the final reckoning. Her last spoken words are 'That isn't the end', and she speaks more aptly than she knows. It is not Judgement Day, only the image of that horror. Before she sees the airman, she hears 'a groan or a grunt'. Much depends on that little word 'or', and it is significant that Mary can't tell whether she hears a groan or a grunt, a human being or a beast. Underneath the phantasm of the airman / Wynn is another of a helpless child trying to get through. When the gun is produced, the mouth goes down 'just like Edna Gerritt's'. 'The head rolled from shoulder to shoulder as though trying to point out something.'

What is it trying to point out? Mary shuts up the airman wailing for the doctor with 'all her small German': 'Nein! . . . ich haben der todt Kinder gesehn' (p. 438). What she has inadvertently said is 'I have seen the dead *children*', not the dead *child*. The truth has come out by mistake and in spite of herself. If she has been covering up Miss Fowler's guilty secret, then to her knowledge there are two children who have been killed by the 'rotten stable.'

One is Edna; the other is Wynn. The carelessness of his parents and the shame surrounding his nativity have sent him into the world with the dice stacked against him and a grievance against women; Miss Fowler has given him money when what he needed was love.

Mary has 'seen' all the broken children who never had a chance – Edna, Wynn, the little Belgians whom she has read about in the newspapers, and, last of all, even the 'small German' that the airman once was, and who also came naked and helpless into the world. She has caught a glimpse of the dead 'Kinder', the kinder law of nature, which pities and renews as well as destroys. As she finishes her grim work, the rain falls more and more heavily. Even as she is thrilling with rapture at the climax of her 'work', the rain is quenching the fire, for her hand has not been able to go all the way with her hatred and she has only *half*-closed the lid of the incinerator against the 'driving wet'. *She* has 'ceased to think'. *She* 'hasn't the mind'. But *sunt lachrymae rerum et mentem mortalia tangunt.* There are tears for Things and mortal objects touch a Mind, as Virgil said.

Kipling wants to say that the Great War *is* Armageddon. He needs to believe and to persuade everyone that the Germans are wild beasts and Absolute Evil. His propaganda insists over and over that only such matching of hate with hate can strengthen the will of the British to defeat the *furor Teutonicus*. But something penetrates the armour and falls through to the other side. And this is Kipling's absolute belief in the goodness of babies. Even the wildest of beasts was once a young cub. And every baby is a 'pagan philosopher small' (*PT*, p. 197).[55] The hero of 'Tods' Amendment' 'was an utterly fearless young Pagan' (*WWW*, p. 310). 'Bloody Pagans' is an alternative name for the Holy Innocents.

And then the final revelation. Miss Fowler will have another story to tell that is not for young people. The story begins with a Great Exhibition, and it also ends with one – with Mary making an exhibition of herself. Lying relaxed on the sofa after her 'luxurious' bath, she becomes a parody of a *poule du luxe*, a *tableau vivant*, an *Olympia Exhibition*. It may be that the 'whole routine' is scandalised because she is meant to be thought of as naked – having seen too far into things. She offers Miss Fowler a self-confrontation; she lies 'on the *other* sofa' (my italics); it is Ithuriel's hour for her mistress too.[56]

7

Kipling and Swinburne: 'A Madonna of the Trenches'

> *Some are best seen in full sun, others under a lamp and a few are only good to be used in dark places where they were made. The women should know this.*
>
> (Introduction to the Outward Bound Edition)

Strictly speaking, this chapter should be headed 'Kipling and Morburnetti', 'Morburnetti' being a coinage on the model of 'MacSpaunday' and intended to epitomise a Pre-Raphaelite ghost compounded of the brilliant generation of 1850s Oxford poets – Morris, Rossetti and Swinburne, each of whom produced some variant of a re-created medieval world. 'Morburnetti' appears in Kipling's early work as a triune poetic model. Louis Cornell was the first to pay close attention to Kipling's adoption of their stylistic mannerisms and subject-matter, which is particularly marked in a manuscript notebook dating roughly from the period 1882–3 called *Sundry Phansies*. As he pointed out, they not only were attuned to Kipling's mood (he was suffering the miseries of unhappy first love at the time), but constituted a poetic avant-garde which any aspiring young poet might have copied.[1] However, as Swinburne is the most prominent of the three in the tale on which this chapter focuses, provided that the reader appreciates that 'Swinburne' stands for a cluster of conflicting emotions connected with an older generation, the apparent exclusion of the others need not worry us here.[2]

Kipling never met Swinburne, though in theory there is no reason why he should not have done so. He was not averse to meeting literary mentors such as Mark Twain and could have had an introduction to him through family connections. Swinburne had been close to Burne-Jones, to whom he dedicated his first series of *Poems and Ballads* and towards whom he cherished amiable feelings for the rest of his life. He was at the wedding-reception

148

for Kipling's parents (though they themselves did not turn up for it!). Beresford reported that Swinburne was shown some of Kipling's imitations of his verse, but had declined to comment on them.[3] Beresford suggested that Swinburne might have been jealous of the precocious schoolboy. No doubt this silence was hurtful, but one suspects that there was a deeper reason for Kipling's lack of communication with the older poet, who lived on at Putney until 1909, and that Kipling had come to distrust the Swinburnian. After 1884, Swinburne in Kipling tends to go underground. T. S. Eliot was responding to this subterranean quality when he commented that *he* could see a Swinburnian influence on Kipling though 'The vocabulary is different, the content is different, the rhythms are different.'[4] (I shall later hazard a guess at one specific example of what he had in mind.) Kipling quotes Swinburne sporadically (mostly in his travel-writing)[5] and there starts to appear in his writing a Morburnetti figure – decadent, blaspheming, self-destructive, *maudit*, whom he is both fascinated with and disowns, an alternative self whom he might have become and who offers him a doubtful literary 'treasure'.

During Kipling's childhood and adolescence Swinburne's reputation went through several phases. Robert Buchanan (the same who later called Kipling the 'Voice of the Hooligan') reviled *Poems and Ballads*. Swinburne's affair with Adah Dolores Isaaks Menken, the 'Female Mazeppa' (whom Kipling mentions *en passant* twice in his early Indian work[6]) made his private life notorious. *Punch* called him 'Mr Swine-born' and he seems to have enjoyed shocking the bourgeois with exaggerated stories about his depravity. Rumours that he kept a jealous monkey-wife were spread by de Maupassant and the Goncourts. His involvement with the Simeon Solomon case drew suspicions of homosexuality upon him. What is certain is that during the late 1870s he nearly drank himself to death, a fate from which he was rescued by his friend Theodore Watts-Dunton. At the same time, his poetry was becoming increasingly more respectable and boring, and getting some kind reviews.[7]

McIntosh Jellaludin, the decayed 'Oxford Man' and 'Virgil in the Shades' mentioned in Chapter 5, is first met drunkenly reciting Rossetti's 'The Song of the Bower' and referring to Charley Symonds's stables. Here we have three-in-oneness: Swinburne's drunkenness, Rossetti's poetry and Morris's wife – Symonds's stables in Holywell Street were the workplace of the father of the gipsyish Jane Morris, 'stunner', and dark lady of the Pre-Raphaelites. (She was the model for Rossetti's *Astarte Syriaca* and *Proserpine*, where she holds a pomegranate.) Jellaludin looks 'nearer fifty than the thirty-five which, he said, was his real age'. The number thirty-five is of course the Dantean midway of life; 'nearer fifty' would fit either Morris or Swinburne in 1885. He recites Swinburne's *Atalanta in Calydon* from beginning to end, no mean feat, as it is well over 2000 lines long. (If he is a type or shadow of Swinburne, his amazing memory becomes more explicable.)

Atalanta, notorious in its time for its blasphemous phrase 'the supreme Evil, God', filters the original Greek plot through the medieval concept of 'druery' (service to a lady). It is a powerful myth of two women destined to destroy the man they both love. Artemis, in punishment for neglect of her altars, sends a wild boar to devastate Calydon, which all the heroes of Greece assemble to slay. First to wound the boar is Artemis's votary Atalanta, who is adored by the leader, Meleager, prince of Calydon. His maternal uncles try forcibly to prevent him from honouring Atalanta with the present of the boar's head, for which he fights and kills them. Whereupon the queen, Meleager's mother and Atalanta's enemy, relights a brand which she had quenched at Meleager's birth, the Fates having predicted that her son's life would last only as long as the brand. As it is consumed, Meleager dies, blessing and cursing his mother: '[I] hail thee as holy and worship thee as just / Who art unjust and unholy'. He is more knightly to Atalanta. No man is to say that 'This man / Died woman-wise, a woman's offering, slain / Through female fingers . . . for thou hast honoured me.' The real culprit is the 'Supreme Evil', who has created the sorry state of things entire and set up a war between flesh and spirit. The mother represents the pull of the flesh and Earth – the cycle of death and birth and the perpetual regeneration of the species through sexuality – while Atalanta represents the pull of the spirit and the Moon, the hope of transcending mortality through ideal love. The meaning of the myth as treated by Swinburne for Victorian readers could be summarised as follows: man makes a sacrifice of his 'brute appetite' when it threatens to become destructive, but in so doing he cuts himself off from Nature and ceases to be a man. The plot of the tragedy Life is that woman is forced to act the part of both creator and destroyer. *Atalanta* is a potent influence on Hardy's *Jude the Obscure*, where the mother–virgin antagonisms are represented by the competing claims of

Arabella and Sue Bridehead, and (in a more attentuated way) on Lawrence's *Sons and Lovers* too.

Jellaludin seems similarly at the mercy of two loves. No doubt he has seen the groom's daughter too, and from then on has been serving a dual dark–bright Venus. He is living with a native woman and suggests to the narrator that through her he has access to a gamut of experiences, including sexual ones, which the narrator is too timid or fastidious to explore in real life. But as he dies, he calls out 'Ethel!' – a name derived from an Anglo-Saxon word meaning 'noble', suggestive of a high-born 'pure white' woman, an Atalanta figure. The narrator waits for the end, knowing that 'in six cases out of ten, a dying man calls for his mother'. However, the narrator seems to lose interest in this matter, and tells us only that Jellaludin 'began mumbling a prayer of some kind in Greek'; his last words are 'Not guilty, my Lord!' which matches Meleager's 'Yet with clean heart I die and faultless hand'. The narrator's failure to satisfy the curiosity that he has raised casts a shadow over Jellaludin's attitude to his mother. The Greek could be a blessing or a curse or might not refer to his mother at all. However, there is a sinister-sounding 'mother' in his work, if not in his life: this is his literary 'treasure', 'the life and sins and death of Mother Maturin'.[8]

The bequest of a 'treasure' that will exceed the *Inferno* relates Jellaludin to Brunetto Latini and so to 'The Strange Ride of Morrowbie Jukes', the fable of which, I suggested in Chapter 5, would have even more point if the Latini figure of the hunter in green contained an allusion to some admired poet who offered a dubious literary precedent. *Atalanta* and 'The Strange Ride' take as their *point de départ* an offence to a moon-goddess; both contain the image of the wasteland and the wild boar. Jukes brandishes his 'hog-sticking spear' at the moon because he is making a bid not to be the moon's servitor and end up like Meleager. Physically, Swinburne, who had red hair and was conspicuously short, does not resemble the tall, sandy-haired hunter, but there is one detail which points to Swinburne having contributed to his make-up. The hunter has a 'long moustache'; 'Algernon', Swinburne's first name, means 'with moustaches'.

Kipling speaks of *Atalanta* in *Something of Myself* as the poem which made him first take notice of Swinburne. The context implies that metrical inventiveness rather than content was what appealed to him (*SM*, pp. 34–5). Yet in the last tale in his last important collection, 'Uncovenanted Mercies', he quotes (imperfectly) from the famous chorus on the nature of man:

> His speech is a burning fire;
> With his lips he travaileth.
> At his heart is a blind desire,
> In his eyes foreknowledge of Death.
> (*LR*, p. 386)

Foreknowledge of death: the lowest common denominator of humanity. Garm, Ortheris's dog, is an honorary human being: when told to perform a trick – 'You're going to die now. Dig yourself your little grave an' shut your little eye' – he obliges; when told he is cured he jumps out, wagging his tail (*AR*, p. 56).

The parallels between the Atalanta myth and some of Kipling's recurrent concerns make it certain that he assimilated themes and imagery from Swinburne's verse drama. In particular we find the Swinburnian 'queen who can do no wrong' (of whom the type is Queen Victoria herself, the Great White Empress who is also the Widow of Windsor, the 'Widdy' or ropehalter.) We also find the mother/virgin creator/destroyer and the boar hunt, though they are never found all together. Kipling's mother-figures die or are inexplicably absent, leaving the world to the tender mercies of a false Madonna or wicked stepmother-figure, often called an aunt. Punch, the child hero of 'Baa Baa Black Sheep', in the 'framing' episode that precedes the news that he is to be sent to England, asks his *ayah* to tell him 'the story about the Ranee that was turned into a tiger' (*WWW*, p. 271). That is the plot in eight words. Punch's mother–queen disappears and is replaced by a cruel devouring mother-substitute – 'Antirosa'. The tiger turns back into a ranee when the mother reappears once more, begging Punch's forgiveness for having unwittingly delivered him to the tiger, and this ten-year-old Meleager, whose innocence is dead for ever, cannot blame her, because she could not do otherwise than she did.

The Atalanta figure, the cold virgin who competes with man, the reluctant destroyer, for whose sake the man emasculates himself, is best exemplified by Maisie in *The Light that Failed*. When we first see her as Dick's childhood sweetheart, practising pistol-shooting with him, she is accompanied by Amomma, a goat who swallows two loaded cartridges. 'Horrid little beast!' says Maisie, as her pistol goes off by accident, nearly blinding Dick. 'Then they'll joggle about inside him and blow up, and serve him right. . . . Oh, Dick! have I killed you?' (p. 6). Dick once promised to make a grass collar for the goat – that is to say, he is to make a halter for his own neck. When he delays in making it, he is rebuked by Maisie. Later he dreams that, when he has won 'all the world and brought it to Maisie in a cartridge-box', all she can say is 'Where is the grass collar you promised for Amomma? Oh, how selfish you are!' (p. 14). When Dick and Maisie meet again as young adults, Maisie tells Dick that Amomma is dead: 'Not cartridges; over-eating. He was always greedy' (p. 57).

Maisie's keeping of Amomma as a pet foreshadows her treatment of Dick, whose inward gunpowder of passion similarly has to smoulder secretly and whose natural appetites she condemns as selfish. Like Atalanta, Maisie competes with men in their own field (she is a woman artist). Dick is an accomplice in the taming of the brute, albeit a rebellious one – he adorns Amomma's horns with 'ham-frills', which symbolic homage to male sexuality offends Maisie. As in the case of Punch's Mamma, the virgin cannot be blamed by the adoring hero, whose role has been determined by the myth aeons before. The Atalanta myth is not the only one operating in *The Light that Failed*, and there are 'private marks' too. Kipling's first love, Florence Garrard, on whom the character of Maisie was based, actually did have a pet goat. One suspects that Esmeralda's goat in Hugo's *Notre Dame de Paris* also plays its part. Kipling reported that he was especially struck with the goat when he read the book as a boy of twelve.[9]

The metamorphosis of the boar-hunt can be more clearly seen in certain stories set in India, where it could be translated into the sport of pig-sticking. In addition to 'The Strange Ride', it can be discerned in 'Pig' and 'Bubbling Well Road'. Of course, Kipling would not be Kipling if he had not somewhere in his *oeuvre* presented the 'recoil of the myth'. So, as we saw earlier, the destructive Maisie is rewritten as Miriam. Similarly, we find a Good Hunting and a truce in the war between flesh and spirit in 'My Son's Wife' (*D of C*).

Of 'My Son's Wife' it has been said that it is spoiled by Kipling's trying to do too much at once; the story has a unifying central idea, however, which is that what the world supposes to be spiritual is frequently carnal and *vice versa*. Franklin Midmore discovers that his London life among the Immoderate Left, which seemed to offer sacred friendship and 'solace', is in fact a nest of squalid little self-deceptions and casual infidelities; while his life in the countryside, which apparently affords satisfaction only to the 'lower centres' – the imagery of dirt, muddy water, pigsties and animals runs throughout – turns out to possess immanent spirituality. The message is that of the preface poem to 'Wireless' (*TD*) – 'Kaspar's Song in "Varda"' – where 'our death' is that the 'preacher' encourages us to go butterfly-chasing in the heavens for evidences of the soul, instead of offering the wise father's advice: go to the kitchen-garden, where the Psyche's origin may be found on a cabbage-leaf, and the world will no longer appear a wilderness of briars.

The boar-hunt is translated into an English fox-hunt, which is played off against what Kipling insists are the really deadly blood-sports of the London jungle. The pattern of (good) absent mother contrasted with (bad) mother-substitute is repeated, but almost in reverse. Midmore's own mother is a shadowy figure, of whom we know not much more than that she has 'embraced a creed which denied the existence of death' – that is, she has 'departed' from engagement with the real world of error and doubt and evil. Midmore's aunt Jenny, by contrast, has left him a house in the country which by taking him 'back to the land' saves his soul, and Rhoda, her former maid, acts as her representative. The elements of 'Baa Baa Black Sheep' are reordered to tell a story of how dayspring mishandled can be restored. The evil 'Aunty Rosa' of 'Baa Baa Black Sheep' is reconstituted as a wise old nurse–housekeeper, whose name, Kipling reminds us, means 'rose' ('There isn't a rose left, Rhoda!' – *D of C*, p. 371).

Atalanta is rewritten as a huntin' county girl, the green-eyed Connie Sperrit, the name indicating that she represents the constant, permanently active spirit of Nature. There is a hint that she might have been a rather wild slip of a girl. When she and Franklin realise that they are in love she says, 'I swear I'll try to be good, dear. I'm not much of a thing at the best. What made *you* – ' Franklin replies, referring to his numerous affairs, 'I'm worse – worse! Miles and oceans worse. But what does that matter now?' This is a sort of inverted Tess–Angel Clare situation. Instead of the catastrophic confession of pre-marital unchastity on the wedding-night, this couple take it for granted that past follies weigh not a jot against their present commitment to one another. 'My Son's Wife' is one of the stories in which Kipling is matter-of-fact about sexual irregularities and illegitimacy, though he cannot quite get away from the double standard: the man's lapses have been 'miles and oceans worse!' than the woman's could ever be. His aunt, Mrs Werf, might have had a 'past' too. Franklin believes that she has destroyed 'all records of her *vie intime*', and her name, Jenny, is one which, following the heroine of Rossetti's poem, Kipling uses elsewhere as shorthand for a 'fallen woman'.[10] The tale encourages and frustrates curiosity about people's 'hidden pasts' in order to assure readers that the new life does indeed cancel out the old.

The most comical feature of this rewriting of *Atalanta* is the diminishing of the rapacious boar into a little white pig 'newly washed and very hungry'. As Franklin and Connie, who do not yet recognise that they are in love, inspect a tenant's cottage, the pig knocks them down sprawling onto the muddy floor. 'The wild boar of Asia could not have cut down a couple more scientifically.' The innocent pig acts as catalyst – most of Kipling's love scenes, such as they are, have an animal witness.[11] He inverts Carlyle's dire words about the roots of the marriage-bower flourishing in dung and replies, as it were, 'So what?'

Next to *Atalanta*, the Swinburne poems which most obsessed Kipling were probably *Dolores* and 'Les Noyades'. Both are important for 'A Madonna of the Trenches' (*DC*).[12] 'Les Noyades' is a source for the motif of love-death by drowning in Kipling's work.

It was numbered among the most shocking and objectionable of Swinburne's 1865 *Poems and Ballads*, and one can see why, combining as it does sado-masochism, necrophilia, egalitarianism and blasphemy with Romantic ecstasy. Freely adapting Carlyle's account of an incident during the Terror and marrying it to the ruling idea of chivalric service to the scornful white mistress, the narrator tells how counter-revolutionists in the Loire were punished by stripping young men and maidens, binding them together in pairs and drowning them, 'naked and wed'. Among them is one 'rough with labour and red with fight' who is thus coupled with a 'lady noble by name and face, / Faultless, a maiden, wonderful, white'. Allowed to make a pre-execution speech, he intercedes for the soul of his executioner, praising him for his 'mercy'. He is even ready to go to Hell in his place. This peasant has yearned for the white lady all his life, but has been unable to declare his love owing to class differences. Now, however, he tells her, 'I shall have you dead.' Praising God for making him the happiest of men, he eagerly anticipates his dissolution: 'I shall drown with her, laughing for love; and she / Mix with me, touching me, lips and eyes.' The narrator then brings the story back to the present. He too has an unattainable love, and, if he had had the chance of the French peasant, he too would have chosen the supreme moment of love in death even if the price was eternal damnation. But no such luck: the gods do not repeat their gifts. (There is a touch of self-parody in the poem which coexists with and intensifies Swinburne's deadly serious claim that Eros is a deity more worthy of self-sacrifice than the Christian God and that *Liebestod* offers the only true liberty.)

Perhaps Kipling's most unusual transmutation of the elements of 'Les Noyades' occurs in 'The Mary Gloster' (*DV*, p. 129), which is my candidate for the poem that Eliot had in mind when making the remark quoted near the beginning of this chapter. Sir Anthony Gloster, a dying self-made shipping-magnate, orders his tomb; his last desire is to be united with his wife, who had died at sea thirty years or so before: he feels reproached by her dead spirit for his philandering with numerous 'hired women' since her death (or perhaps before – the point is not entirely clear). His son is to promise to enable him to fulfil this yearning; his body is to be placed on board the *Mary Gloster*, one of his freighters:

> you'll find her a lively ship;
> And you'll take Sir Anthony Gloster, that goes on 'is wedding-
> trip,
> Lashed in our old deck-cabin with all three port-holes wide,
> The kick o' the screw beneath him and the round blue seas
> outside!

His son is to have the ship brought to the Macassar Straits and scuttled at the precise compass-bearing where the dead wife's body was committed to the deep, so that his dead father may 'kiss my girl on her lips! / I'll be content with my fountain. I'll drink from my own well, / And the wife of my youth shall charm me.'

The poem contains the emblem of the man and woman being bound together and drowning in a final 'marriage'; the ship represents the woman – 'Mary Gloster' is the name of both wife and ship; the wife died aboard her and Sir Anthony's corpse is to be 'lashed' to the ship in the cabin bedroom they once shared; Swinburne's dying bodies are changed by Kipling into a lively female ship and a male cadaver animated by the 'kick o' the screw beneath him'. Kipling went direct to Carlyle for one detail. The first *noyade* had involved packing a boat with victims and then holing it when in the middle of the Loire. The method described in the poem was later adopted because it saved expense, a practical detail of no interest to Swinburne.[13] The dying businessman is very aware that to sink a costly ship is an extravagance, but such is his obsession that expense be hanged. The wife is another of Kipling's dual-natured Marys; she is his 'Lady' who has made a man of him, and whom at one point he calls 'mother' but she also pulls the old pagan downwards towards life-in-death, a fate he embraces partly (one is given to understand) as an act of expiation.

If 'The Mary Gloster' contains one of Kipling's most indirect allusions to 'Les Noyades', 'A Madonna of the Trenches' (*DC*) contains his most overt, for two verses form the epigraph and lines from these are quoted by the leading characters. The relevant verses are the first and the last but five; Kipling indicates an omission through suspension points:

> Whatever a man of the sons of men
>   Shall say to his heart of the lords above,
> They have shown man, verily, once and again
>   Marvellous mercies and infinite love.
>
>   . . . . . .
>
> O sweet one love, O my life's delight,
>   Dear, though the days have divided us,
> Lost beyond hope, taken far out of sight,
>   Not twice in the world shall the Gods do thus.

I believe that Kipling supplied the Swinburnian epigraph as a kind of back-up clue to the meaning of the story – that is to say, the story itself supplies its own directions as to how it should be read, but it helps if the reader can bring the entire Swinburne poem to bear on it. 'A Madonna of the Trenches' has been, in my opinion, radically misread by most critics.

'Madonna', like 'Fairy-Kist', has a doctor detective as leading character. He is the same compassionate, irritatingly hearty, somewhat Philistine Robert Keede, who is able to offer effective help because he keeps a tight control over his imagination. (Keede's cheery clubman manner is, of course, a cover-up for a far greater self-identification than he admits to.) He has to deal with a case of post-war hysteria in a Masonic lodge. Young Clem Strangwick suddenly bursts out, 'Oh, My Aunt! I can't stand this any longer', during a boring lecture on the Orientation of Solomon's Temple (p. 241). The name 'Clem' is significant, suggesting both the regional 'clemmed' (starved) and 'to clam up'. The source of Strangwick's disturbance emerges under the influence of a 'Paregoric' medicine and Keede's questioning. Kipling is playing on two senses of 'paregoric', which is (literally) a pain-relieving drug or (metaphorically) the soothing effect of unburdening one's mind in speech.[14]

Strangwick was a 'runner' in a particularly hellish area of the trenches, 'faced with dead bodies' which 'were like gruel in a thaw' and which creaked as he ran over them during a freeze. He would negotiate his way by such signposts as 'the two Zoo-ave skel'tons' and 'Butcher's Row where the *poy-looz* was laid in six deep each side' (p. 253). (For laconic grimness Kipling never surpassed these descriptions; 'faced', for instance, could scarcely be bettered for economy of appalling suggestion.) Strangwick at first pretends that it is the dead bodies that are on his mind, but Keede refuses to accept this explanation. Eventually it transpires that his aunt Bella Armine and his platoon sergeant, John Godsoe, who also happens to be his courtesy 'uncle', have been secretly in love for years. She hides 'a gatherin' in her breast' and sends a message to Godsoe in the trenches via Clem: 'Tell Uncle John I hope to be finished of my drawback by the twenty-first [of January], an' I'm dying to see 'im as soon as 'e can after that date' (p. 251).[15] On the 21st, after an especially horrific run, Clem sees in Butcher's Row 'somethin' ahead on the duckboards' which partially covered the dead bodies underfoot. It resembles his aunt, but 'In 'alf a second I saw it was only the dark an' some rags o' gas-screen.'

Godsoe's response when his 'nephew' tells him of this hallucination is to return to Butcher's Row. At the precise spot as before, the apparition of Bella is seen again, this time by both men. She stretches out her arms to Godsoe: 'An' 'e was looking' at 'er as though he could 'ave et 'er, an' she was lookin' at 'im the same way.' Godsoe takes two lighted braziers into a dug-out, invites the ghost inside, and then, in front of the stupefied Clem, shuts and wedges up the door. The next day Godsoe is found suffocated from charcoal fumes, and Clem hears later that Aunt Armine died on the morning of the 21st. The effect of this experience is to throw him into turmoil. 'It knocked out everything I'd believed in. . . .

An' she nearer fifty than forty an' me own Aunt! . . . All that time Auntie Armine stood with 'er arms out – an' a look in 'er face! *I* didn't know such things was or could be!' (p. 256). 'If the dead *do* rise – and I saw 'em – why – why *anything* can happen' (p. 258). He refuses to marry his fiancée, with whom he had previously 'got as far as pricin' things in the windows together' (p. 250), so she institutes a breach-of-promise action against him. Since his glimpse of the love of Bella and Godsoe he has felt a revulsion against settling down with a 'good little wife'; the shop window with its tempting display of purchasable domestic objects has become for him emblematic of meretricious shows of this world (lawful love must be paid for with money), when set beside the immortal love of his elders: 'he killing 'imself before my livin' eyes so's to carry on with 'er for all Eternity – an' she 'oldin' out 'er arms for it! . . . The reel thing's life an' death. It *begins* at death, d'ye see. *She* can't understand' (p. 259). Keede says that the truth has now emerged and that Clem will now be able to sleep. He consigns Clem to the care of his sponsor at the Masonic lodge, who turns out to be the husband of the late Bella Armine, and thus Clem's uncle by marriage; he, of course, is ignorant of his wife's secret passion. 'All [Clem] wants now is to be kept quiet till he wakes', says Keede, with which words the story ends.

Most critics read the tale as a quasi-Christian one, and take the theme to be the triumph of love over death. Many of them then proceed to regret that a powerful story is spoiled by a portentously banal message. 'The ingeniously obfuscatory revelation of "the horror" turns it at last into nothing more than the comforting popular sentiment that a great love goes beyond the grave', says Bayley. Angus Wilson complained that Kipling had equated the 'enduring through a lifetime of undeclared passion with St Paul's suffering' and had thus confused 'a staple of high romantic literature' with 'the centre of Christian belief. . . . There is plain sentimentality clothed in a metaphysical authority which it does not possess.'[16]

Sandra Kemp stood Wilson's complaint on its head, and argued that what he sees as a weakness is in fact the story's strength: the 'unselfish love' of Godsoe and Bella (they have seen each other alone only once 'in all these years') will be rewarded by the resurrection of the body. 'Kipling brings together the two traditions of transcendent love, the "sacred" and the "profane" ("Mary" and "Isolde"): a vision of perfect love, not in traditional terms as virgin love but as a love that is both spiritual and sexual.'[17] Kemp has considerably advanced discussion of the story in her stress on the physicality of the love of Godsoe and Bella, and its relationship to medieval *fin amour*, but I think that her conclusion, that the relationship of Bella and Godsoe is offered as a daring vision of *perfect* love, is true only from Godsoe's angle, and in any case will not satisfy those who say that the story is sentimental.

'Madonna' is one of the Masonic stories that Kipling wrote after the First World War. He had become a Mason in 1886, and found in its discipline, comradeship, secret rituals, respect for all men's craft and symbolism of the building of the temple a refuge from anarchy and nightmares. In 'Madonna' Freemasonry is associated with qualities which enable the mentally war-wounded to learn to trust life again, a precondition of their eventually marrying and becoming the fathers of families once more. The Lodge is a halfway house. Swinburne is associated with the opposite pull – downwards towards escape from the world and extinction. The pull is presented in seductive terms; the death-instinct disguises itself as a victory over death. The story is about the fight between these two opposed principles, and is, I think, among the finest short stories in English about the psychic effects of the First World War.

Like T. S. Eliot, D. H. Lawrence and Virginia Woolf, Kipling intuits that among its most damaging after-effects is the corruption of the sexual imagination of the young generation that has survived the carnage; the experience of living in a charnel-house, in which one has been surrounded day after day by the sight and stench of rotting corpses has associated 'disgusting images with the act of the sexual instinct' (Shelley's definition of obscenity).[18] The experience has struck at the very centre of man's generative impulses and capacity for tender affections. One effect of this is the state of mind depicted in Wilfred Owen's 'Greater Love', where the sexual act is seen as a mockery (in both senses of the word) of real death:

> Your slender attitude
> Trembles not exquisite like limbs, knife-skewed
> Rolling and rolling there
> Where God seems not to care;
> Till the fierce love they bear
> Cramps them in death's extreme decrepitude.

Another reaction is that depicted by Kipling: a sensitive young man makes an ideal out of the perverted and distempered projections of his imagination. Strangwick's 'cover-story', that he was hysterical because of his recollections of the dead bodies creaking underfoot, turns out to be a partial truth.

The view that Kipling is exalting the *Liebestod* of Bella and Godsoe rests largely on a certain interpretation of the relation of the preface and *envoi* poems of 'Madonna' to the story itself. The first, 'Gipsy Vans', ironically praises the law-abiding citizen. The trap is sprung in the last verse: the gipsies tell the conformist that after death 'your God and your wife / And the Gipsies 'll laugh at you! / *And then you can rot in your burying-place*'. The poem praises lawlessness and seems at first to be endorsing Godsoe's brand of profane love. But, as readers of Lavengro's famous dialogue with Jasper Petulengro learn, the gipsy creed is a materialist one which does not admit of transcendent love or the resurrection of the body.[19] 'Life is sweet, brother', and the only gipsy life is that of the physical body on earth. Kipling's gipsies have nothing but contempt for the doctrine that self-denial and self-sacrifice are the gates to a superior plane of existence. They do *not* recommend that you should 'Lose your life for to live your life.' Godsoe would be the target of their scorn for being too timid to flout convention while Bella was alive, and for imagining that his voluntary death could be an open sesame to 'carryin' on for all Eternity'.

The *envoi*, a fragment of 'Gow's Watch', the verse drama which Kipling never completed, seems at first less equivocal than 'Gipsy Vans'. It contains a story which parallels 'Madonna' in situation (an old soldier who – probably – commits suicide upon hearing of the death of his lifelong secret love) and theme (Love's religion as a challenge to orthodoxy). The young queen pronounces judgement: 'I have seen Love at last. / What shall content me after?' But there is an important difference. Gow dies with his mission completed, the decisive battle won and the rightful queen on the throne. There is no conflict between love and duty. Godsoe *deserts* the fighting to join his 'immortal' love with the outcome still hanging in the balance. The disparity opens up the possibility that 'Gow's Watch' is a counter-statement to a prose story about 'How a Man may go to see Life and meet Death there'.[20]

A feature which seems to support Wilson's (and Kemp's) reading is the pervasive pressing into service of the language of the Bible for erotic purposes. John Godsoe's name, for instance, is clearly intended to recall John 3:16: 'God so loved the world that he gave his only begotten son, that whosoever believeth in him should not perish, but have everlasting life.' On his way to Butcher's Row, Godsoe (it would seem) quotes the words of St Paul in the Burial Service: 'If after the manner of men I have fought with beasts at Ephesus, what advantageth it me if the dead rise not?' Together they suggest that the sergeant is a Christ-figure who has been prepared to lay down his life, fighting the German wild beasts, as a ransom for many, and thus deserves a heavenly reward in the arms of his Madonna. Ephesus is also the location of the shrine of Diana, and 'Great is Diana of the Ephesians'. 'Fighting with wild beasts' can therefore stand for 'subduing the mutinous passions'. That temperance is both a Christian and a pagan virtue means that at 'Ephesus' there can be a *rapprochement* between the two.

However, Clem also overhears Godsoe repeating lines from Swinburne's 'Les Noyades', and he keeps shouting them for three days after the death of his uncle until treated for hysteria by Keede. Keede now asks him to recall them:

> '. . . that hymn you were shouting till I put you under. It was something about Mercy and Love. Remember it?'
>
> 'I'll try,' said the boy obediently, and began to paraphrase, as nearly as possible thus: ' "Whatever a man may say in his heart unto the Lord, yea verily I say unto you – Gawd hath shown man, again and again, marvellous mercy an' – an' something' or other love." ' (*DC*, p. 246)

The narrator is recording as nearly as possible Clem's paraphrase (or is it that Clem is paraphrasing as accurately as he can Godsoe's original utterance?) of his recollection of Godsoe's quotation, and we can't know how accurate *that* was. What is noteworthy is the euphemising of Swinburne's original – the alteration of 'the gods' into 'Gawd' and the addition of the biblical 'yea verily I say unto you'. What is being muffled by this process of oblique transmission is that Swinburne's 'marvellous mercy' and 'infinite love' are ironic blasphemies; the words mean precisely the opposite of what they would to a Christian. 'Mercy' is being used as in 'leaving X to Y's tender mercies'. God is praised in much the same way as the blinded Dick Heldar expresses gratitude to the Almighty for allowing him the stupendous luck of arriving just in time for a battle so that he can be shot and thus put out of his misery. 'Oh God has been most good to me!' (*LF*, p. 287). Another model is

Uncle Remus's Brer Rabbit thanking Brer Fox for throwing him in the briar-patch; the victim outwits the aggressor by inducing the latter to inflict what he believes to be the ultimate punishment, which the victim then claims is what he wanted all along.

The Swinburnian original contains a blasphemous distortion of St Paul and supplies a reason why the Burial Service and Swinburne are juxtaposed in Godsoe's mind. One stanza contains the Pauline idea that a reward in the hereafter makes worthwhile the hand-to-hand fighting with the enemies of God on earth; the petitioner asks God for a boon, pleading that he has fought the good fight:

> Lord, if I loved thee – Lord, if I served –
> If these who darkened thy fair Son's face
> I fought with, sparing not once, nor swerved
> A hand's-breadth, Lord, in the perilous place. . . .

(The hoped-for reward in his case being the right to go to Hell in the place of his murderer.) At the climax of Clem's confession, the Christian gloss abruptly peels away; Clem quotes Swinburne accurately; he speaks the language of paganism: 'Not twice in the world shall the *Gods* do thus' (my italics).

The Swinburnian element, therefore, works against a Christianising interpretation and makes it possible to read inversely all expressions of gratitude to the Christian God; similarly the Madonna celebrated in Kipling's story is closer to Our Lady of Pain than the Mother of God. Indeed, what is 'A Madonna of the Trenches'? At first glance it seems to convey the idea of transference into 'ordinary' life of an archetype on the lines of 'A Village Romeo and Juliet' or 'A King Lear of the Steppes'. But it could also be ironic, as in Henry James's 'The Madonna of the Future', the point of which lies in an artist's choice of an unworthy woman as the model for the religious masterpiece he intends to paint. The deluded artist is quite unable to see that his 'ideal' is venal, vulgar and old. A trench Madonna might be the negation of a real Madonna – the Queen of Hell. However, before one comes down in favour of one or the other, there are further ambiguities to explore.

'Bella Armine' is a most peculiar name, to which Kipling draws our attention by making Clem say that her real name was Bella, but that the children always called her 'Auntie Armine', because it 'sounded more like her – like somethin' movin' slow, in armour'

(*DC*, p. 249). This is Kipling's signal that the reader is being offered
a pseudo-explanation. Why, if you elide the names, do you get
'Bellarmine'? An irrelevant coincidence? A bellarmine is a handled
earthenware ale jug, resembling in some degree the human body.
Bella Armine's role, then is that of Valkyrie; she is a magnificent
Wagnerian semi-divine warrior ('A biggish woman, an' had been
'andsome' – ibid.) whose task it is to convey the bodies of heroes
to Valhalla and revive them with refreshing draughts.

But, as we have seen in 'Mrs Bathurst', woman as the vessel
that quenches male thirst is an unstable symbol, and this is inherent
in the name 'Bellarmine'. The jug acquired the name from a Jesuit
cardinal famed in the sixteenth century for his map of Hell. He is
to be found in D'israeli's *Curiosities of Literature*.[21] Bellarmine is one
of the zealots who 'exhausted their ink-horns in building up a Hell
to their own taste, or for their particular purpose'. In *Omniana*
(owned by Kipling) Coleridge begins the entry 'Hell' with the
words 'Bellarmin makes sweating and crowding one of the chief
torments of Hell.' The *Oxford English Dictionary* supplies the
additional information that he was the particular enemy of the
Protestants in Flanders.[22]

Thus, like Mrs Bathurst, she may have a dual nature: benign
and nurturing in life, demonic and devouring after death. 'Bella'
means 'beautiful' or 'fair'. It is the name Godsoe greets her by
when she appears for the second time – 'Why, Bella! Oh, Bella!'
Or, rather, he is greeting the 'rags o' gas-screen' out of which the
hallucination has been constructed. In other words, Godsoe is like
the Fool in 'The Vampire' who made his prayer to a 'rag and a
bone and a hank of hair' and called her his 'Lady Fair'. Her name
is vampiric too. 'Amine' is Sidi Nouman's ghoul-wife in *The Arabian
Nights*; she disappears into the graveyard to devour dead flesh.[23]
Bella looks at Godsoe as though she could *eat* him; Godsoe has to
die so that the consumption may take place.

Indeed, the more curiously one considers the matter, the less
this love seems a comforting sentimentality. Clem has accepted as
his 'ideel' of immortal love vampirism *à deux*. (Godsoe has the
same devouring look on his face; each could say with the man in
'Les Noyades', 'Now I shall have you dead.') Moreover, the love-
object is a woman old enough to be his mother. There is more
than a suggestion of incestuous love here; an 'aunt' can also be a
doxy in Elizabethan slang. Her garments conceal a diseased breast
('She never talked of her body much to anyone' – *DC*, p. 250),

which makes the fair lady akin to the witch Geraldine in Coleridge's *Christabel*:

> Behold! her bosom and half her side –
> Are lean and old and foul of hue.
> A sight to dream of, not to tell!
> Oh shield her, shield sweet Christabel!

The diseased breast, like the cancerous ulcer in 'The Wish House', is the outward eruption of Eros denied. What Clem euphemistically calls ''ousekeepin'' (the word causes him to burst out laughing 'horribly', giving the lie to his later claim that he has never laughed since that 21 January) takes place behind the shut door of the dug-out, which is a parody of the nuptial chamber, as the braziers emitting poisonous black smoke parody the symbolism of the hearth. The effect on Clem of the experience is not merely to shatter his safe world-picture, bounded by, in A. G. Sandison's words, 'family squares, rituals of love and marriage'.[24] The devils have entered into the vacancy thus created. He has resolved to embark on a career of self-destructive promiscuity, seeking to enact again and again the experience of Butcher's Row. At least this is one meaning of the broken sentences that Clem utters at the climax of his 'sudden insane fury', when, we are to understand, his suppressed self speaks at last: 'She [his fiancée] don't know what reel things mean. *I* do – I've 'ad occasion to notice 'em. . . . *No* I tell you! I'll 'ave 'em when I want 'em, an' be done with 'em, but not till I see that look on a face . . . that look . . . I'm not takin' any' (*DC*, p. 259). Clem in his fury has changed his vowels. He now says 'reel' whereas at the beginning of Keede's therapy he cried out 'Nerves? It's real! It's real!' (p. 243). The change of letter is crucial. Clem has replaced the 'real' with the 'reel', the projected film-loop of illusion.[25] What are we to suppose Clem means to ''ave' when he wants and 'be done with' and 'take' when he sees 'that look on a face'? They could be the 'things' that he and his fiancée have been 'pricing' in shops; one day he will want to buy furniture and settle down, but not until he has found the embodiment of his ideal. But this does not make very good sense of ''ave done with 'em'; the predatory language suggests that it is women as sex-objects that he will ''ave' when he wants, provided that they are 'reel' vamps out to devour him, and that he will throw away the shell when he has eaten the kernel; or, more horribly, since bared teeth also are found in the rictus of death, he is looking for that sign in the faces of the women he will ' 'ave'. Of such mental states are made Jack the Rippers.[26]

After the confession, Keede takes a purgatorial 'flamboyant' robe from a robe-press and lays it over the boy. But, as Clem himself asks at the beginning, 'What'll I do? What'll I do about it?': Keede has exorcised the devils, but what man in his senses would willingly marry a girl who has pursued him with a breach-of-promise suit?[27] Brother Armine says that 'she'd make him a good little wife too, if I'm any judge' (p. 261). Reliable judge he is not, since he has been blind to his wife's adulterous passion. In refusing to be dragged into wedlock by the threat of pauperisation, Clem (we are made to feel) is saving himself from a milder Butcher's Row.[28]

Keede's last words – 'All he wants now is to be kept quiet till he wakes' – hint at something that Clem is still trying to hide from his consciousness. T. C. Swinton wrote discerningly,

> There seem to be clear hints that Strangwick's aunt and uncle are closer than he thinks. . . . When we remember Helen Turrell in 'The Gardener' [the last tale in DC], whose tragedy was that she could never acknowledge openly . . . that the nephew killed in action was really her son, we can fairly infer that the lovers Strangwick saw with his own eyes preparing to carry on for all eternity were his own mother and father.[29]

A closer look would, I think, persuade most people that Swinton is right;[30] those unpersuadable could still agree that Armine and Godsoe are parent-figures whom Clem seems to have loved better than those whom he called Dad and Ma. What does it mean? And how is this theme related to that of war?

Clem has been able to control his imagination throughout all the horrors he has witnessed by doing his duty and being literal-minded. He represses his growing awareness that he is a bastard. When his mother dies of cancer, his mingled feelings of love and hate surface and he turns the rags into a vision of his mother. Sexual intercourse is a devouring by an old woman with a diseased breast, but, because he loves his parents, the repellent becomes the supremely alluring, to the tune of 'Les Noyades'.

Behind 'A Madonna of the Trenches' lie the metaphors that we are Nature's bastards and that war is Mother Earth devouring her children. These are the deadest of clichés; the mind ceases to respond to them. But clichés become terrifying when imaged as literally true. Why children's imaginations are so vulnerable is that for them figures of speech have not yet become cliché. A case in point is Kipling's horror as a small boy when his aunt jokingly said that she wished she could cut herself in half so as to remain upstairs saying goodnight while being downstairs as well. 'I have just seen her cut in half', he gasped to his cousin, who realised that he had 'visualised his aunt cut in two with extraordinary intensity, and with horrible glimpses of lacerated internal organs'.[31] In 'A Madonna of the Trenches' Kipling has produced a symbolical grotesque comparable to the dream-sequence in Bunuel's *Los Olvidados*, where the starving slumboy asks his mother for food, and the mother rises, smiling and holding out to him a dripping cut of raw meat.

The Swinburnian quotation can now be seen as integral to the story. The Great War is the triumph of the death-instinct, a visitation of the sins of the fathers upon the children, the nineteenth century's corpse outleant into the twentieth, the ultimate perversion of love. And the decadent poets of an older generation have played their part, insidiously feeding the heart on fantasies.

But Kipling knows that this vision of nature is only part of a symbol system, and hopes to drive it out by a contrary symbol system, that based on the building of Solomon's temple. The struggle is on for the boy's mind, with the Masonic fellowship offering a period for rest and recuperation; the story comes out in favour of Browning's 'It's better to be sane than mad', though whether the healing powers will win is left open. The tale ends on much the same note as 'At the End of the Passage', which closes with a misquotation from Browning's 'Time's Revenges':

> There may be Heaven, – there must be Hell.
> Meantime, there is our life here. We-ell?

'Heaven', 'Hell' and 'our life here' correspond to three man-made enclosures in the story, all of which have doors or drawers that conceal. These are the domestic cabinet, the dug-out and the Masonic robe-press, respectively. The dug-out conceals Hell; the press containing 'some flamboyant robe' is Purgatory – 'our life here' – but it is easy to miss the glimpse into Heaven.

One of Clem's childhood memories is that Godsoe 'had a sittin' room full o' Indian curios that him and his wife used to let sister an' me see when we'd been good' (*DC*, p. 247). 'Indian curios' evoke everything that 'India' could mean to a reader of Kipling – delusive peris, disease, filth, suttee and Kali. But they also 'may be heaven': the delights of the senses, colour, endless diversity, seen under Eastern light in the pride of one's youth. The curios too, are 'real/reel' things that Clem has 'had occasion to notice', and, placed in curio-cabinets in a respectable English home, represent all the miseries and splendours that can exist behind the façade of 'ordinary' married life. Armine makes cabinets (p. 248) and thus is a hider of ugliness, disguising from himself his wife's infidelity. But cabinets can also protect Edens from prying eyes.

Keede says, 'That's all that's wanted!' upon hearing that Armine is Clem's uncle. He has seen that, although Clem has lost both parents, he still has relatives: a half-sister, an aunt. All that was wanted to make a Family Square of four – Kipling's symbol of domestic solidarity – was a substitute father, and now he has been found. The words are also spoken by Robert Keede in his detached role of RK the artist, who delights in such symmetries.

Clem's uncle is a simple man, but he is one of the Craft and a maker. And he is named 'Brother Armine' to remind the reader that the list of connotations – armour, Valkyrie, deviser of torments, ghoul – is incomplete. The Arminians or anti-Calvinists 'asserted that God bestows forgiveness and eternal life on all who repent and believe; that He wills all men to be saved'.[32]

One of the dangers which a study of literary indebtedness runs is that it may make its point so thoroughly that the defining features of the subject's art are lost. In the case of Kipling, however, indebtedness is itself a defining feature, and, as we have seen, there are many uses to which he puts voices other than his own. They may be used to suggest the unsayable; they may dissent from the main thrust of a propagandist intent, or speak in the tongues of the pagan. They offer a partial freedom from the limited narrative viewpoint of 'I', while possessing something of I's authority. They are like Chaucer's 'myn author' or framers of the *sententiae* in his tales. In Kipling's dialogue with the past, he finds a substitute for the good collaboration which be sought but never actually found; even more than Stevenson and Conrad, he was attracted to the idea of joint-authorship. *Quartette*, in which 'The Strange Ride' appeared, was a collaborative effort by the Family Square. 'On Greenhow Hill', according to his sister's testimony, owed as much to Kipling's father as to Kipling himself. *The Naulahka* was written with Wolcott Balestier. Kipling seized chances to become involved in the genesis or rewriting of another's book, as in the case of Charles Warren Stoddart's *Misty City*, or the plot-outlines he devised with Rider Haggard.[33] He wrote a play – *The Harbour Watch* – with his daughter Elsie, a school history of England with C. R. L. Fletcher.

Kipling never found even an *il miglior fabbro* – there is no equivalent in his life to the Eliot–Pound partnership. Partly this must be because collaboration is an unstable mode of literary production in an age which promotes the figure of the artist writing out of the integrity of his lone soul, for all the wistful glances it may cast back to the idea of the communal voice of the ballad-maker, to the guild, the *atelier*. The search by Kipling for community and collaboration among his contemporaries was always undermined by a contrary voice telling him that 'the race is run by one and one'. But always available to him was 'patching', the incorporation of voices from the past into the new fabric of words.

There are some things which Kipling wrote where no seams can be found between his voice and that of his literary ancestors. 'The Way through the Woods' has the reputation of being 'so far outside its author's usual range'[34] that one would never have expected him to write it. It is of such immediate and haunting charm that one can carry it around in one's head for years without realising that it is also a multi-inwoven emblem of 'Fiction . . . built on fiction'.

> They shut the road through the woods.
>   Seventy years ago.
> Weather and rain have undone it again,
>   And now you would never know
> There was once a road through the woods
>   Before they planted the trees.
> It is underneath the coppice and heath
>   And the thin anemones.
> Only the keeper sees
>   That, where the ring-dove broods,
> And the badgers roll at ease,
>   There was once a road through the woods.
>
>   (*RF*, p. 87)

The wood, a synecdoche for Nature itself, also means 'a literary miscellany, a collection', as in the Latin *silva* and Jonson's *The Forest, Underwoods* and *Timber, or Discoveries*. It was a conceit borrowed by Stevenson. Kipling dreamed of building 'a veritable three-decker out of chosen and long-stored timber' (*SM*, p. 228). 'Cold Iron' in *Rewards and Fairies* 'gave me my underwood: "What else could I have done?" – the plinth of all structures' (*SM*, p. 190).

One imagines the poem as spoken by an old man. Seventy years is the 'natural span' of human life; 'They' are unknown 'powers' that placed the artist's stranger soul amidst the diversity and profusion of material phenomena. 'Weather and rain' – the circumstances of mortal life – cause the casualties and conflicts within the 'wood' which obscure the artist's way. 'If I had your book to write', Kipling is reported to have said in 1898 to the author of a *History of English Literature in the Victorian Era*, 'I would attempt in a final chapter to discover the path which may lead from the present chaotic conditions of our literature.'[35] But, if the way forward is dubious, so is the way back. The keeper – that part of the personality which acts as the custodian of our literary heritage – is able to discern continuities amidst diversity, but cannot actually carry us into the past. The 'thin anemones' are surely, as they are in Shelley, poetic thoughts, and the badgers are like the 'labour' which sports 'like tame beasts' in 'life's green grove'.[36]

> Yet, if you enter the woods
>   Of a summer evening late,
> Where the night-air cools on the trout-ringed pools
> Where the otter whistles his mate,
>   (They fear not men in the woods,
>   Because they see so few.)
> You will hear the beat of a horse's feet,
> And the swish of a skirt in the dew,
>   Steadily cantering through
>   The misty solitudes,
> As though they perfectly knew
>   The old lost road through the woods. . .
> But there is no road through the woods.

The *silva* is not a teak jungle or a *selva oscura*; there are no harpies or predatory animals, nor is it the haunt of the shikarri, the pursuer of venery who slaughters beasts. The wood does not run wild but is managed, kept for coppice, which is not allowed to grow into big trees but is regularly cut down to meet 'a temporary need' of the age and springs up again (*BW*, p. 285).

Yet desire stirs with memory. Dante's descending vortex is replaced by the rings of the rising trout, the preliminary in 'The Brushwood Boy' to George's courtship ride with Miriam. The swish of the skirt in the misty solitudes supplies the onlooker's need for assurance that there is a female presence – but is it the True Romance drawing a veil lest we see too far into things, or a deceitful fairy queen? The onlooker entertains momentarily the fancy that this presence may provide some way out of the natural, finite world into the infinite, but the temptation to follow 'Natural Supernaturalism' out of Nature is resisted. The mood is a holding-together in tension of the enchanted and the disenchanted; the calm and the restless, a sense of possession and a sense of loss.

The poem is a drawing of the writer's private map of one literary life. Of course it is wonderful that Kipling – or anyone – wrote it, and this analysis does not account for its being as it is and not otherwise. Yet one can see, too, that the elements were there all the time waiting to slide into his mind 'smoothly and orderly as floating timber on a bank-high river'. And, once one thinks about it, this is not really surprising, coming from a man who wrote to his son, 'It may be some help to know that another man has had to face something of the same sort (I mean loneliness *plus* news of a pal's death, *plus* dirt, *plus* a general feeling that the world is a wicked place, which it isn't)' (*OBK*, p. 178).

Appendix I
Hector Macdonald

Kipling would have heard of Macdonald before the Boer War. He claimed to know 'every step of [Roberts's] career by heart' and congratulated him on his 1897 memoirs. These contain details of the exploits of Colour-Sergeant Hector Macdonald during the Afghan campaign and highlight his name in the chapter headings and index.

In February 1900, Kipling was on the train picking up the casualties of Paardeberg, the battle that won Bloemfontein for the British. Many were from Macdonald's Highland Brigade, which lost heavily. An account of Macdonald's tactics may be found in volume III of L. S. Amery's *The Times History of the War in South Africa* (1905). Kipling and Macdonald were in Bloemfontein at the same time (c. 20 March – 20 April), though it is unlikely that they met, as Macdonald was crippled with a foot wound. Kipling was then editing the Bloemfontein *Friend* for Roberts. Among the contributors was Bennet Burleigh, the *Telegraph* correspondent who took Kipling to the skirmish of Karee Siding, and who had been Macdonald's most fervent publicist in Britain after Omdurman. Another war-correspondent admirer of Macdonald and friend of Kipling (not at Bloemfontein) was Conan Doyle.[1]

Macdonald's suicide, I believe, was a factor in Kipling's depression over the outcome of the Boer War. As said before, there is a *latent* political allegory in 'Mrs Bathurst'; the location of the story shifts all over the world – England, Canada, New Zealand, the South Pacific, and finally South Africa. The desertion of a woman of the Empire has its counterpart in the betrayal of an imperial ideal, *Pax Britannica*, feeder of lame ducks and crusher of scorpions. The journey ending in the jungle seems to me to reflect his fears for the abortion of Rhodes's dream of a Cape-to-Cairo railway.

The linking of elements of Macdonald's story to the tale of a wronged woman might have had its origin in the circumstances of Macdonald's secret common-law marriage. Macdonald never publicly acknowledged his wife, probably for fear of jeopardising his career. But I think that Kipling was also struck by the fact that

172

he shot himself on Lady Day (25 March) and that the Paris hotel was named the 'Regina'. Perhaps he thought that it wasn't a coincidence and that Macdonald was making a statement about his service to the late Queen Victoria.

The significance of the name 'Macdonald' cannot be discounted. Macdonald was Kipling's mother's maiden name, and though the two men were not related, Kipling regarded himself as a member of the clan. He adopted the name when travelling incognito during a period of ill-health in May 1891. According to an editor of the *Kipling Journal*, he was 'always interested in reading or hearing anything about the clan Macdonald, and proud of descent therefrom through his mother'. A Boer War anecdote reports his joking remark to a wounded Highlander in Rondebosch hospital, 'Oh, I am a Macdonald on my mother's side, and she taught me never to like a Campbell.' It is a safe conjecture that Kipling would have been especially alert to the story of any clan member who brought infamy upon the name.[2]

On 5–6 February 1913, six weeks short of the tenth anniversary of Macdonald's suicide, the Kiplings stayed at the Regina on their way to Egypt. The Regina was a modern (1900) grand luxury establishment, the cheapest in its class according to the 1907 *Baedeker*. Situated at the present Place des Pyramides, it was quite well placed for the Gare de Lyon, gateway to Marseille and the Orient. According to the present *caissier* it had no particular reputation as a stop-over for travellers to the East, but it would have been a convenient choice. As far as I can discover, he never stayed there again, preferring the Hotel Brighton and the Meurice (*OBK*, pp. 145–7, 199; Carrington, p. 592). One might regard the matter as just a curious coincidence but for known cases of Kipling's feeling compelled to visit places despite their associations of pain or horror. Such are his return to the Gau-Mukh at Chitor after having experienced a sense of 'moral choke-damp' there and his 1920 trip to Lorne Lodge, where the old horror came back.[3]

Appendix II
Kipling and Blake

How much of Blake did Kipling know? 'The Tyger' obviously impressed him; he uses it as a key text in *The Naulahka* (pp. 137, 220); a chapter in *The Jungle Book* is called 'Tiger! Tiger!'. He garbles slightly a stanza of 'The Shepherd' in *Departmental Ditties* (*DV*, p. 35). Tompkins noted that *The Light that Failed* and 'Dayspring Mishandled' read like expansions of the fables of 'The Clod and the Pebble' and 'A Poison Tree' respectively, but she was pointing out an affinity, not claiming a conscious influence.[1] I also detect Blake's influence on the rhythms of 'Blue Roses', the epigraph to chapter 7 of *The Light that Failed*. On the basis of the above, a nodding acquaintance with some of the poems in *Songs of Innocence and of Experience* is indicated.

But there are traces of more extensive knowledge. 'Sure, folly's the only safe way to wisdom', says Mulvaney, in 'On Greenhow Hill' (*LH*, p. 80), which sounds like a hybrid of two of Blake's 'Proverbs of Hell': 'If the fool would persist in his folly he would become wise' and 'The road of excess leads to the palace of wisdom'. 'When a Woman kills a Chicken / Dynasties and Empires sicken' (*D of C*, p. 13) resembles an outgrowth from 'A dog starv'd at his master's gate / Predicts the ruin of the state' ('Auguries of Innocence'). 'It is right it should be so; / Man was made for joy and Woe' from the same poem is inverted by 'Eenee, Meenee, Mainee, Mo! / Man is born to toil and woe' (*LST*, p. 281). Most intriguing of all is a reference in that most painterly of his books, *The Light that Failed*. Dick observes as he turns over the pages of his 'Nungapunga Book', a compendium of visionary nude drawings and verse featuring his friend the Nilghai, 'What a fortune you would have been to Blake, Nilghai! . . . There's a succulent pink-ness about some of these sketches' (*LF*, pp. 126–7).

Where may Dick be supposed to have got the idea that Blake is a luscious flesh-painter? Though not exactly untrue, it is not the first attribute that springs to mind. Nor, though Blake was often celebrated as an original *colourist*, was it a commonplace of Blake criticism in the late Victorian era. But it *is* prominent in Dante

Gabriel Rossetti's 'Supplementary Essay' on Blake's art. This was appended to volume I of both editions of Alexander Gilchrist's *Life of Blake* (1863 and 1880). Rossetti stated that evidence for Blake's 'brotherhood with all the great colourists' may be found in the 'lovingly wrought and realistic flesh-painting which is constantly met with in the midst of his most extraordinary effects' (pp. 417–18). (Dick may be supposed to have taken Rossetti's advice in that essay to study Blake in the British Museum's Print Room.) Indeed, I would say that Blake is one of the many artists 'present' in *The Light that Failed*. Its theme – the frustration of youthful joys and powers by mind-forged manacles – is a very Blakean one. Rossetti praised *The Song of Los* for the 'almost miraculous expression of the glow and freedom of air in closing sunset, in a plate where a youth and maiden, lightly embraced, are racing along a saddened low-lit hill, against an open sky of blazing and changing wonder'.[2] This seems to me, *mutatis mutandis*, to lie behind the 'sunset' imagery in the first chapter of *The Light that Failed* and the description of Dick and Maisie as their later day by the sea draws to a close:

> They ran inland across the waste to warm themselves, then turned to look at the glory of the full tide under the moonlight and the intense black shadows of the furze-bushes. It was an additional joy to Dick that Maisie could see colour even as he saw it, – could see the blue in the white of the mist, the violet that is in gray palings, and all things else as they are, – not of one hue, but a thousand. (*LF*, p. 113)

In that chapter (7), Dick's thrilling description of 'little heavens' which he would show Maisie after 'weeks of crashing through water as black as black marble because it's so deep' (p. 101) might be an unconscious reminiscence of a passage in *The Book of Los* where Los's pent-up energies rend 'with a crash from Immense to Immense' the 'vast solid' 'black as marble of Egypt' in which he has been bound.

Gilchrist's *Life of Blake* was not simply a biography. It provided a generous selection of his poetry, prose and graphic work and an annotated catalogue of his paintings. Until Yeats's 1893 edition, the Gilchrist *Life* and W. M. Rossetti's 1874 edition of the *Poetical Works* were the chief channels by which knowledge of Blake was diffused. Every single definite and apparent allusion to Blake in

Kipling can be accounted for by the supposition that he had read the *Life*. Rossetti's 'Supplementary Essay' highlighted the idea that Blake found truth in extremes and referred students to Blake's *Descriptive Catalogue*. This was reproduced in volume II of the *Life*, as is the Canterbury-pilgrimage engraving.

No collected Blake exists among the contents of Bateman's library or Wimpole Hall, but Kipling had a very retentive memory. Would he have had access to Gilchrist's *Life*? It appears so. There was a heavy emotional commitment to the promotion of Blake on the part of the 'Oxford' Pre-Raphaelites and the Arts and Crafts movement. For them he represented the integrity of the artist-craftsman, the marriage of word and image, the 'two-fold vision' of the everyday world. His hatred of blurring and preference for the 'wiry bounding line' was in conformity with the Pre-Raphaelite dislike of 'Impressionism' and love of clear outline. Gilchrist's *Life* was a favourite book of Burne-Jones, on whose art Blake was an acknowledged influence.[3] After Morris died in 1896, 'Aunt Georgie' recorded that she and Burne-Jones took comfort in reading aloud in the London studio:

> A book that we chose by instinct at this time . . . was Gilchrist's *Life of Blake*, and again Edward said what he had said before about Chaucer and Morris: 'There is so much that is alike in all those great creatures. Blake and Morris resemble each other in so many things – in their splendid simplicity above all.'[4]

I have not traced the edition of Gilchrist owned by Burne-Jones, but the probabilities favour its being the original 1863 edition, which Burne-Jones had helped Rossetti to publish. Possibly he owned the rather more sumptuous 1880 edition too. Kipling, incidentally, would have read the above words, though not before 1904, the year that his aunt's *Memorials of Edward Burne-Jones* appeared. (There is a copy in Bateman's library, with some marginal linings.)

Some signs of the influence of Blake on Kipling's own graphic work may be detected. Ruskin's *Elements of Drawing*, owned by Kipling, recommended the beginner to study the Job engravings for their imaginative power and light effects. I believe that the design of the 'Behemoth and Leviathan' plate, reproduced in Gilchrist,[5] reappears in the *Just So Stories*, playfully turned through an angle of ninety degrees. He also owned Walter Crane's *The*

Decorative Illustration of Books (1896), which reproduces (p. 111) Blake's 'A Cradle Song'. The lettering of Lockwood Kipling's menu-card for Rudyard's birthday[6] has Blakean features, as does Kipling's holograph of 'Imperious, wool-booted sage'.[7]

Affinities between Kipling and Blake are easy to find – the mixture of the esoteric and the simple, the recurrence of symmetries and contrary states of the human soul, innocence and experience being the chief polarities, inversion of the received values of angel and devil, celebration of primal energy, the persistence of the mother–virgin–whore figure, first noted in Swinburne's 'Essay on Blake'. In short, the case for Kipling's finding Blake a good artist to steal from is reasonably strong, and perhaps can be taken further.

Notes

Unless otherwise stated, place of publication is London, and references to the works of Kipling, Chaucer, Ruskin and Swinburne relate to the editions indicated in the Note on Texts (p. ix) and, for Kipling, also in the List of Abbreviations (p. x), which specifies the abbreviations used for Kipling's works. In addition, the notes below use short forms for a number of other sources, as follows.

Ackroyd   Peter Ackroyd, 'Chameleon Genius in the Black Void', *The Times*, 22 Jan 1987, p. 13.
AJM   *Aunt Judy's Magazine*.
Bayley   John Bayley, 'The Puzzles of Kipling', *The Uses of Division* (Chatto and Windus, 1976) pp. 51–81.
Beresford   G. C. Beresford, *Schooldays with Kipling* (New York: G. P. Putnam's Sons, 1936).
Birkenhead   Lord Birkenhead, *Rudyard Kipling* (Weidenfeld and Nicolson, 1978).
Blake   William Blake, *The Complete Writings*, ed. Geoffrey Keynes rev. edn (Oxford: Oxford University Press, 1966).
Bodelsen   C. A. Bodelsen, *Aspects of Kipling's Art* (Manchester: Manchester University Press, 1964).
Brewer   E. C. Brewer, *The Dictionary of Phrase and Fable*, 9th edn (Philadelphia: Claxton, Remset and Haffelfinger, n.d).
Brogan   Hugh Brogan, 'Kipling after Fifty Years', *Journal of the Royal Society of Arts*, cxxiv (Apr 1986) 321–33.
Carrington   Charles Carrington, *Rudyard Kipling*, rev. edn (Harmondsworth: Pelican, 1970).
Cary   *The Vision of Hell by Dante Alighieri, translated by the Rev. Henry Francis Cary, M.A. and illustrated with the designs of M. Gustave Doré* (New York: A. L. Burt, 1890).
Cohen   Morten Cohen, *Rudyard Kipling to Rider Haggard, the Record of a Friendship* (Hutchinson, 1965).
Cornell   Louis Cornell, *Kipling in India* (Macmillan, 1966).
D'israeli   Isaac D'israeli, *Curiosities of Literature* (Routledge, 1867).
DNB   *Dictionary of National Biography*.
Dunsterville   L. C. Dunsterville, *Stalky's Reminiscences* (Jonathan Cape, 1928).
Eliot   T. S. Eliot, 'Rudyard Kipling', introduction to *A Choice of Kipling's Verse*, pbk edn (Faber, 1963) pp. 5–36.
ELT   *English Literature in Transition*.
Ewing   Juliana Ewing, *Six to Sixteen, a Story for Girls*, Uniform Edn (SPCK, 1897).
Gilbert   Elliot Gilbert, *The Good Kipling* (Manchester: Manchester University Press, 1972).

Gilchrist	Alexander Gilchrist, *Life of William Blake*, 2nd edn, 2 vols (Macmillan, 1880).
Henderson	Philip Henderson, *Swinburne: Portrait of a Poet* (Routledge, 1972).
Jarrell	Randall Jarrell, *Kipling, Auden & Co.: Essays and Reviews 1935–1964* (New York: Farrar, Strauss and Giroux, 1980).
KC	Norman Page, *A Kipling Companion* (Macmillan, 1984).
KJ	*Kipling Journal* (1927–).
Kemp	Sandra Kemp, *Kipling's Hidden Narratives* (Blackwell, 1988)
KNR	Edmund Wilson, 'The Kipling that Nobody Read', *The Wound and the Bow*, rev. edn, pbk (Methuen, 1961) pp. 94–161.
Lewis	Lisa A. F. Lewis 'Technique and Experiment in "Mrs Bathurst"', *KJ*, Dec 1980, pp. 36–8.
MacMunn	Lt-Gen. Sir George MacMunn, *The Underworld of India* (Jarrolds, 1933).
MEB	Georgiana Burne-Jones, *Memorials of Edward Burne-Jones*, 2 vols (Macmillan, 1904).
OED	*Oxford English Dictionary*.
Omniana	S. T. Coleridge and R. Southey, *Table Talk and Omniana*, ed. T. Ashe (Bell, 1888).
Orel	Harold Orel (ed.), *Rudyard Kipling: Interviews and Recollections*, 2 vols (Macmillan, 1983).
Page	Norman Page, 'What Happens in "Mary Postgate"?', *ELT*, xxix, no. 1 (1986) 41–7.
Raine	Craig Raine, Introduction to *A Choice of Kipling's Prose* (Faber, 1987).
RG	*The Readers' Guide to Rudyard Kipling's Work*, ed. R. E. Harbord and R. L. Green, 8 vols (Canterbury: privately printed, 1961–72).
Rutherford	Andrew Rutherford (ed.), *Kipling's Mind and Art* (Edinburgh and London: Oliver and Boyd, 1964).
Sandison	Alan Sandison, 'Rudyard Kipling', in *British Writers*, 8 vols, gen. ed. Ian Scott-Kilvert (New York: Charles Scribner's Sons, 1983) vi.
Sartor	Thomas Carlyle, *Sartor Resartus, with Lectures on Heroes and Hero-Worship, Chartism and Past and Present* (Chapman and Hall, 1888).
Swinton	T. C. W. Swinton, 'What Really Happened in "Mrs Bathurst"?', *Essays in Criticism*, xxxviii (Jan 1988) 55–74.
TLS	*The Times Literary Supplement*.
Tompkins	J. M. S. Tompkins, *The Art of Rudyard Kipling* (Methuen, 1959).
Tompkins, Saga	J. M. S. Tompkins, 'Kipling and Nordic Myth and Saga', *English Studies*, lii (Apr 1971) 147–57.
Weygandt	Ann Weygandt, *Kipling's Reading and its Influence on his Poetry* (Philadelphia: University of Pennsylvania Press, 1939).

Wilson   Angus Wilson, *The Strange Ride of Rudyard Kipling* (Secker
                  and Warburg, 1977).

INTRODUCTION AND ACKNOWLEDGEMENTS

1. Quotations in this paragraph from *DV*, p. 587; Wilson, p. 342; *Letters
   of John Keats*, ed. Robert Gittings (Oxford University Press, 1970);
   p. 157; Ackroyd.
2. Brogan, p. 328.
3. Poe and Dickens are two authors whose importance to Kipling is
   confirmed by letters and interviews, but who are seldom mentioned
   in his work. See *KJ*, July 1949, pp. 1–2; Mar 1980, pp. 13–25.
4. See *OED*, s.v. Metagrobolise, which cites Rabelais. In *SC* the word
   means 'mystify' (pp. 107, 119). 'My theory is . . . *The Light that Failed*
   was a sort of inverted, metagrobolised phantasmagoria based on
   Manon' (*SM*, p. 228); cf. the Assistant's comments on the events of
   'At Twenty-Two', a transference of Zola to the Giridih coalfields:
   '*Germinal* upside-down' (*ST*, p. 292). Introduction to the Outward
   Bound Edn (New York: Charles Scribner's Sons, 1897–1937) i, xi, xii.
5. For instance, in 'Mrs Bathurst' the 'cocoanut-woman' whom Spit-Kid
   Jones married (*TD*, p. 343) makes instant sense to anyone recalling
   the line from 'McAndrew's Hymn' about the 'Living God' who 'swells
   the ripenin' cocoanuts an' ripes the woman's breast' (*DV*, p. 123).

CHAPTER 1   THE SIGNIFICANCE OF THE SAHIBA'S
FOREFINGER

1. Bodelsen, pp. 105–17. For 'clou' see *SM*, p. 72. My nomination for the
   clou of 'A Wayside Comedy' is 'if we except Major Vansuythen, who
   is of no importance whatever' (p. 44), for reasons which this book
   should make clear. Randall Jarrell's choice was the name 'Ted'.
2. For example, *KC*, p. 153; Edward Said, Introduction to *Kim* (Harmondsworth: Penguin, 1987) p. 12.
3. Jarrell, p. 360.
4. Raine, p. 28.
5. Wilson, pp. 167–8. Challong is also Browning's Caliban in *Caliban upon
   Setebos*. See *SC*, p. 52, for the impression this made upon Kipling at
   school. For a recent discussion of Kipling's treatment of the 'double'
   see Kemp, pp. 11–28.
6. The story contains imagery drawn from Masonic ritual. Kipling
   frequently draws analogies between disloyalty to the Queen, cursing
   one's mother and betraying the Masonic Mother Lodge. Cf. 'The
   Madness of Private Ortheris', where Ortheris is at pains to deny that
   he cursed Queen Victoria (*PT*, pp. 292–3). For 'traffic' in the sense of
   commerce between man and woman see *OED*, Traffic, sb. 4c. Cf. Olive
   Schreiner, *The Story of an African Farm* (pbk Edn, Harmondsworth:
   Penguin, 1939, pp. 155–6): 'Marriage for love is the beautifullest external

symbol of the union of souls; marriage without it is the uncleanest traffic that defiles the world.' See also *The Tempest*, II.i.143–62, for Gonzalo's ideal commonwealth, which entails the abolition of 'all traffic', including marriage.

7. *Kim* p. 166; *LH*, p. 163. 'The Eye of Allah', *DC*, p. 366: 'You have made her all Jewess' – 'What else was Our Lady?' See also Ch. 2, note 21.
8. Kipling owned a very worn copy of *Typee*. He quotes *White Jacket* in *A Fleet in Being*, his record of his trips with the Channel Squadron. Daniel Karlin sees the influence of *Moby-Dick* in *Captains Courageous* (address to the Kipling Society, 24 Apr 1988). A manuscript cancellation refers to Hawthorne's *The Scarlet Letter* in 'The Propagation of Knowledge'.
9. W. W. Robson, 'Kipling's Later Stories', in Rutherford, p. 260.
10. Ibid., p. 261.
11. John Bayley, 'The Tall and the True', *TLS*, 27 Mar 1987, 317–18.
12. Brogan, 329. See, for example, two interesting essays, William J. Scheik, 'Hesitation in Kipling's "The Phantom 'Rickshaw"', and Terry Caesar, 'Textuality, Entanglement and Revenge in Kipling's 'Dayspring Mishandled"', *ELT*, XXIX, no. 2 (1986) 48–63.
13. Jarrell, p. 358; D. M. G. Roskies, 'Telling the Truth in Kipling and Freud', *English*, XXXI (1982) 4.
14. Cornell, p. 23.
15. For an echo of this see 'The Files', *DV*, p. 351. For Joyce's opinion of Kipling in 1907, see *Selected Letters of James Joyce*, ed. R. Ellmann (Faber, 1975) p. 142: 'If I knew Ireland as well as R. K. seems to know India I fancy I could write something good.'
16. Reproduced in *EV*, p. 25.
17. Bodelsen, pp. 98–9 and n., 129n.
18. I. Masquerier was an early-nineteenth-century history painter. The Pinecoffins are among 'the Devonshire people that were old when the Armada was new'. See the *Youth's Companion* version of *LST*'s 'An English School', 19 Oct 1893 (press-cutting in the Kipling Library); Orel, I, 99; II, 214.
19. *SM*, pp. 109–110; Birkenhead, p. 107.
20. Cohen, p. 64 and plate following p. 56; 'Influence of Names' in D'israeli's *Curiosities of Literature*, apparently read by Kipling at school in the standard one-volume edition and tenaciously retained by his magpie mind, was used in 'The Propagation of Knowledge', *DC*, p. 286. It treats of the power of names to create expectations of certain behaviour in fact and fiction. Several dictionaries of names are in the Library at Bateman's: for example, H. Harnson, *Surnames of the United Kingdom* (Eaton Press, 1911); R. Ferguson, *Surnames as a Science* (Routledge, 1883).
21. Jarrell, p. 339.
22. Kipling's words reported in Mme Schekevitch's *Time Past*, in *KJ*, June 1936, 76.
23. Kipling mentions Jack the Ripper in 'The Smith Administration' (*SS*, II, 427) and 'Fairy-Kist': 'Wollin was on the break of life, and, given wounds, gas and gangrene just at that crisis, why anything – Jack the

Ripperism or religious mania – might come uppermost' (*LR*, pp. 164–5). The Ripper case is evidently behind 'Bertran and Bimi' (*LH*).

24. See Roger Taverner, 'Python Pal Throws Film Lifeline to Sad Cleese', *Sunday Express*, 17 Apr 1988: 'Jones, 45, has written the screenplay for an adult version of "Gulliver". The new approach to the children's favourite is sure to cause controversy.' Bonamy Dobrée, broadcast talk on the Third Programme, reported in *KJ*, Dec 1952, 9–11.

25. *KJ*, June 1932, 49.

26. Søren Kierkegaard, *The Concept of Irony*, tr. Lee M. Capel (Bloomington: Indiana University Press, 1965) pp. 266, 270.

27. *Century Magazine*, III (1882) 83–6; x (1886) 318–19. Frank Stockton, 'The Lady or the Tiger?' and Other Stories, ed. Francis R. Gemme (New York: Armont, 1968) p. 6.

28. Stockton, a short-story writer remembered chiefly for his 'Rudder Grange' books, belonged to the genteel East Coast tradition of American letters. He had editorial duties on both *St Nicholas* and *Century* magazines, as well as being a frequent contributor. Both magazines published Kipling's fiction during the 1890s; Kipling unsuccessfully tried to place 'The Dusky Crew' with *St Nicholas* as a schoolboy in 1879. Kipling met Stockton, at that time a *Century* man, at a publishers' luncheon on 13 February 1892. See C. M. Wright, 'How "St Nicholas" Got Rudyard Kipling', *Princeton University Library Chronicle*, xxxv (1974) 263–4. The zenith of Stockton's fame was the period 1880–95. The title 'The Disturber of Traffic' may echo Stockton's 'The Discourager of Hesitancy', and 'Cupid's Arrows' (*PT*) may owe something to 'Our Archery Club'.

29. Tsvetan Todorov, *The Fantastic*, tr. Richard Howard (Ithaca: Cornell University Press, 1973). See also Rosemary Jackson, *Fantasy: The Literature of Subversion* (London: Methuen, 1981): '"Meanings" recede indefinitely with "truth" as a mere vanishing point of the text' (p. 38). Unlike Jackson I do not consider that fantasy rules out an allegorical interpretation; this seems to me to be one of the alternatives open to the hesitating reader, especially when nineteenth-century painting and writing is under consideration.

30. That Stockton's story was seen as a comment on marriage was not lost on some contemporary readers; see '"The Lady or the Tiger?" or Both?', *Century*, IV (1883) 318–19. This includes the lines: 'Which door to open? Death or life? / A beast of prey! A lawful wife! / No wonder if he gasped and tarried. / We all do, when we're killed – or married.'

31. See Burton Pollin, 'Poe and Kipling: A "Heavy Debt" Acknowledged', *KJ*, Mar 1980, 13–25. Kipling's copy of *Tales of Mystery and Imagination*, seemingly acquired during the 1890s, shows most signs of wear at 'Thou Art the Man'.

32. Hemingway, *A Moveable Feast* (London: Jonathan Cape, 1964) p. 75. *RG* and Jeffrey Meyers independently noticed a similarity between Kipling's and Hemingway's descriptions of their 'omission' techniques. Meyers argued cogently that Hemingway had derived it from his study of Kipling. See Meyers, *Hemingway* (London: Macmillan, 1986) pp. 114, 139.

33. The relationship of the conventions of Kipling's stories to the rituals of *tableaux vivants*, romps such as 'Kissing the Queen of Sheba', word-games, rebuses, the Punch and Judy show, and so on, would be worth investigating.

CHAPTER 2 AUNT JUDY, RUSKIN, CARLYLE

1. See also Tompkins, *Saga*; Carrington, p. 69. A letter at Wimpole Hall from Joel Chandler Harris replying to an inquiry from Kipling theorises that 'Miss Meadows' represents Nature. Kipling was to use this idea in 'The United Idolators'.
2. Kipling's library holdings of myth, folklore and related studies are too numerous to detail, but include W. Crooke, *An Introduction to the Popular Religion and Folklore of Northern India* (1894); H. Bayley, *The Lost Language of Symbolism* (1912); Tawney and Penzer, *The Ocean of Story*; Charlotte Burne, *Handbook of Folklore* (1914). (Bateman's.)
3. See J. W. Gleeson White, *English Illustration: 'The Sixties': 1855–70* (London: Constable, 1897) p. 114; *SM*, p. 33.
4. Lady Gregory, *Journals* (1946), entry for 20 July 1919, in *KJ*, July 1948, 17; *SM*, p. 7. The 1876 volume's 'Little Brown Girls' by S. M. Gidley contains extracts from a glowing tribute paid by senior girls at a Lahore mission school to the kindness and able teaching of 'Mr Kipling [i.e. Rudyard's father], of the School of Design' (699). The 1879 volume also appears to have been read by Kipling at some point. It contains poems 'From the Swedish of Stagnelius'; Kipling gives 'Kaspar's Song in "Varda"' (*TD*, p. 212) the identical subtitle. 'The Dog in History' mentions a 'Learned Dog' whose act climaxes in feigning illness and death (p. 297). This might have been the germ of 'Garm' (*AR*). Kipling owned H. R. F. Gatty's *Juliana Horatia Ewing and her Books* (Bateman's).
5. *AJM*, xiv (1876) 479–82, 516–21.
6. The folklorist Andrew Lang's article 'Mythology' for the 1911 edition of the *Encyclopaedia Britannica* critically summarises the approaches of contemporaneous British mythological systems, concentrating on Max Müller (whom he regards as completely exploded), Herbert Spencer and Frazer. For some references to Max Müller in Kipling see *PT*, p. 267; *KI*, pp. 176, 205; *DV*, pp. 29, 80. Muller of 'In the Rukh' (*MI*) has been given some of his qualities, notably a tendency to Hellenise India. Kipling met Frazer in 1921 when they received honorary degrees from the Sorbonne; he owned a volume of Frazer's *Folklore in the Old Testament*, 3 vols (1918), and his annotated translation of Apollodorus (Bateman's). The 'Neminaka café' in 'Dayspring Mishandled', which treats the literary world as a cut-throat priesthood, probably derives from Chapter 1 of *The Golden Bough*, which sets out to investigate the mysterious origin of the custom at Nemi by which the priest of Diana was stalked and killed by his successor. Kipling advises Haggard to read Tylor's *Primitive Culture* for confirmation of the theory that 'the world's *very* limited modicum of thinking was done millions of years

ago' (Cohen, pp. 138–9), but it is not clear from the context whether he himself had done so.

7. See George P. Landow, *Victorian Types, Victorian Shadows* (London and Boston, Mass.: Routledge and Kegan Paul, 1980), esp. pp. 47–50; F. L. Cross and E. A. Livingstone (eds), *The Oxford Dictionary of the Christian Church*, 2nd edn (Oxford University Press, 1974), s.v. Allegory, Types.

8. George P. Landow, *The Aesthetic and Critical Theories of John Ruskin* (Princeton, NJ: Princeton University Press, 1971) pp. 349–51.

9. Kipling gave his daughter Elsie most of Juliana Ewing's books (Wimpole Hall Library). 'The Last of the Stories' (1888) evidences his knowledge of *Jackanapes* (*AF*, p. 317).

10. *AJM*, xvii (1879) 707.

11. Cornell, p. 35; and *EV*, *passim*.

12. For example, Holman Hunt, *The Hireling Shepherd, Claudio and Isabella, The Awakening Conscience, The Light of the World*; D. G. Rossetti, '*Ecce Ancilla Dei*'; Hughes, *April Love*. See *The Pre-Raphaelites* (Tate Gallery and Penguin, 1984) for descriptions of the frames.

13. Christabel Maxwell, *Mrs Gatty and Mrs Ewing* (Constable, 1949) pp. 220–2.

14. *SM*, pp. 11–14; Kipling, 'An English School' (see Ch. 1, note 18).

15. *MEB*, *passim*; John Christian, 'Ruskin and Burne-Jones', in Leslie Parris (ed.), *Pre-Raphaelite Papers* (Tate Gallery, 1984) pp. 184–205. For Aunt Georgie's 'bringing tidings of comfort from *Fors Clavigera* to some gnarled unlettered old woman' or thinking that '*The Seven Lamps of Architecture* on every working man's table' would improve the world, see Angela Thirkell, *Three Houses* (Oxford University Press, 1931); in Orel, ii, 308–9. Sara Anderson was secretary successively to Ruskin, Burne-Jones and Kipling (Birkenhead, p. 407).

16. Ruskin, 'Mythic Schools of Painting', Lecture ii, *The Art of England; Works*, xxxiii, 290–1.

17. In Bateman's; *PT*, p. 314. The story subjects Ruskin's 'woman worship' to criticism. See *Kim*, p. 326, for a Ruskinian echo: Kim pictures a woman freed 'from the shows of this life . . . desiring nothing, causing nothing'.

18. See also *DC*, p. 98. In *SC* and *SM*, Kipling implies that M'Turk was the Ruskin reader, but Beresford suggests that Kipling was the enthusiast. Beresford, p. 150: 'Gigger flung Ruskin into it'. Dunsterville wrote of Kipling's attempts to improve the taste of his compeers, '*Fors Clavigera* and *Sartor Resartus* we absorbed in silence.' See Orel, i, 27–8; *KJ*, June 1932, 53; *KJ*, Apr 1945, 4.

19. Which four? One suspects Kipling of a pointed allusion here. My guess is that they include Letters lxxix and lxxx (July, Aug 1877), where Ruskin attacks Whistler and usury respectively. They have a general relevance to the Stalky story 'The Impressionists'. See also *DC*, p. 98.

20. In a little-known story, 'The Legs of Sister Ursula', Kipling imitates the style in which Ruskin retells the legend of St Ursula.

21. *Sartor* i.vii, p. 30. Ruskin, *Works*, xxvii, 397: 'Mother-naked sits Theseus', in *Fors*, Letter xxiii, 'The Labyrinth', which seems to

have particularly lodged in Kipling's memory. It reprints a verse-skit purportedly written by a 'mangled convict' called Cohen, whose 'gentle mother dear' had taught him to write (cf. 'Miriam Cohen') and a fearsome description of the geography of Dante's hell.

22. Birkenhead, p. 356.
23. See Dunsterville, p. 40. For references to Carlyle in Kipling's work see 'The Files' (*DV*, p. 351), 'A Burgher of the Free State' (Sussex Edn, xxx, 154), and *SM*, p. 21. Kipling's set of Carlyle was the Boston Edn (n.d.), in the library at Bateman's.
24. See Cohen, p. 40, Kipling to Haggard, 1925: 'Like olives and caviare and asafoetida, I'm an acquired taste.' The last item suggests that he considers himself a bit Teufelsdrockhian.
25. Tompkins, p. 88.
26. For example Cohen, p. 157: Kipling refers to 'The Gardener' as a 'yarn'. See also Cornell, p. 135, on Kipling's fondness for clothing-imagery; and L. A. F. Lewis, 'Some Links between the Stories in Kipling's *Debits and Credits*', *ELT*, xxv, no. 2 (1982) 77.
27. Wilson, pp. 342–3.

CHAPTER 3   PIGS, SERPENTS, CANNIBALS, BATS AND BEES

1. Cornell, p. 133.
2. Among others are '.007', where the Great Overseer is like unto a station-yard master, and 'The Horse Marines' (a garage-owner). 'The Bull that Thought' wittily develops the proposition that 'God is a Frenchman'. A fairly civilised God, the landowner 'M. Voiron' owes his charm to his mother, who is both the Vierge Marie and Marianne, the pleasant land of France.
3. For example, in the First Shepherd's Play, in the Wakefield Cycle, the Christ child is given a 'spruce coffre' to symbolise his mortal body.
4. For example, in 'The Strange Ride of Morrowbie Jukes', 'False Dawn', 'The Broken Link Handicap', '"Sleipner" Late "Thurinda"'. 'Lived in the pigskin' (i.e. 'in the saddle') was a phrase used by Kipling's editor E. Kay Robinson (*KJ*, Mar 1932, 19). In *Fors*, Ruskin confessed to hating his name because it meant 'pigskin'.
5. See 'The Undertakers' (*JB2*.) 'The Veterans' (1907) commemorates the Mutiny survivors (*DV*, p. 305).
6. See also 'The Arrest of Lieutenant Golightly' (*PT*). See analysis in Gilbert, pp. 52–60, who could have gone further. The 'hero' is revealed as a putrefying mushroom on a dunghill.
7. Rutherford, p. 258.
8. See MacMunn, pp. 50, 96–102, on the ubiquity of the stone lingam in Hindu temples and domestic altars as it struck a contemporary of Kipling, whose awareness also emerges in *LF*, pp. 127–9. Dick draws the naked Nilghai shining up Nelson's Column surrounded by many wives. 'Observe the virtuous horror of the lions!'
9. The composition date fits my hypothesis that the story originated in

the Kiplings' inability to mourn publicly the death of Wolcott Balestier. The epigraph poem, about a blind sea-serpent and his bride, evidently refers to a different serpent pair, as the setting is the South Seas. For a possible source see H. K. F. Gatty, 'Sea Giants', *AJM*, xiv (1876) 462, 469: 'Why is it that when there is "nothing in the papers", the Great Sea Serpent, or some other fabulous monster, is fished up from unfathomable depths . . . ?' True natural history would 'enable the Sea Serpent to rest in the obscurity that is his due, – if only wonder-seekers would learn to take as much interest in strange facts, as they do in sensational fictions'.

10. Tompkins, p. 131; Philip Mason, *Kipling: The Glass, the Shadow and the Fire* (London: Jonathan Cape, 1975) p. 211; *KJ*, Oct 1940, p. 23.

11. Birkenhead, p. 301. Cohen, p. 107: '[Kipling] added that his experiences during the war had not raised his opinion of the Press!'

12. For the origin of the masked, bat-carrying Harlequin in the medieval demon Hellequin and his troupe, and Hellequin's wooing of the Fairy Morgue, see Enid Welsford, *The Fool*, pbk edn (New York: Anchor, 1961) pp. 291–3. *AJM*, xvii (1879) 26–7, recounts the link between the Wild Huntsman and the 'Maisne Hellequin'. Brewer (in the library at Bateman's) cites under 'Wild Huntsman' traditions identifying him with the Wandering Jew and a German aristocrat. The narrator in 'The Village that Voted' derives the 'Gubby Dance' from Hone's *Every-Day Book*. The entry for 8 May 1826 (ii, 324–5) describes the Helston 'Furry', clearly the source. The Hone index entry immediately preceding 'Helston, Cornwall' is 'Hell, a pageant representation of'. This refers to the 'Cow-mass' of Dunkirk, which included a Hell-mouth, Lucifer leading a chained archangel Michael, a Harlequin, and a huge dancing figure of a jewelled female, whose 'eyes and head turned very naturally' (ibid., pp. 435–7). See William Hone, *The Every-Day Book*, 3 vols (Tegg, n.d.). It is worth looking up as a pointer to Kipling's creative use of source-material.

13. Kipling was strongly impressed by *Lear*. See 'The Propagation of Knowledge', *DC*, esp. pp. 277, 289.

14. Carrie Kipling's diary records Kipling working on it in 1914, but his preface says he wrote it in 1913 (*KC*, pp. 132–3); this I see not as evidencing Kipling's bad memory but as a direction to read it as 'a tale of 1913'. His first draft may date from then.

15. Nellie Farren (1848–1904) died in West Kensington, not Africa, *pace* Masquerier, who is ignorant about genuine artists. One of her triumphs was the burlesque *The Forty Thieves*. See *DNB*, 1901–1911 Supp.

16. *Dictionary of American Biography* (1930 edn), v, entry for Joseph William Drexel. Note the Drexelius who 'estimated the total of the damned at one hundred thousand millions' (*Omniana*, s.v. Hell; Kipling's copy is in the library at Bateman's.

17. See entries for Astarte in *Lemprière's Classical Dictionary* and Brewer; Milton, *Paradise Lost*, i. 437–9.

18. 'Huckley' is intended to suggest 'Ugly', 'Hughli' and perhaps 'Hockley i' the Hole', the Restoration bear-pit. The 'village' has no bounds of time or space. See *EV*, p. 489: 'Till the Hughli silts on the plains of Wilts'.

19. Jarrell, p. 357.
20. Birkenhead, p. 339.
21. For Penfentenyou as Canadian see Bodelsen, p. 16. See also *The Cambridge History of the British Empire* (Cambridge: Cambridge University Press, 1959) III, 416–32. Kipling endorses Jameson's judgement of Laurier 'that dam' dancing-master' (*SM*, p. 196). See Michael Brock, 'Outside his Art', *KJ*, Mar 1988, 20 and n. 43, for Kipling's alarm at Canada's reciprocity agreement with the United States (1911).
22. The *Encyclopaedia Britannica* (1911) gives the area of England as 50, 851 square miles and the area of the Bombay Presidency as 122, 984 square miles.
23. The 'Black Thought' is 'a horror of great darkness which *drops upon a man unbidden*, and *drives* him to think *lucidly, connectedly, with Cruikshank detail* of all the accidents whereby, through no fault of his own, he may be cut off from his work, and forced to leave those he loves defenceless to the world' (*BW*, p. 14, my italics). See Haggard's diary, 1918: 'He has an active faith in the existence of a personal devil' (Cohen, p. 99). For literary antecedents, see Kipling's use of Lesage's *Le Diable boiteux*, 'My Christmas Caller', *KI*, pp. 125–35.
24. For example, in 'On the Gate' (*DC*) and 'Uncovenanted Mercies' (*LR*).
25. Cf. 'You're always so extreme' (*D of C*, p. 394); 'Oh, but you're so-o extreme' (*SM*, p. 197).
26. See Milton, *Paradise Lost*, I.768–75. Pope, *The Dunciad*, IV.79–84, on the followers of the Goddess of Dulness: 'Not closer, orb in orb, conglob'd are seen / The buzzing Bees about their dusky Queen', while others 'Gently drawn, and struggling less and less, / Roll in her Vortex, and her power confess'. For Kipling's familiarity with Pope, see *EV*, p. 57; *DC*, pp. 281, 285.
27. Horace, *Satires*, I.ii.24, Kipling was a lifelong rereader of Horace.
28. Wilson, p. 156.
29. For Kipling's interest in Byron and especially *Don Juan*, see *SS*, I, 22, and II, 234, 247, 248; *SC*, p. 227; 'To the Address of W. W. H.', *EV*, pp. 404–8; *KI*, p. 124.
30. See Nina Auerbach, *Woman and the Demon* (Cambridge, Mass.: Harvard University Press, 1982) for a detailed treatment of the mythic power of the Victorian victim woman.
31. Louis Cornell, Introduction to 'The Man Who Would Be King' and Other Stories* (Oxford: Oxford University Press, 1987) p. xxxvi.
32. See Matthew 12:36.

CHAPTER 4   KIPLING AND DANTE (I): 'MRS BATHURST'

1. Carrington, p. 436.
2. Bodelsen, ch. 12 (title); Richard Holmes, 'My Unknown Kipling', *Sunday Telegraph*, 4 Jan 1987, p. 14; Carrington, p. 435; Wilson, pp. 296–9. For a summary of the problems, see *RG*, IV, 1806–10. See *KJ*, nos 34, 43, 47, 48, 90, 91, 95, 96, 97, 109, 164.
3. *KJ*, Dec 1967, p. 14.

4. *KJ* Oct 1938, pp. 91–5. Hall theorised that Vickery had had concussion with amnesia. He and a friend signed a contract with Kipling to produce a play of 'Mrs Bathurst', but the friend had a nervous breakdown.
5. Raine, pp. 14–18.
6. Hermione Lee, Introduction to *Traffics and Discoveries* (Harmondsworth: Penguin, 1987) p. 24.
7. Keats to Brown, 30 Sep 1830.
8. Tompkins, pp. 89–91; Bodelsen, pp. 124–54; Gilbert, pp. 94–117. See also Sandison, p. 194.
9. Gilbert, pp. 115–17.
10. Ibid., p. 90.
11. Ibid., p. 102.
12. Bodelsen, p. 135.
13. Possibly we are to think she has died from an abortion; Vickery's face reminds Pyecroft of 'things in bottles in those herbalistic shops at Plymouth – preserved in spirits of wine. White an' crumply things – previous to birth as you might say' (*TD*, p. 355). Vickery has also deserted his fifteen-year-old daughter. 'Who's to look after the girl?' is an unanswered question posed by the story. A future on the streets is a likely scenario, given her age.
14. Gilbert, p. 104.
15. The Mars-Venus myth is followed through in Carpenter Rigdon's curious nickname 'Crocus'. *Crocus Martis* and *Crocus Veneris* were alchemical names for oxides of iron and copper respectively. Crocus leaves the ship when ''oisted out with a winch' (*TD*, p. 354), which recalls the net (a 'crocus bag' is an alternative name for a gunny sack) in which Mars and Venus were hoisted to Olympus. Crocus is the link-man between Mrs Bathurst and Vickery – he takes Vickery to the circus – and his name 'links' iron and copper. It also means 'a quack doctor' (*OED*).
16. Tompkins, p. 90; Bodelsen, p. 128.
17. M. Harrison and B. Waters, *Burne-Jones* (New York: G. P. Putnam's Sons, 1973) pp. 96–100. The liaison lasted from 1867 to 1871, causing great suffering to Georgiana. See Jan Marsh, *Pre-Raphaelite Sisterhood* (Quartet, 1985) pp. 270–6. Kipling's disapproval of the *ménage à trois* and the emphasis in his work on covering up family scandals may derive in part from this. His aunt's discreet *MEB* appeared in the same year as 'Mrs Bathurst'.
18. Ovid, *Heroides*, Loeb Classical Library edn. See for example ii.74: est, cuius amans hospita capta dolo est' ('This is he whose wiles betrayed the hostess that loved him'); and ii.132–3: 'Est sinus, adductos modice falcatus in arcus; ultima praerupta cornua mole rigent' ('There is a bay, whose bow-like lines are gently curved in sickle shape; its outermost horns rise rigid and in rock-bound mass'). Cf. 'Mrs Bathurst': 'At either horn of the bay the railway line cut just above highwater mark, ran round a shoulder of piled rocks, and disappeared' (*TD*, p. 340). Ovid, *Opera Omnia*, ed. Weise, 3 vols (Leipzig, 1887), is in the library at Bateman's. Kipling refers to Ovid's *Tristia* (*PT*, p. 327) and quotes from the *Metamorphoses* (*DC*, p. 378). *RG*, IV, 1789, suggests

that 'Phyllis' is Kipling's mistake for 'Fillis', a Johannesburg circus-owner. But the narrator is reporting what he *hears*; 'Phyllis' might be his understanding of Pyecroft's 'Fillis'. In any case, Kipling was using his sources creatively. He changed 'M'Benji' siding to 'M'Bindwe' (*RG*, IV, 1796).

19. Kim Landers pointed out the Chaucerian parallel. Cf. 'Tess's country' in 'My Sunday at Home' (*DW*, p. 343), a tale about disorder underlying the green orderliness of England. 'Tess's country' is haunted by the spirit of the sacrificed woman, who, turned witch-like, plays fantastic tricks.

20. This derives from Ewing, VII, 69. The narrator's great grandmother 'took off a watch and chain and hung them on my neck. It was a small French watch with an enamelled back of dark blue, on which was the word "Souvenir" in small pearls.'

21. Gilbert, p. 110; Sandison, p. 194.

22. C. W. Stoddard quoting RK during the Naulakha period: 'Do not, if possible, create a completely new set of characters to fill yacht in last chapter, but gather in people mentioned incidentally all along the book; thus the reader has not to meet new people late in the day' (Orel, II, 214).

23. Gilbert, p. 108.

24. Bodelsen, p. 141.

25. Ibid., p. 144.

26. Bodelsen, pp. 153–4. Kipling to Haggard, 1905: 'Pity one can't sprinkle lime over illustrators – same as slugs' (Cohen, p. 59). 'With the Night Mail' was the sufferer. See Lewis, pp. 36–8.

27. Bodelsen, p. 145n.

28. Swinton (pp. 64–5) proposed a corporeal spirit which could be struck by lightning and buried. This is stretching the concept of 'spirit' a little far.

29. Information on the *Cape Times* from Jeremy Lawrence.

30. *DNB*, 2nd Supp., 3 vols, II. For a contemporary, partisan, Scottish view see David Cromb, *Hector Macdonald* (Stirling: Eneas Mackay, 1903) esp. pp. 41–2, 57–8, 79–85, 92, 115. Trevor Royle, *Death before Dishonour: The True Story of Fighting Mac*, (Edinburgh: Mainstream Publishing, 1982), is a well-researched account; see pp. 91, 108, 125.

31. Carrington, p. 377; Wilson, p. 232.

32. Hilton Brown, *Rudyard Kipling* (Hamish Hamilton, 1945) p. 137.

33. For example, 'What, exactly, are all these "prophylactics" you've ordered *for*?' A concern with the incidence of venereal disease in the armed forces appears sporadically in Kipling's work: Larry Tighe in 'Love o' women' (*MI*); 'The Army of a Dream' (*TD*, p. 262); *SM*, p. 56. See also *LR*, p. 282. But the hypothesis that Vickery has syphilis (*RG*, IV, 1810) lacks support; he has none of Tighe's symptoms.

34. Raine, p. 16.

35. 'The Immortal Exile', *AJM*, XIII (1875) 45.

36. In the library at Bateman's.

37. Cary, p. 72.

38. Robert Buchanan, 'The Voice of the Hooligan', *Contemporary Review*,

LXXVI (Dec 1899) 774–89; in R. L. Green (ed.), *Kipling: The Critical Heritage* (Routledge, 1971).

39. Cary, p. 90.
40. Ibid., p. 81.
41. Ibid.
42. Treated by Spenser (*Faerie Queene*, II.x) and Swinburne (*Locrine*, 1887), it contains the 'two women in one house' theme.
43. 'Mormonistic' in the *Windsor Magazine* version, so 'Mormonastic' is deliberate. See *DC*, p. 89, for 'monastic microbes'.
44. Lewis, p. 37. She tentatively theorised that Boy Niven 'stands for a homosexual variety' of 'lawless love'; the argument of this chapter and her *aperçu* were reached totally independently of one another, which bears out my contention that Kipling 'solutions' are attainable by many pathways, just as Kipling said.
45. John Shearman has suggested to me that we may be intended to think that the tramp is a Cape coloured. Perhaps the men are supposed to diverge in their identification of the 'mate'. Whereas Pyecroft has Niven on his mind – he is the one who knows Niven's whereabouts – Pritchard is bothered by the 'unnaturalness' of Capetown. This would fill out the sentence 'Pritchard covered his face with his hands for a moment, like a child shutting out an ugliness' (*TD*, p. 365). RK's impression of Capetown in 1891 was of an abundance of *hubshees* of the sort that his *ayah* had told him 'slept in such posture as made it easy for the devils to enter their bodies' (*SM*, p. 95). A fearful thing to tell a child.
46. Hooper refers to 'your Mr Vickery' (*TD*, p. 348) at a point when all that he has been told about the deserter is that he is 'a warrant' oo's name begins with a V.' (p. 345); he has put two and two together from reading a 'wanted' description.
47. The 'Devil's Farm' is found in Coleridge's 'The Devil's Walk'; Kipling recommended Coleridge to the young A. W. Baldwin for his 'habit of approaching the ordinary at extraordinary angles' (Orel, II, 301–2). The Boy Niven episode has its origin in a Vancouver land-deal in which Kipling was cheated by an 'English Boy'; see *SM*, p. 107. *SS*, II, 56, clearly refers to the same incident, though there is a curious discrepancy in the dates.
48. From the *TD* version Kipling dropped a *Windsor Magazine* sentence describing the teak forest: 'It's all black, boggy soil' (*Windsor Magazine*, Sept 1904, 385), which had related the jungle more closely to the barren island. But he strengthened the toad-like qualities of Niven. Cf. ''e stopped in that bog full o' ferns' (*Windsor*) and ''e 'opped about' (*TD*). Kipling's tinkerings show, I think, an attempt to make things neither too difficult nor too easy for the reader.
49. Cf. the death of McIntosh Jellaludin, *PT*, pp. 333–5.
50. One of Kipling's earliest extant poems, unpublished by him, was 'Job's Wife', a dramatic monologue spoken by a tempter to suicide (*EV*, p. 49).
51. Lewis, p. 37.
52. Or with partial second sight; the totally blind heroine of 'They', placed

between 'The Army of a Dream' and 'Mrs Bathurst' in *TD*, has total access to the spirit world.
53. *OBK*, p. 127; Birkenhead, pp. 274–5.
54. Carrington, p. 565.
55. See the preface verse to the *Harper's Weekly* version of 'Children of the Zodiac' (*RG*, III, 1274): ' "Now whom shall I kiss?" said Venus, / And "What can I kill?" said Jove, / And "Look at the forge" said Vulcan, / And "Smut's on my wings" said Love.'

CHAPTER 5   KIPLING AND DANTE (II): HOME AND FRIENDS

1. *AJM*, xvII (1879) 713.
2. See Michael Lynch, ' "Here is Adhesiveness": From Friendship to Homosexuality', *Victorian Studies*, xxIx (Autumn 1985) 67–96.
3. See Christopher Ricks, *Tennyson* (Macmillan, 1974) pp. 218–19; Ricks, I think, overstresses Tennyson's unself-consciousness about the potential dangerousness of the 'double-natured' ideal, but he does show that such unself-consciousness became more difficult to maintain as the century wore on. Alfred Austin in 'Mr Swinburne', *Temple Bar*, xxIv (July 1869) 457–74, holds Tennyson's example partly responsible for Swinburne's 'effeminacy'.
4. Birkenhead, p. 87.
5. Carrington, p. 69.
6. Whitman's influence on Kipling is important, but I do not know of any detailed account of it. In Kipling the eight-legged beast is an image of bisexuality, sometimes dangerous, as in the 1888 ' "Sleipner", Late "Thurinda"' (Haining, pp. 156–63). It is linked to the trickster figure of Loki: 'His legend includes animal metamorphoses of the most obscene character. In the shape of a mare he became the mother of the eight-legged horse of Odin [i.e. Sleipner]' (Andrew Lang, entry for Mythology in the *Encyclopaedia Britannica*, 1911). In 'Stream Tactics' (*TD*) the artist's joyous freedom from the limitations of gender is represented by forcing a policeman to take a ride in a (female) car called 'the Octopod', the driver, 'Kysh', standing for Kipling's personal Daemon. Tompkins, *Saga*, was the first to link Sleipner to 'Steam Tactics'. Interestingly, in 'A really good Time', written during the early period of his lionisation in London during 1890, Kipling represents himself as attracting speculation about where he stands on the 'Woman Question', whether he is a literary imposter and whether his style is 'hermaphroditic'. (*AF*, pp. 242–4.)
7. Carrington, p. 435.
8. *Kipling's Horace*, ed. C. E. Carrington (privately printed for the Kipling Society, 1980) p. 61.
9. See *SS*, I, 114. See also ibid., p. 310 (where he sees Doré as a suitable illustrator of a city of *devils*); *LH*, p. 376; Cohen, p. 152.
10. *ELT*, xxIx, no. 2 (1985) 124. See also Elsie B. Adams, 'No Exit: An Explication of Kipling's "Wayside Comedy" ', *ELT*, xI, no. 3 (1967) 180–3; and Hugh Haughton, who in his introduction to *Wee Willie*

Winkie (Harmondsworth: Penguin, 1988) comments 'It [i.e. "A Wayside Comedy"] is a colonial Wayside Inferno' (p. 27).

11. Other factors aiding self-identification with Dante include the following. Rossetti's father had advanced an (untenable) theory that Dante had been a Freemason and that *The Divine Comedy* was a Masonic allegory; Kipling may have learnt of this through his family or Masonic histories. Dante was around five or six when his mother died, the same age at which Kipling was separated from his mother. Lastly, Doré's frontispiece gives Dante a very Kiplingesque cleft chin!

12. Cornell, p. 94; 1891 version of *The City of Dreadful Night* (the Calcutta travel diary, not the *LH* short story) p. 40. In the *SS* version (II, 234) the Dantean allusion is not so clear.

13. Cary, p. 75.

14. *AF*, p. 298. See also 'The Phantom 'Rickshaw', *WWW*, p. 148; *KI*, pp. 83, 122–4; *OBK*, p. 124; *LR*, p. 381: 'Usen't there to be a notice hereabouts requesting visitors to leave all their hopes behind them?'

15. Cary, pp. 25–8.

16. Tompkins, p. 195, on 'The Crab that Played with the Sea' (*JSS*).

17. *West Indies Committee Circular*, 15 May 1930.

18. Cary, p. 66.

19. L. A. F. Lewis, 'The Historical Background to the Eye of Allah', unpublished talk given to the Kipling Society.

20. Dante, quoted in D'israeli, p. 336.

21. Cary, pp. 56–7. 'Teem' (*TSD*) is set in Cahors; Teem the dog, like Dante, exercises his finest art in the darkest places.

22. That is, he sees the threesome as if they were the 'three military men' in the Circle of the Sodomites, who 'whirled round together in one restless wheel' (canto XVI; Cary, p. 83.)

23. Birkenhead, pp. 41–2.

24. In 'The United Idolaters' the suspicions of 'Mister' (German for 'crapper') *have* created evil among the boys. The housemasters refuse to see anything in the 'Tar Baby' cult, in which 'Miss Meadows's' bed-cord is strained to the utmost, but an outbreak of 'animal spirits'. Stalky knows better.

25. Cornell, pp. 96–7; *KI*, p. 84. MacMunn, writing about the Kipling era, singled out Lucknow, Lahore and Peshawar as notorious for 'a street of . . . eunuch courtesans who dressed as women and farded as such, play a strange perverse and demoniacal profession' (p. 201).

26. 'Typhoid at Home' (*KI*, pp. 69–77) was written during this period. This should be borne in mind when assessesing the objectivity of Kipling's report on the state of Lahore's cow-byres.

27. Wilson, p. 72.

28. See items in *EV* written 1882–4: marginalium to 'A Dedication', (p. 117); 'El Dorado' (pp. 168–9); 'The City of the Heart' (pp. 224–5). These contain some of the raw material for 'The Strange Ride'.

29. Evelyne Hanquart, 'Kipling and Dante', *KJ*, June 1985, 18–26.

30. Cary, pp. 78–9 n. 1.

31. Ibid., p. 82.

32. Except, just possibly, in the monogram Kipling placed at the beginning of the pocket edition.

33. 'Gunga-Wallah' was early-twentieth-century Forces slang for male prostitute (Partridge, *Dictionary of Slang and Unconventional English*). See also 'Gonga'.

34. Browning's 'Gold Hair: A Tale of Pornic', the source of the name, employs the same pun, but in order to draw attention to the meretricious beauty of the dead girl who hides money in her hair.

35. *DV*, p. 63; Cornell, p. 170, printed in the Allahabad *Pioneer* on 16 Dec 1884. Dass fuels a fire with 'dried bents, sand-poppies and drift-wood'. The poppy symbolised in Kipling the promise of young love; cf. the use of drift-wood, grass-tufts and a 'yellow sea-poppy' in *LF*, p. 8.

36. Hanquart (see note 29) believes that the dog derives from the speckled panther, symbolic of pleasure or luxury, in *Inferno*, I.

37. Kipling refers to this quotation in 'Watches of the Night' (*PT*, p. 92).

38. There is a similar oddity about time in 'The Mark of the Beast', by which Kipling intends to unsettle the reader about whether the torturing of the leper has really taken place or has been imagined by the drunken narrator.

39. See 'The Undertakers', 'The Elephant's Child'.

40. See 'An Indian Ghost in England', Haining, pp. 58–61; originally published in the *Pioneer*, Christmas 1885.

41. Charles Dickens, *Little Dorrit*, pbk edn (Harmondsworth: Penguin, 1967) pp. 767, 772.

42. 'The Strange Ride' is a Christmas story: Mary and Joseph go up to Bethlehem to be taxed, and Jesus is born; Morrowbie Jukes goes down to Bedlam to be taxed, and is reborn. 'The Strange Ride' was begun immediately after 'The Dream of Duncan Parrenness' (*LH*), which was first published on Christmas Day 1884, the day on which Jukes is rescued from the pit, assuming that a naturalistic time-scale is operating. Kipling took pains over both tales; they both contain an encounter with an older, corrupt *possible* self whom the narrator fears to become, or whose life he fears to repeat.

43. *KJ*, Dec 1985, 30–2, reproduces a version of White's chart.

44. Cornell, pp. 96–7. Kipling seems to have given this novel the alterna-tive name of *The Book of the Forty-Five Mornings* (Wilson, pp. 159–60). In *The Naulahka* the Indian necklace has forty-five stones (p. 252). In 'The Strange Ride' the notebook has the 'First forty-five pages blank' (p. 196). I suggest that the blank pages stand for *The Book of the Forty-Five Mornings/Mother Maturin*, which he first conceived while writing 'The Strange Ride'. In *The Naulahka* Tarvin gives back the Indian necklace – the central stone has an ominous dark red heart, implying that to keep it means death; I take the subtext of the novel to be Kipling's explanation of his failure to write *The Book of the Forty-Five Mornings*, 'treasure' standing for 'works'; he has renounced the writing of an authentic Indian book in favour of a 'wholesome' life.

45. The *Quartette* version makes this more pointed by including a reference to the Ilbert Bill.

46. The landscape with its burrows derives from the links at the Burrows, Westward Ho!, which is arrived at after 'Gallantry Bower' and 'the

homes of the Carews and the Pinecoffins'. 'The Burrows, lying between the school and the sea, was a waste of bent rush and grass running out into hundreds of acres of fascinating sandhills called the Bunkers where a few old people played golf . . . even then golfers wore red jackets' ('An English School', *LST*, pp. 255–6, with some details from the *Youth's Companion* version). RK has Indianised the landscape, with the golfers' red jackets becoming the salmon-coloured cloth. See *LR*, p. 391, for a sinister golfer.

47. Ackroyd, 13.
48. Cf. for instance, 'To Be Filed for Reference' with Grant Allen's viciously racist 'The Reverend John Creedy' in *Strange Stories* (1884). Allen seeks to prove that even the 'best' – i.e. Oxford-educated – black man is a savage at heart. Kipling's 'reply' is that everyone is.
49. Carrington, p. 551; *SC*, p. 218.
50. Hermione Lee, Introduction to *Traffics and Discoveries* (Harmondsworth: Penguin, 1987) p. 20. See also Wilson, pp. 218–20.

CHAPTER 6   KIPLING AND CHAUCER: MARY POSTGATE

1. For example, 'He shares the early English poet's eye for wayward detail, the odd character, the slice of life, the amused sense for human foibles and joys' – Edward Said, Introduction to *Kim* (Harmondsworth: Penguin, 1987) p. 15. See also the *Atlantic Monthly*, LXXXIV (Nov 1899) 714–16; *KJ*, June 1933, p. 42 ('He is the modern Chaucer'); Wilson, p. 129.
2. 'An Excellent Reason', 'The Justice's Tale', 'The Consolations of Memory' and 'Prologue to the Master-Cook's Tale'.
3. Pollard is very worn and used; Kipling also owned G. G. Coulton's *Chaucer and his England* (Methuen, 1908).
4. 'Kipling's Schooldays', *KJ*, Mar 1927, 32. In his book Beresford gives Froissart and Langland equal weight (Beresford, pp. 13, 233; in Orel, I, 39.)
5. Dryden, Preface to *Fables*.
6. Hazlitt, 'On Chaucer and Spenser', *Lectures on the English Poets*, II; Leigh Hunt, *Wit and Humour*; Arnold, 'The Study of Poetry'; Meredith, 'The Poetry of Chaucer'.
7. Ruskin, *Lectures on Art* (1870); *Works*, xx, 29–30.
8. See Blake, pp. 566–75.
9. Chaucer, *Knight's Tale*, l. 2206.
10. See Weygandt, p. 23 n. 69; *KJ*, Mar 1970, 30–1; Joseph Jacobs (ed.), Preface and notes to *Indian Fairy Tales* (London: David Nutt, 1892).
11. Several of Kipling's early stories dealing with chance, dice and cards also show the imprint of *The Pardoner's Tale* – for example, 'The Joker' (1889), Haining, pp. 170–4. Death says to the card-players, 'Three-handed euchre, was it? . . . Two combining against one when one is too successful? I think I know something about that game.' When 'beer and bones' – 'which deceive not' – are introduced together in a story, this is generally the signal that some illusion is about to be

practised, which brings together the Pardoner's deceits, his 'pigges bones' and the 'corny ale' he drinks before his tale.

12. Another is Pope's Sporus. In Kipling, sexually ambivalent names often indicate villainy, as in the case of Mr Groombride in 'Little Foxes' (*AR*).

13. See for instance J. Winny, Introduction to *The Miller's Tale* (Cambridge, 1971); Angela Carter, 'Alison's Giggle', in E. Phillips (ed.), *The Left and the Erotic* (London: Lawrence and Wishart, 1983) pp. 53–68.

14. I don't mean that medieval theologians censored this question, but no more than anyone else did they come up with a satisfactory answer. The orthodox explanation was that God wishes to keep man humble.

15. See Trix Fleming's anecdote (Birkenhead, pp. 77–8) of the girl with bad breath; it reveals Kipling's habit of thinking of the human body as a world.

16. The sequence (a visit to a 'cow's mouth'; a slippery path ending in a trap consisting of a pierced stone wall overlooking a tank or slime in which stands a man or lingam, 'the Loathsome Emblem of Creation'; a chuckle; behind or beneath the wall a secret chamber in which women have been mutilated or burnt alive) is found in *Letters of Marque* (*SS*, I, 99–105) and *The Naulahka*. See also 'Bubbling Well Road' (*LH*) and 'Typhoid at Home' (*KI*, pp. 69–77).

    MacMunn, a founder member of the Kipling Society and an old India hand, though not a close friend of Kipling, wrote, commenting on the omnipresence of the symbolism of yoni and lingam in Indian art, but seemingly unaware of Kipling's association of it with evil, 'Gao-mukh and "Bubbling Well", the subject of one of Kipling's stories, is really the *Gao-vulva* whence pours the life-giving and sin-purging liquor, the urine of a cow' (MacMunn, p. 98).

17. *Kim*, pp. 313, 366; *Cook's Tale*, l. 4422. I think this sheds some light on the difficulty John Bayley articulates (Bayley, pp. 58–9), i.e. whether Kipling has unwittingly 'compounded a howler' or is 'testing the reader'.

18. Mrs Fettley calls her 'Gra''. Kipling's grey women are usually baleful, like the Grey Sisters in Kingsley's *The Heroes*. Chaucer's Wife is at one point compared to a 'grey goos' in her rapacious search for a mate (*Wife of Bath's Tale*, ll. 269–70). 'The Wish House' is a Visitation in reverse; it is Elizabeth (Liz) who comes to visit the Mary figure, cruelly 'magnified' by her ulcer and ambivalently 'full of grace'. For the title 'The Wish House' cf. Carlyle, *Heroes and Hero Worship*, Lecture I: 'The noblest god [i.e. of Norse myth] is . . . Wish. The God *Wish*; who could give us all that we *wished*! Is not this the sincerest and yet rudest voice of the spirit of man? . . . Higher considerations have to teach us that the God *Wish* is not the true God' (in *Sartor*, 1888, Chapman and Hall edn p. 198).

19. Rupert Croft-Cooke, 'Bateman's', *KJ*, June 1963, 5–10, in Orel, II, 364; Maggs's catalogue no. 379, 1919: *Early English Literature Comprising Poetical and Prose Works by Authors Born before 1700*. The Chaucer manuscript is plate III, item 1053. Maggs's catalogue adds, 'Special arrangements can be made for sending books on approval to America and abroad.' Maggs is a source for 'Dredd', the black-letter booksellers

in 'Dayspring Mishandled', who likewise send books to America. My thanks are due to John Dench of CCAT for the gift of the Maggs catalogue and to Julian Wiltshire for matching the catalogue illustration to the original at Bateman's.

20. Blake, p. 572.
21. Modern texts read 'gat-tothed', but 'gap-toothed' as an attribute of the Wife had been current since Dryden.
22. *Civil and Military Gazette*, 6 June 1888, in *KJ*, July 1940, 15–18.
23. Charles Nodier, *Contes fantastiques* (Paris: Charpentier, 1861). Kipling uses the song from *La Fée aux miettes* as the epigraph to 'Dayspring Mishandled'. The editor's 'Notes sur les fées et la littérature féerique' identifies fairies with the Fates and literary figures such as Gloriana: 'Parques, nymphes, junones, déesses mères, druidesses, prophétesses gauloises, furent pour les François crédules, pour les poètes . . . des êtres identiques.' The folk 'les désigna plus spécialement par le nom de fata, sous lequel ses ancêtres avoient honoré les Parques identifiées aux déesses mères'. The line had come to the end with 'la Manto, l'Alcine, la Mélisse d'Arioste, la Titania de Shakspeare, la Gloriane de Spencer [sic]' (pp. 272–3). There is no copy of Nodier at Bateman's or Wimpole Hall, so it would be hard to prove that Kipling read that particular edition, but the editor was not being original.
24. 'Mary Postgate' was started in March 1915 (*KC*, p. 106) but not published until September 1915. The Germans first used poison gas on the Western Front in April. The *Lusitania* was sunk on 7 May.
25. Bodelsen, p. 102; *KJ*, June 1970.
26. Page, p. 46.
27. Jarrell, p. 363 ('The German pilot isn't really there, of course, except in our desire, but his psychological reality is absolute'); Bayley, p. 66. Bayley has since been convinced by Page but now argues that it does not make sense to ask whether the airman is real or not. See John Bayley, *The Short Story* (Brighton: Harvester, 1988) pp. 86–93.
28. Page, p. 42.
29. Boris Ford, 'A Case for Kipling?', *Scrutiny*, xi (1942–3) 23–33.
30. We may infer that her 'unofficial' name was Kafoozalum, 'The Harlot of Jerusalem'. Kipling regarded the song as a 'work of art' (Wilson, p. 147), possibly because he saw that it is an analogue of *The Miller's Tale*.
31. See M. P. Hamilton, 'Echoes of Childermas in the Tale of the Prioress', *Modern Language Review*, xxxiv (1939) 1–8. If 'Mary Postgate' is, as I suggest, a Childermas story and Edna Gerritt has died on 28 December, Wynn was buried on the 23rd (the funeral took place five days before). This is the date on which Morrowbie Jukes falls into the pit, which illustrates Kipling's self-referentiality and lifelong brooding on the mysteries of birth and death.
32. The most detailed treatment of the influence of Jane Austen upon Kipling is to be found in L. A. F. Lewis, 'Kipling's Jane: Some Echoes of Austen', *ELT*, xxix, no. 1 (1986) 76–82.
33. Dates and ages are emphasised; one can work out that Mary is born

in the year of the Franco-Prussian War (1870) and that Miss Fowler was 'nearer fifty than forty' when Wynn was conceived (1893–4). For the 'dangerousness' of this age see 'My Rival' (*DV*, p. 22), which Kipling's sister said did *not* refer to their own mother, and 'A Madonna of the Trenches'.

34. 'Teem', published in the January 1936 number of the *Strand Magazine*, appeared either just before or just after Kipling's death.

35. *KNR*, p. 35.

36. John Evelyn's *Sylva*, a favourite of Kipling's, mentions the association of bay laurel with true visions, poetic fury, the Delphic tripos and the Dodonian oracle. That the Pythian Sybil was intoxicated with common laurel is found in Erasmus Darwin. Kipling had a special interest in plant drugs and could have gathered information about the common laurel from many sources. Two possibilities are the *OED* and Barton and Castle's *The British Flora Medica*, which he owned in a revised edition of 1877. 'Portugal' may carry a private mark. Birkenhead reports (p. 16), apparently from a communication with Kipling's sister, that there were 'three speckled Portugal laurels' in the little garden of Lorne Lodge, but Portugal laurels are not speckled. Could she have meant the aucuba or *Japanese* laurel? Did she say 'Portugal' because of private knowledge that the shrubbery in 'Mary Postgate' ultimately derived from the 'House of Desolation'? Punch is frightened by 'the rustling of the laurel-bushes' in Antirosa's garden (*WWW*, p. 302). But I suspect a coded public message as well, and that 'Portugal' alludes to the May sinking of the *Lusitania*. The manuscript shows 'Portugal' already in place, but the story is at a late stage of composition and the script is undated. That the fury provoked by the sinking will conquer the *furor Teutonicus* is an idea which may be symbolised by the breathing in of a Lusitanic *furor*. Portugal is 'our oldest ally'.

37. One of Kipling's earliest fears was of a 'darker room full of cold, in one wall of which a white woman made naked fire, and I cried aloud with dread, for I had never before seen a grate' (*SM*, p. 4).

38. Kipling took a lot of trouble over this passage (manuscript evidence).

39. Page, p. 45.

40. Bayley, pp. 66–7. Mary may be supposed to have derived her notions of how a German speaks French from *Trilby*.

41. 'Conventionality', from Kipling's first collection, *Schoolboy Lyrics*. (In Outward Bound and Sussex editions, and *EV*, p. 91.)

42. A. G. Gardiner, in *Prophets, Priests and Kings* (London: Alston Rivers, 1908) pp. 296–7, had described Kipling's world as composed of 'not men, but the baleful caricatures of men; not women, but Maenad sisters with wild and bloodshot eyes and fearful dishevelled locks'. Kipling returns the gibe with interest. Gardiner's phrase about Kipling's art, 'the terrible gaiety of despair', is very discerning, though he means it as blame.

43. In 'The House Surgeon' (*AR*, p. 267), the onset of insanity is imaged as a little shadow floating *inside* the brain.

44. From Swinburne's 'Itylus'.

45. Miss Sichliffe ('The Dog Hervey', also in *D of C*) is the other camel-

like woman in Kipling's work. She says that, although her mother calls her Marjorie (pearl), 'my real name is Moira' (i.e. Fate; p. 143). But she is a kind Fate, presenting men with orchids and goldfish – that is, restoring their virility. She is a 'patcher up' of lame dogs, animal and human, a female *Resartor*, an archwife whose trade is to make good and mend the cloth of life, a Saviour to Mary Postgate's Paviour, a pre-war woman like Connie Sperrit.

46. Page, p. 45.
47. *RG*, VII, 3346.
48. Cf. the closing line of *Hedda Gabler*, 'But people don't *do* such things', which RK used in 'The Mother Hive' (*AR*, p. 85); and Pope: 'Narcissa's nature, tolerably mild, / To make a wash would hardly stew a child' (*Epistle to a Lady*, ll. 54–5). Though accepting the existence of the airman, Robson saw 'the essential identity – symbolic, of course, not literal – between the dying airman and Wynn' (Rutherford, p. 274).
49. Found, for instance, in Peacock's *The Misfortunes of Elphin*. Beetle discovers Peacock in the Head's library (*SC*, p. 217).
50. I have not found a real 'Vegg's Heath' (the site of Wynn's landing).
51. Carrington, pp. 467–8; Wilson, pp. 199–200.
52. Kipling declined to meet Baroness Orczy in 1933 (Wilson, p. 330).
53. There are signs in the manuscript that all passages containing coded indictments of England's negligence were added at a late stage.
54. Cohen, p. 171. Kipling on his love for Flo Garrard: 'I can't imagine a man deliberately keeping sacred letters' (Birkenhead, p. 76).
55. A variant reading of 'Imperious Wool-booted sage' (*EV*, p. 435), originally written for *Edna* Florine Irwin, gives 'Oh Pagan philosopher' instead of 'Oh fluffy philosopher'. The holograph is in Marlboro College Library, Vermont (Howard C. Rice collection).
56. Cf. the shock ending of Zola's *Nana*, of which I think this is a 'metagrobolisation and inversion'. Between 1865 and 1915 Manet was known in England chiefly as the painter of *Olympia*. Memories of the 1865 furore over *Olympia*'s Salon exhibition were stirred in 1907 when it achieved the status of a French national treasure by its transference from the Luxembourg to the Louvre – a 'mild sensation' according to the *Daily Telegraph*, 7 Feb. It had been bought by subscription after its exhibition at the Paris Exposition Universelle of 1889, which Kipling visited (*SF*, p. 12). 'Little Victorine' (*D of C*, p. 182) may allude to Manet's model for *Olympia*. Miss Fowler has previously 'scandalised' the establishment (i.e. reduced it in size, as in *scandalising* a sail). 'Mary Postgate' contains a series of buried puns on the meanings of 'scandalised', as 'Mrs Bathurst' does on 'inversion'.

CHAPTER 7   KIPLING AND SWINBURNE: 'A MADONNA OF THE TRENCHES'

1. Cornell, pp. 30–5.
2. Swinburne is a marginally more visible influence than Browning on Kipling's poetry up until 1884; *EV* contains at an estimate at least

thirty-three definitely Swinburnian poems including parodies, as against about twenty Browningesque ones.

3. Birkenhead, p. 8; *KJ*, Mar 1933, 20. Swinburne's contemptuous 1908 reaction upon being passed over for the Nobel Prize was, 'I have not been offered the honour of taking a back seat behind Mr Rudyard Kipling' (Henderson, p. 282).

4. Eliot, p. 8.

5. Weygandt, pp. 124–7, spotted Kipling's quotations from 'Song in Time of Order', 'Félise', 'A Leavetaking' and 'Dolores', and reference to 'Faustine'. He parodies 'Hertha' in 'O Baal, hear us!' (*EV*, p. 411). 'The Leper' lies behind the early poem 'Paul Vaugel' (*EV*, p. 101) and 'Dayspring Mishandled'.

6. *EV*, p. 285; *KI*, p. 182. Menken (d. 1869) performed her act strapped to a horse. That Kipling in 1885–7 should allude to her at all is odd, and is, I think, better evidence of *his* special interest in Swinburne than of *her* posthumous fame. She may have determined Kipling's choice of 'Ada' as the name of Mrs Bathurst's niece; the circus-motif would support this. The niece is a loose end; I believe we are to see her as an 'aider' of her dead aunt's revenge in some unspecified way – giving her watch to Boy Niven, perhaps. I considered the possibility that Ada has joined 'Phyllis's circus' as an equestrienne and that she has beguiled Vickery into the jungle in a re-enactment of the Swinburne–Menken relationship. But it is stressed that Vickery never sees the 'natural' performing animals, only the 'unnatural' biograph.

7. Henderson, pp. 126, 131–2, 140–50; Clyde Hyder, *Swinburne's Literary Career and Fame* (New York: Russell and Russell, 1963) p. 192.

8. A film of *Mother Maturin* was planned in the 1920s. Kipling ordered that Mother Maturin was to be depicted as a 'voluptuous honey-coloured Fate' in 'red or green native slippers' (Orel, II, 379).

9. Birkenhead, p. 51; *SF*, p. 5.

10. For instance, in the poem 'The Liner She's a Lady', and *SS*, I, 278–87.

11. In Ewing's 'Father Hedgehog and his Neighbours', *AJM*, XIV (1876), a hedgehog witnesses a love-declaration. See also Ewing, xxv, 253: 'The subject of my first painting is settled . . . A spotted pig in the middle of the field. The sun at its meridian; the pig asleep. Motto, "Whatever is, is beautiful."'

12. There is a running pun on 'Doll' throughout Kipling's work through which he expresses the idea of pain arising out of the ruin of innocence – the child's toy (the 'dear little doll') becoming the worker in the 'dolly-shop', Dolores, who is both the sorrowing mother and Our Lady of Pain, and ''Dal' = 'Dol', with an American accent. A similar multiple pun invests 'Lyde of the music-halls' ('A Recantation', *DV*, p. 369), who, besides recalling Marie Lloyd, Harry Lauder and Horace's Lyde, is a Cockney 'Lady', the Mater Dolorosa and *Leid* (German for 'pain' or 'sorrow').

13. Carlyle, *The French Revolution*, v.iii ('Destruction').

14. See Elaine Showalter's *The Female Malady* (Virago, 1987), especially pp. 169–76, on the treatment of male hysteria during and after the First World War. Keede resembles W. H. R. Rivers in his humane use of 'paregoric' methods. Showalter notes that in the 'shell-shock'

literature following the First World War 'men's quarrels with the feminine element in their own psyches become externalised as quarrels with women'. She does not mention Kipling's fictive depiction of male hysteria from 1884 onwards, surely a notable exception to her argument that the condition was generally unrecognised.

15. 21 January is St Agnes Day; 'A Madonna of the Trenches' is a nightmare version of Keats's *Eve of St Agnes*.

16. Bayley, 70–1; Wilson, p. 315.

17. Sandra Kemp, Introduction to *Debits and Credits* (Harmondsworth: Penguin, 1987) pp. 22–3.

18. *Shelley's Prose*, ed. D. L. Clark (Albuquerque: University of New Mexico Press) p. 223.

19. For Kipling's knowledge of *Lavengro*, see *SC*, p. 217.

20. Heading of chapter 8 of *From Sea to Sea* (SS i, 278).

21. 'The Propagation of Knowledge', which immediately follows 'Madonna' in *DC* makes extensive use of D'israeli.

22. D'israeli, p. 77; *Omniana*, p. 37. 'Madonna' is set just over the Flanders border in the ancient province of Artois, but in Bellarmine's lifetime both Flanders and Artois belonged to the Spanish Netherlands.

23. Kipling knew *The Arabian Nights* well and the story is summarised in Brewer under 'Amine'. The skeletons are another mockery of 'unity in death'; presumably they are known to be 'Zoo-ave' (a pun) through their rags of gay uniforms. See also *LR*, p. 327, for Martin Ballart's obsession with a photograph of a 'young man in a trench dancing languorously with a skeleton'.

24. Sandison, p. 195. Rita Howes, a former student at my college, has suggested in class discussion that Kipling intends the reader to think that Bella has died of an abortion; it would account for her referring to her 'draw back' as her 'little trouble' and is consistent with her expressed relief at not having a child during the war. This seems very possible to me, and does not rule out her having cancer as well.

25. The imagery of the movies links 'Madonna' with 'Mrs Bathurst' and another *DC* story – 'The Prophet and the Country'.

26. See Ch. 1, note 23. One critic who may have read 'Madonna' in this way is Edmund Wilson: 'In "A Madonna of the Trenches" and "The Wish House" – gruesome ghost stories of love and death that make "The End of the Passage" and "The Mark of the Beast" look like harmless bogey tales for children – cancer serves as a symbol for rejected or frustrated love' (*KNR*, p. 158).

27. See 'Kidnapped' (*PT*, p. 134), where the jilted Miss Castries shows how lady-like she is by refusing to file a breach-of-promise suit. Perhaps Kipling felt that it was a vulgar, regrettable, but necessary social contrivance in an imperfect world where the jilted woman often was unfairly blamed for a broken engagement and rendered unmarriageable.

28. For an association between love and 'The Butcher's Row' see the poem of that name by Edmund Gosse, *Century Magazine*, v (1883–4) 563. The poet and his love, who is dressed in 'laughing white', wander down 'the Butcher's Row' in Limoges on St Maura's Day. The girl's

purity is evidently intended to be a shocking contrast to the butcher shops. Gosse, an early admirer of Kipling, was a witness at his wedding (Birkenhead, p. 134).

29. Swinton, p. 59.
30. 'Then Uncle John says something to me about seein' Ma an' the rest of 'em in a few days, an' had I any messages for 'em? Gawd knows what made me do it, but I told 'im to tell Auntie Armine I never expected to see anything like *her* up in our part of the world' (*DC*, p. 254).
31. Birkenhead, p. 23.
32. Brewer, entry for Arminians.
33. Cohen, pp. 181–7.
34. *Rewards and Fairies*, ed. Roger Lewis (Harmondsworth: Penguin, 1987) p. 276, quoting Kingsley Amis, *Rudyard Kipling and his World*.
35. E. W. Martindell, 'Kipling among the Early Critics', in *KJ*, Apr 1941, 9–12.
36. Shelley, *Prometheus Unbound*, iv.404–5. Shelley is an influence on the lyric style of Kipling, who owned, surprisingly, three copies of his works. I find in Kipling's *oeuvre* evidence of knowledge of *The Revolt of Islam*, 'Prince Athanase', *Prometheus Unbound*, *Adonais* and *Hellas*. A passage in *Queen Mab* denouncing commerce has a line pencilled down the margin.

APPENDIX I   HECTOR MACDONALD

1. *SM*, p. 155; Julian Ralph, *War's Brighter Side* (London: Arthur Pearson, 1901) p. 221; Lord Roberts, *Forty-One Years in India* (London: Bentley, 1897) ii, vii, 200, 221, 515.
2. *KJ*, Oct 1941, 22; Dec 1940, 3; 'Victorian' (pseud.), 'Boer War Incidents', *KJ*, Apr 1942, 13.
3. *SS*, i, 104; Birkenhead, pp. 290–1.

APPENDIX II   KIPLING AND BLAKE

1. Tompkins, pp. 13, 151.
2. Gilchrist, i, 419.
3. *MEB*, ii, 271.
4. Ibid., p. 290.
5. Gilchrist, i, 336.
6. Birkenhead, plate 8.
7. See Ch. 6, note 55.

Index